THE LIFE OF BISHOP WILFRID
BY EDDIUS STEPHANUS

The *Life of Wilfrid* offers us a graphic portrait of one of the most forceful characters in the history of the English church: a man courageous and energetic yet at the same time litigious, ostentatious and overbearing, his life punctuated by restless travels and the most violent quarrels. Of noble birth, Wilfrid (c.634–709) gained his first experience of monastic life as a boy at Lindisfarne. Thereafter we find him at various times, crossing Gaul, staying in Lyons, visiting Rome, back in England at York, Ripon or Hexham, preaching to heathens in Sussex or Frisia, quarrelling with kings and bishops, imprisoned in Northumbria, again in Rome seeking papal support for his claims, founding monasteries in the Midlands and at last, in his old age, reconciled to those with whom he had earlier quarrelled so bitterly. Partisan but highly detailed, the *Life* was probably written within a decade of the saint's death. It is a remarkable account of a powerful personality who aroused affection and dislike in almost equal proportions.

THE LIFE OF BISHOP WILFRID
BY EDDIUS STEPHANUS

TEXT, TRANSLATION AND NOTES BY

BERTRAM COLGRAVE

formerly Reader in English, University of Durham

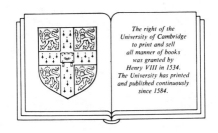

The right of the
University of Cambridge
to print and sell
all manner of books
was granted by
Henry VIII in 1534.
The University has printed
and published continuously
since 1584.

CAMBRIDGE UNIVERSITY PRESS

CAMBRIDGE

LONDON   NEW YORK   NEW ROCHELLE

MELBOURNE   SYDNEY

Published by the Press Syndicate of the University of Cambridge
The Pitt Building, Trumpington Street, Cambridge CB2 IRP
32 East 57th Street, New York, NY 10022, USA
10 Stamford Road, Oakleigh, Melbourne 3166, Australia

First published 1927
First paperback edition 1985

Printed in Great Britain by Redwood Burn Limited, Trowbridge, Wiltshire

Library of Congress catalogue card number: 85-16625

British Library cataloguing in publication data
Eddius Stephanus
[Vita Sancti Wilfridi Episcopi Eboracencis.
English & Latin]. The life of Bishop Wilfrid.
1. Wilfrid, *Saint* 2. Christian saints –
England – Biography
I. [Vita Sancti Wilfridi, Episcopi Eboracencis,
English & Latin] II. Title III. Colgrave,
Bertram
270.2′092′4   BX4700.W5

ISBN 0 521 30927 1 hard covers
ISBN 0 521 31387 2 paperback

PREFACE

No apology is needed for a fresh edition of the text of Eddius Stephanus's Life of St Wilfrid. The last two editions, that of Levison in the *Monumenta Germaniae Historica* and that of Raine in the Rolls Series, are accessible only on library shelves. In addition, the accuracy of the latter's text leaves very much to be desired. It is therefore obvious that there is a real need for a fresh text which claims at least to be reasonably accurate and accessible. The translation is unpretentious and is intended only as a help to the increasing number of students who desire to study the history of the seventh century from the original documents but are hindered by the difficulties of Eddius's crabbed style. This, together with the notes, may perhaps serve to introduce students to one of the most striking figures in the history of the Church in the North. The period in which he flourished was a time of great activity in Northumbria in the realms of religion, politics, art and literature, and a careful study of the life of St Wilfrid forms one of the best introductions that a student could have to the ecclesiastical and social history, not only of Northumbria, but of the other English kingdoms too, while Wilfrid's ceaseless wanderings connect him closely with the history of contemporary Western Europe.

I have not attempted in the introduction to go into any details as to the character, influence and position of St Wilfrid. It may be possible later on to make a separate study of his life, putting him as far as possible in his true historical background and attempting to complete what Bishop Browne so ably began thirty years ago in his *Theodore and Wilfrith*.

I have received much help which I gladly acknowledge. In the first place my debt to the two great leaders in the study of this period, Plummer and Bright, will be obvious throughout In addition to my detailed acknowledgments in the proper places, it is only right to make here a general acknowledgment of the common debt which all students of the period owe to their labours. My thanks are also due to many friends for help of various kinds: to the Rev. Christopher

Wordsworth of Salisbury; to my colleagues, Professor How, Mr E. V. Stocks the University Librarian and Mr J. Meade Falkner, Librarian of the Chapter Library, Durham; to the staff of the Bodleian Library, Oxford, and especially to Dr Craster, who put into my hands a copy of the correspondence which enabled me to solve the puzzle of the lost Salisbury MS; and to the staff of the Cambridge University Library, who were always ready to bring their expert knowledge to my aid. I have also to thank Mr T. G. Benson, Assistant Master at Harrow School, for help in difficult points in the translation, and Mr Bruce Dickins of Edinburgh University for many valuable suggestions.

But most of all my thanks are due first to Professor H. M. Chadwick of Clare College, Cambridge, for suggesting to me the task which I have attempted to fulfil and for constant advice throughout, and secondly, to my colleague Dr Edward Pace, Reader in Divinity in the University of Durham, for carefully revising my translation, for reading through the proofs and for continual encouragement and suggestions. Whatever value this little book may have, will be largely due to their help, so generously given.

Lastly, may I thank the Syndics of the Cambridge University Press for undertaking the publication of this work and for all the help given by the staff and the proof-readers in the course of its production.

BERTRAM COLGRAVE

HATFIELD COLLEGE
  DURHAM
  October 1926

CONTENTS

INTRODUCTION

EDDIUS'S *Life of Wilfrid* is, with the exception of the *Anonymous Life of St Cuthbert*, and Bede's Metrical Life of the same saint, the earliest piece of biography we possess. In fact it is almost the earliest considerable piece of literature written in this country. Its importance is obvious for it gives us a contemporary picture of a man who was a great figure in the political and ecclesiastical life of the seventh century. The Church was definitely moulded into shape during Wilfrid's lifetime, and Wilfrid himself played a leading part in deciding what that shape should be. He was largely instrumental in converting the whole of Northumbria to the Roman form of Christianity; he brought the north definitely into contact with the Mother Church by his journeys to Rome and by his appeals to the Apostolic See; he built churches which were the wonder of the western world; he exercised a great influence on the art and architecture of the times[1], and, more important even than all these, by his defiance of kings and princes he asserted the authority of the Church in so definite a manner that as a result no less than twenty-six of the forty-six years of his episcopacy were spent in exile. He died worn out by the struggle, but he had triumphantly proved that the Church was no mere appendage to the throne.

This work has always been attributed to Eddius Stephanus, though the actual evidence is far from strong. The preamble to the Fell MS in the Bodleian Library states that it was written by a certain Stephanus, a priest. On the Cottonian MS there is written in a sixteenth-century hand, possibly that of Sir Robert Cotton, "per Heddium Stephanum monachum Cantuar. An° 720." This is all the evidence we have from the MSS themselves[2]. William of Malmesbury also declares that the Life is the work of the priest Stephanus (*Gesta Pontif. Anglorum*, III, Prol.).

---

[1] For instance he put glass into the church windows at York some years before Benedict Biscop did the same at Jarrow. See ch. XVI, note.

[2] The story told by Mabillon, AA.SS.O.S.B. saec. IV. pt I. 672, that the Salisbury MS contained the full name of Eddius Stephanus is of course inaccurate, as I have shewn below that the mythical Salisbury MS which has caused the editors so much trouble, is simply the Fell MS masquerading under another name.

There is a reference in Bede which helps to identify this Eddius Stephanus. He says (*H.E.* IV. 2), "Except James above mentioned, the first singing master in the churches of the Northumbrians was Aedde surnamed Stephen invited from Kent by the most reverend Wilfrid." This quotation explains the reference in ch. XIV of the present work where we are told that Wilfrid returned from Kent to Northumbria bringing with him the singers Aedde and Aeona. So it has always been held that this Aedde or Eddius is the author of the work[1]. This is the only place in which the name is mentioned, and it is possible to gather but little information about Aedde in the work itself. He probably came north in 669. Raine (*H.C.Y.* p. xxxi, Pref.) declares for no very obvious reason that Eddius was present at *Ouestraefelda* in 702; but at any rate it is probable, by his use of the first person in his description of the last journey to Rome, that he was with Wilfrid on that occasion (cf. chs. LII–LIII). He returned later to Ripon as is clear from the reference in ch. XVII, where he speaks of the treasures which Wilfrid gave, which "are preserved in our church until these times as a witness to his blessed memory; here too his remains rest." It was here presumably that he wrote the Life of his master. There are also various other indications that he was a monk at Ripon (cf. chs. XLV, LXII–LXVIII).

It seems probable that the anonymous Life of St Cuthbert which appeared between 698 and 705 inspired the community at Ripon to urge Eddius to produce an account of his own patron. The fact of the existence of a Life of Cuthbert, whom the community must have regarded as in a certain sense a rival of their own great founder, would undoubtedly stir them up to produce a Life of Wilfrid.

We do not know the exact date of the Life but it is clear that it cannot have been written very long after Wilfrid's death. Eddius came up north with Wilfrid in 669 and must at that time have been at least twenty years old and in all probability was more, seeing that he was even then an accomplished musician. So at the lowest computation Eddius would be sixty years of age when his patron died. It is highly probable therefore that the Life was produced within the next ten years—that is to say, before 720. The tone of the last few

---

[1] Levison, however, is inclined to doubt the identification on the ground that if Eddius had been speaking about himself in ch. XIV he would have used the first person. But Eddius's use of the first person is so very casual that this objection bears little weight (see *S.R.M.* VI. 180).

chapters and the details about the first anniversary of his death also tend to shew that the Life was produced shortly after Wilfrid died (cf. also chs. XVII, XXII, XXIII, XXVI, XXXVII).

Eddius would have no difficulty in gathering together the materials for his history. He had been intimately associated with Wilfrid over a period of forty years and besides that he was in close touch with Acca and Tatberht. It was Acca for whom Wilfrid asked when he recovered consciousness after his illness at Meaux and to whom he revealed his vision (ch. LVI); Tatberht was his kinsman and he told him the story of his life probably as he rode south to Oundle on his last journey (ch. LXV). All this, and the many reminiscences of the monks who had followed him, were at Eddius's disposal.

It is easy to criticize Eddius—to point out his partisanship, and his mistakes in historical fact, to call him credulous and to cast doubts on the historical value of his work. All this has been done[1], and it is impossible to deny the truth of many of the criticisms which have been made. But in spite of all this the Life presents a living picture of St Wilfrid such as we certainly do not get in Bede. It is scarcely fair to expect Eddius to be anything else but partisan; it is extremely difficult for the modern biographer to escape from the snare with the experience of 1200 years of biography-writing behind him. Eddius, on the other hand, had probably only one example to imitate. Besides all this Eddius's aim was to extol his patron, even if he had to twist the facts in order to do it. So it is not surprising to find that Eddius judges all men by their attitude to his hero. Aldfrith's death, for instance (ch. LIX), is due to his treatment of Wilfrid; Ecgfrith so long as he lived at peace with Wilfrid was victorious, but when disagreement broke out between them, the king's power rapidly diminished (ch. XIX; compare also ch. XX, note)[2]. But we must not condemn Eddius as being utterly unscrupulous. Take for instance the gap which occurs in the Life between the times when Wilfrid left the north in 692, after he was driven out by Aldfrith, and the conference at *Ouestraefelda* in 703. It may well be that Eddius, having no means of finding out the details of his life during that period,

[1] See especially B. W. Wells and R. L. Poole, "Eddius' Life of Wilfrid," *E.H.R.* VI. 1891, 535 ff.; *E.H.R.* CXXXIII. 1919, 1 ff.

[2] Yet sometimes Eddius can praise Wilfrid's opponents. He speaks highly of Chad (chs. XIV, XV), he emphasizes Aldfrith's prudence (chs. XLIV, XLV, LIX) and describes how Iurminburg afterwards became a reformed character (ch. XXIV).

preferred to keep silence. He does not hesitate to explain the motives for Wilfrid's two expulsions, while Bede is content merely to quote the facts. In both cases the reasons given (chs. xxiv and xlv) are likely enough—except for the story of the bribing of Theodore—and they are not altogether creditable to Wilfrid, at any rate from our point of view. But, apart from all questions of the credibility of Eddius as a historian, the value of the biography is to be found in the account given of the building and renovation of the churches of York, Ripon and Hexham, the glimpse we get of the significance of Wilfrid in the history of the times, and an extremely interesting picture of life in England and on the continent in the late seventh century. Concerning the accusation made against Eddius that he was credulous, little need be said. He believed in miracles as Bede did, and sometimes over-emphasized the miraculous element. It was natural to his age, and, like all other religious and orthodox people of his time, he readily believed in stories of supernatural interposition in the everyday affairs of life.

A few words may be said concerning the relation between Bede's account of Wilfrid and that of Eddius. Bede obviously uses Eddius though he does not acknowledge it. As in his borrowings from other sources[1] he alters the language while keeping closely to the sense. He has, however, added fresh details. On the subject of Aethilthryth he got his information from Wilfrid himself (*H.E.* iv. 19). Other details of Wilfrid's life he may easily have obtained from his friend Acca, such as Wilfrid's stay with Willibrord on his last journey to Rome (*H.E.* iii. 3), the picturesque account of the way in which Wilfrid relieved the famine in Sussex (*H.E.* v. 11), or the consecration of Oftfor and Suidberht (*H.E.* v. 11). It is clear throughout his account that he is not altogether favourable to Wilfrid; one fact alone may be mentioned to illustrate this point; he describes only one miracle connected with Wilfrid—the vision of St Michael; it is noticeable that in this miracle his friend Acca plays an important part. But when he is writing the Life of St Cuthbert, a man especially dear to him, it is noticeable that the miraculous element is more than usually great. But in spite of all this we know from Bede's other writings that he was a careful and scrupulous historian, and, after

[1] Cf. his borrowings from the *Anonymous Life of St Cuthbert* in his prose Life of that saint, and from the anonymous monk of Lindisfarne in his *Lives of the Abbots.*

a detailed comparison of Eddius's narrative with that of Bede, one is forced to the conclusion that Bede, especially on points in which they differ, is a more dependable authority[1] (see e.g. notes on chs. XI, XXIV, XLI, XLIII, etc.).

The style of Eddius's Latin, though not so good as that of Bede, is nevertheless very much better than that of other (continental) Latin writers of the period. His sentences often hang together badly, his genders and cases are sometimes mixed, he is capable of mistakes in declensions and conjugations, an active form is invented for deponent verbs, and words are used in wrong, or at any rate very unusual, senses. But in spite of all these things the narrative is on the whole clear and straightforward and the number of obscure passages is not very much greater than we find in Bede.

There are two manuscripts of the Life. C, the first, is at the British Museum in the Cottonian collection (Vespasian, D. VI). It is part of a volume which apparently once belonged to the Canterbury library, judging from an inscription on fol. 2. The size of the MS is $5\frac{1}{4}$ in. $\times$ $7\frac{1}{4}$ in. The book consists of two parts, the first of which (fols. 2–77) belongs chiefly to the ninth century with a few eleventh-century additions, while the latter part (fols. 78–125) contains the life of Wilfrid in a hand of the eleventh century. On the last page (fol. 125) are a few exercises in penmanship which belong to the twelfth century. From some of these it would appear that the volume was removed from somewhere in Yorkshire to Canterbury[2]. The chapter headings are written in red or purple ink and in a few places there are rather crude attempts at ornate capitals (e.g. chs. XV, XXXVII, XXXIX, XL, XLVIII, LI, LX, LXIV, etc.) some of them with roughly drawn faces or animal designs. Two of the leaves of the MS are missing and consequently there is a gap extending from the end of ch. XV to the middle of ch. XVIII (see note a.l.).

[1] For a detailed study of the whole question see R. L. Poole's article in *E.H.R.* CXXXIII. 1919, 1–24.

[2] It reads as follows: "Reverentissimo domino suo et amico in Christo dilectissimo A. de N"; then lower down on the same page: "Will(elmus) de Neut(on). Willelmus Dei gratia rex Ang(lorum) dux Nor(manni)e dominus Ib(erni)e comes Ant(gav)ie et Aquit(ani)e vic(ecomiti) Ebor(acensi) salutem." Then after a space: "Dilecto amico suo G. fil. G. suus Ada de Neut(on) salutem et dileccionem. Precor vos pro amore mei et servicio, quatinus unum equum mihi acomodetis, unde nuncium meum apud Ebor(acum) agere valiam. Valete." Below in an early fourteenth-century hand is written: "Nomen scriptoris Robertus plenus amoris."

There is a copy of this made by Thomas Gale, a High Master of St Paul's School, in the seventeenth century, preserved in the Bibliothèque Nationale, Paris, No. 13, 791. It is a somewhat careless piece of work.

On the first folium is the following inscription: "Heddius cognomento Stephanus de vita Wilfridi archiepiscopi Eboracensis (hanc inscriptionem habet codex Cottianus, unde haec descripsimus sed manu recentiori. Jacobus Usserius qui ista codici Cottiano affixit, hanc ipsam vitam Heddii attribuit ex codice ecclesiae Sarensis; v. eius...)." The book, whose title is omitted here, is Ussher's *Discourse of the Religion Anciently professed by the Irish and Brittish*, 1631, where he speaks of the MS at Salisbury and declares that he read on it the name of Stephen and not that of Eddius. So much for Gale's inaccuracy which is very marked all through this piece of work.

F, the second MS, is in the Fell Collection at the Bodleian Library, Oxford (vol. III. 34 a–56 b, originally vol. I). It forms part of a volume of Saints' Lives and is clearly written in a late eleventh- or early twelfth-century hand. The capitals of a number of the chapters are missing. Evidently they had been left to be put in later by another scribe. The MS is $8\frac{1}{4}$ in. × $12\frac{3}{4}$ in.

When Mabillon edited the Life in 1677 he only had a copy of the Cotton MS, but later on Dr Thomas Gale had obtained a copy of a MS belonging to the Salisbury Cathedral Library from which he supplied the defects of the Cottonian MS and through Professor Bernard, Professor of Astronomy at Oxford at the time, sent them on to Mabillon, together with a list of variant readings which Mabillon published in another part of the same volume published in 1680 (AA.SS.O.S.B. saec. IV. pt II. pp. 550–553). Since then editors have been puzzled to know what has become of this Salisbury MS— Codex Sarensis as Mabillon calls it. Only two MSS are known at present. Raine suggested that the Fell and Salisbury MSS might possibly have been identical, while Levison, the most recent editor, denied this and declared the Codex Sarensis to have been another MS now lost. The question however can easily be solved. In the first place all editors have noticed the close similarity between the variants preserved by Mabillon from the Salisbury MS and those from the Fell MS. As a matter of fact, by far the greater number of the readings are identical, and those which are not, look more like careless slips of the

pen than actual variants. But there is some correspondence among the Salisbury Muniments which explains the whole matter. In 1640 the Archbishop of Armagh, Dr Ussher, borrowed six books from the Church Library at Salisbury. Of these, three can be identified by the descriptions given as MS Fell, I, II, and III. In 1650 Dr Baylie, Dean of Salisbury, demanded their return and four of them were sent to the Bodleian Library. Of the other two volumes, "His Grace of Armagh testified that they were plundered and lost." The Salisbury authorities allowed the rest of the volumes to remain at the Bodleian until they called for them. In 1679, the late Librarian of the Bodleian, by this time Bishop of Lincoln, acknowledged that these four books, belonging to Salisbury, had been placed in the Library during his time but only three of them could now be found. Later on the Bishop of Oxford, Dr Fell, had them on loan to be "collated and compared." He died in 1686 and the three volumes were returned to the library in the form of a bequest from the Bishop! Hence it is simply a matter of different names for the same MS.

In the Bodleian Library there is also a beautifully written copy of the Fell MS made by a nephew of Dr Fell (MS Jones, II). This was probably made during the period when the books were in the Bishop's possession before his death. There are various conjectural readings in the margin.

What is the relation between the two MSS? It is clear that neither one is a copy of the other because in several places one MS omits words and phrases which the other one inserts (cf. chs. I, VI, XIII, XVIII, XXX, LIII, LV, LVII), while certain proper names are spelt with consistent differences in each. On the whole it looks as though they were both copies of another MS which was not the archetype. This seems apparent owing to the fact that in both there are obvious mistakes which appear to be due to the copy that the scribes were using, as e.g. in the chapter-heading of Chap. XXV. On the whole the scribe of F seems to have done his work more carelessly, and, if there is anything to choose between them, preference should be given, not, as Raine says, to F, but to C[1].

In the text I have not attempted to reproduce slight orthographical differences, which, so far as one could tell, were due largely to the idiosyncrasies of the scribes. Thus -ae is written sometimes -ae, sometimes -e, and sometimes -ẹ. I have adopted the usual spelling.

---

[1] See *S.R.M.* VI. 185 ff.

In the same way I have rejected spellings such as *michi, nichil, ancxiatum,* and have also adopted the assimilated forms of prefixes in verbs such as *affirmare* for *adfirmare, illucescente* for *inlucescente.* Both types are found indifferently in the MSS. I have preserved all variants which have the slightest value, but I have only in specially interesting cases noted those which are merely differences in spelling, such as I have just described, or are undoubtedly nothing more than a slip of the pen on the part of the scribe.

The Life has been edited, either in part or entirely, by the following:

1. JOHN LELAND. *De Rebus Britannicis Collectanea.* Tom. III, pp. 169–170. (Edited Thomas Hearn, Oxon. 1715, vol. IV. pp. 109 ff.) He quotes about ten chapters, making use of a MS which is now apparently lost.

2. JAMES USSHER, Archbishop of Armagh, quotes various passages from C, in all about four chapters, in his book, *A Discourse of the Religion Anciently professed by the Irish and Brittish,* London 1631, pp. 102, 104–106, and also two chapters in his work called *Britannicarum Ecclesiarum Antiquitates,* Dublin, 1639, pp. 78, 922, 931.

3. JEAN MABILLON. *Acta Sanctorum Ordinis S. Benedicti,* saec. IV. pt I. Paris, 1677, pp. 676–722. He was the first to publish the whole Life. It was produced from the copy of C made by Thomas Gale and now preserved in the Bibliothèque Nationale, Paris (see above). Later on the parts missing in C were supplied from the Codex Sarensis (really F, see above) and some variant readings were added, saec. IV. pt 2, pp. 550–553, *a.* 1680.

4. THOMAS GALE. *Historiae Britannicae, Saxonicae, Anglo-Danicae Scriptores XV.* Oxon. 1691. Pp. 51–90. This was from C but he declared in the preface that it was "ad codicem MS Sarisburiensem emaculatam et auctam." Actually it scarcely differs from the text published by Mabillon.

5. J. A. GILES. *Original Lives of Anglo-Saxons.* Published for the Caxton Society, London, 1854. Pp. 198–277. A reprint of Gale's text.

6. JAMES RAINE. *The Priory of Hexham.* Vol. I. (Surt. Soc. vol. XLIV.) Durham, 1864. Appendix, pp. iv, v. The chapters referring to the building of Hexham. From C.

7. N. E. S. A. HAMILTON. *Willelmi Malmesbiriensis. De Gestis pontificum Anglorum libri quinque* (Rolls Series, vol. LII.) London, 1870. Pp. 222–226. Four chapters from C.

8. A. W. HADDAN and W. STUBBS. *Councils and Ecclesiastical Documents relating to Great Britain and Ireland.* Vol. III. Oxon. 1871. Edits those parts concerned with ecclesiastical law. C and F collated.

9. JAMES RAINE. *Historians of the Church of York.* Vol. I. (Rolls Series, vol. LXXI.) London, 1879. Pp. 1–103. The full text of the Life. Based on F but collated with C; a very inaccurate piece of work. The critical notes on the text are amazingly inadequate.

10. J. T. FOWLER. *Memorials of the Church of St. Peter and St. Wilfrid, Ripon.* Vol. I. (Surt. Soc. vol. LXXIV.) Durham, 1882. Pp. 4–5, 7–11, 14–19, 21–26. Edits the parts dealing with the church at Ripon, based on Raine's text.

11. WALTER DE GRAY BIRCH. *Cartularium Saxonicum.* Vol. I. London, 1885. Pp. 72–73, 103, 159–161. Wilfrid's petition and the decrees of Pope John and Archbishop Theodore. From C.

12. W. LEVISON. *Monumenta Germaniae Historica. Scriptores Rerum Merovingicarum.* Vol. VI. Hanover and Leipzig, 1913. Pp. 163–263. Contains the whole Life with an accurate text based on a careful collation of C and F. It also has a valuable critical apparatus, notes, and introduction.

LIST OF ABBREVIATIONS

A.E.E.	G. Baldwin Brown. *Arts in Early England.* London, 1903–25.
A.S.C.	Earle and Plummer. *Two Anglo-Saxon Chronicles Parallel.* Oxon. 1892–99.
Bede, *H.A.*	Bede. *Historia Abbatum.* See *H.E.* below.
Bright, *E.E.C.H.*	W. Bright. *Early Chapters in English Church History.* 3rd ed. Oxon. 1897.
Cath. Enc.	*Catholic Encyclopædia.* New York, 1907–14.
Chad. *O.E.N.*	H. M. Chadwick. *Origin of English Nation.* Cambridge, 1907.
D.C.B.	Smith and Wace. *Dictionary of Christian Biography.* London, 1877–87.
D.N.B.	*Dictionary of National Biography.* London, 1885–1908.
Ducange.	Ducange. *Glossarium mediae et infimæ Latinitatis.* Niort, 1883–87.
E.E.T.S.	Early English Text Society. London, 1864 etc.
E.H.R.	*English Historical Review.* London, 1886 etc.
En. Brit.	*Encyclopædia Britannica.* Cambridge, 1911.
E.R.E.	J. Hastings. *Encyclopædia of Religion and Ethics.* Edinburgh, 1908–21.
H.E.	Bede. *Historia Ecclesiastica Gentis Anglorum.* Ed. Plummer. Oxon. 1896.
Mab. *AA.SS.O.S.B.*	Mabillon. *Acta Sanctorum Ordinis Sancti Benedicti.* Saec. IV. Pts i and ii. Paris, 1677.
Migne.	*Patrologiae Cursus Completus.* Latin series. Paris, 1844–64. Greek series. Paris, 1857–1912.
Raine, *H.Y.*	*Historians of the Church of York and its Archbishops.* Edited by James Raine. Rolls Series, vol. LXXI (vol. I). 1879.
S.R.M.	*Scriptores Rerum Merovingicarum.* Vol. VI. (1913.) Ed. Dr W. Levison. Hanover and Leipzig.
Surt. Soc.	Publications of the Surtees Society. Durham, 1835 etc.
Vit. Anon. Cuthb.	*Anonymous Life of St Cuthbert. Bedae Opera Historica Minora.* Ed. J. Stevenson. E.H.S. 1841.
Vit. Cuth.	Bede's *Prose Life of St Cuthbert. Bedae Opera Historica Minora.* Ed. J. Stevenson. E.H.S. 1841.

THE
LIFE OF
BISHOP WILFRID

[PRAEFATIO]

IN nomine domini nostri Christi Iesu. Incipit de humili excusatione Stephani presbiteri scribentis de vita sancti Wilfrithi Deo digni episcopi[1].

Praeceptorum vestrorum magnitudine, O venerabiles domini Acca episcopus et Tatbrehtus[2] abbas, *totiusque*[3] *familiae* arbitrio[4] superatus, *utinam ut tam effectu parere valeam quam voto. Est enim et hoc opus arduum et meae intelligentiae* et eloquentiae *facultas exigua; quae tamen, etsi ministerium*[5] *minime expleret iniunctum, certe debitum oboedientiae exsolvit obsequium. Maximum enim indicium erga vos meae reverentiae est imperiis vestris*[6] *amplius me impendere voluisse quam possim. Quod si dignum aliquid vestrae electioni confecero*[7]*, id erit profecto divini muneris, quia nec dubitatur ipsorum fide perficiendum quorum est adhortatione susceptum. Quisnam erit qui*[8] *non intellegat vestris orationibus praesumptum esse, quod etiam per me creditis implendum*[9]*? Etenim ingens mihi*[10] *lucrum est atque utilitas hoc ipsum, quod* beatae memoriae Wilfrithi[11] episcopi *recordor. Est siquidem perfecta via ad virtutem illum scire, quis fuerit. Ideo, ut breviter dicam, omnia quae de eo sermo referentium*[12] *iactavit, credite et minima vos estimate de maximis audisse, quia non ambigo nec eos potuisse omnia cognoscere. Obsecro itaque eos qui lecturi sunt, ut fidem dictis adhibeant**, relinquentes antiqui hostis millenos invidiae stimulos et recolentes, quod eloquentia pertonabat. Semper enim in propatulo fortitudo emulos habet: *feriuntque summos fulgora montes.*

Neque enim me quicquam audaci temeritate, *nisi quod compertum et probatum a fidelibus sit, scripsisse arbitrentur; alioquin tacere quam falsa dicere maluissem*†. Coeptum orationibus vestris nos iter carpamus.

[1] *Preface from* F. C *has only* De humili excussatione scribentis *and in addition in a later hand (possibly that of Sir R. Cotton)* per Heddium Stephanum Monachum Cantuar. An° 720   [2] Tatberchtus C   [3] et totius C   [4] ambitu C   [5] misterium F   [6] *omit* F   [7] conficero C *and* F   [8] Quis namque C   [9] inplendum C *see Introduction*   [10] michi C *see Introduction*   [11] Wilfridi *and so throughout* C (*except that occasionally* V *is interchanged for* W)   [12] reverentium F

* V. Cudbercti prol.   † V. Cudbercti prol.

PREFACE

IN the name of our Lord Christ Jesus. Here begins the humble apology of Stephen the priest, who writes concerning the life of St Wilfrid, the bishop worthy before God.

Constrained as I am by the weight of your commands, my venerable masters, Bishop Acca, and Abbot Tatberht, and by the urgency of the whole community, I would that the result might be as good as my intentions. For this task is great and my powers of understanding and eloquence are small; but, although these faculties are ill able to perform the task you have allotted me, at any rate they will have fulfilled the debt of obedience I owe you. For what greater proof could there be of my respect for you, than that it is my wish to devote myself to your commands, even though they exceed my powers? So, if I produce anything which shall justify your choice, it will assuredly be by the help of the divine gift; because there is no doubt that it will be brought to a successful close, thanks to the faith of those at whose request it was taken up. Who will fail to understand that the task undertaken at your request was one which you believe even me to be capable of carrying through?

In fact, this very task of preserving the blessed memory of Bishop Wilfrid is of great gain and value to myself. Indeed it is in itself a ready path to virtue to know what he was. So, to be brief, even though you believe all the claims that popular report has made for him—and you may well do so—yet be sure that even then you have heard very little about matters that are very great, for I am certain that no one could know them all. So I beseech my readers to believe my report, neglecting the thousand envious pricks of the ancient foe and reflecting on what has been eloquently proclaimed. For boldness ever has its rivals in public places—"the lightnings strike the tops of the mountains." Nor let it be thought that I have written rashly anything which has not been received on good authority and tested by trustworthy men. Else I would rather hold my peace than state what is false. And now let us start upon the journey which we have undertaken at your request.

CHAPTER I

Explicit praephatio Stephani presbiteri. Incipit de nativitate et prodigio sancti Wilfrithi episcopi[1]

Igitur[2] beati Wilfrithi pontificis, Deo adiuvante et sanctis meritis eius, vitam scribere exordiar, quem Dominus secundum egregii doctoris verba[3] et[4] *praescivit et praedestinavit et vocavit, iustificavit et glorificavit**. De utero enim matris suae valde religiosae ita eum sanctificatum a Deo prodigium demonstravit, sicut Hieremias audivit a Domino dicente: *Priusquam te formarem in utero, novi te; et antequam exires de vulva sanctificavi te; prophetamque in gentibus posui te*†. Nam cum mater eius dolore parturientis fatigata in domo sua iaceret et mulieres circa se mansissent, viderunt viri foris stantes domum illam extimplo quasi ardentem et flammam usque ad caelum elevatam; omnes undique concito cursu pavidi[5] advenerunt, flammam minuere aquis hominesque de incendio eripere cupientes. Quibus mulieres de domo obviarunt dicentes: "Sustinete, stabiliter expectantes; ecce modo infans huic natus est mundo." Illi vero stupefacti, videntes magnalia Dei, sicut Moyses in rubo vidit flammam sonantem nihilque consumentem, agnoverunt. Nos autem fratres, frequenter legimus spiritum sanctum in igne apparuisse, quia *Deus ignis est, consumens*‡ peccatores et illuminans iustos; quod lumen non sub modio sed super[6] candelabrum Dominus poni iussit. Et hoc per beatum pontificem nostrum[7] omnibus paene Brittanniae ecclesiis palam effulsit, sicut praesagia[8] futurorum prodiderunt et rei eventus postmodum probavit.

CHAPTER II

Explicit primum miraculum. Incipit[9] *de eo, quod in pueritia Deum elegerit*

Cum ergo puerilis aetatis esset, parentibus oboediens, omnibus carus, pulcher aspectu, bonae indolis, mitis, modestus, stabilis, nihil inane more puerorum cupiens[10], sed secundum apostolum Iacobum

---

[1] De nativitate sancti Wilfridi et prodigio C   [2] *The capital letter is missing here in* F, *also at the beginning of over twenty other chapters*   [3] sententiam C
[4] *omit* C   [5] pavide C   [6] supra F   [7] Wilfridum episcopum *for* po. no. C
[8] presagi C   [9] Expl.... Incipit *omit* C   [10] cupiens *after* inane C

* Rom. 8. 29, 30.   † Jerem. 1. 5.   ‡ Heb. 12. 29.

CHAPTER I

End of the preface of Stephen the priest: of the birth
of Saint Wilfrid the bishop and of a portent. [634 A.D.]

So, with the help of God, and by the merits of the Saint himself,
I will begin the life of the holy Bishop Wilfrid, whom the Lord, in
the words of the most excellent teacher, "foreknew and predesti-
nated, called, justified and glorified." For even from the womb of his
most pious mother, a sign from God proved him to be sanctified,
even as Jeremiah heard the Lord's word saying, "Before I formed
thee in the belly I knew thee: and before thou camest forth out of
the womb I sanctified thee, and I ordained thee a prophet unto the
nations." For while his mother, worn out by the pain of her travail,
was lying in her house with the women about her, some men who
were standing outside suddenly saw the house apparently on fire,
the flames rising to the heavens. They all came running from every
direction in excitement and terror, eager to quench the flames with
water and to rescue the inhabitants from the fire. But the women of
the house met them and said, "Stand back and wait, for an infant
has just been born into this world." When they saw this they were
amazed and recognized the mighty works of God, even as Moses saw
the flame which was roaring in the bush and yet consuming nothing.
Now, brethren, we frequently read that the Holy Spirit has appeared
in the form of fire, for God is a fire consuming sinners and enlighten-
ing the righteous. This light the Lord has commanded to be set, not
under a bushel, but on a candlestick, and through our blessed bishop
it has shone openly upon almost all the churches of Britain, even as
the omens foretold: and events afterwards gave proof of them.

CHAPTER II

End of the first miracle: How he chose God
in his boyhood. [648]

During his boyhood he was obedient to his parents and beloved of
all men, fair in appearance, of good parts, gentle, modest and firm,
with none of the vain desires that are customary in boyhood; but
"swift to hear, slow to speak," as the Apostle James says: he always

*velox ad audiendum, tardus ad loquendum**, omnibus in domum patris
sui venientibus humiliter aut regalibus sociis aut servis eorum semper
edocte ministravit ut[1] secundum prophetam *omnes Dei docibiles
essent*[2]†. Postremo tamen quarto decimo anno in corde suo cogitabat
paterna rura deserere, iura[3] celestia quaerere. Privigna enim sibi,
matre sua mortua, molesta et immitis[4] erat; tamen arma et equos
vestimentaque sibi et pueris[5] eius adeptus est, in quibus ante[6]
regalibus conspectibus[7] apte stare posset. Cumque benedixisset eum
pater eius, sicut Isaac Iacob et Iacob filios suos, ut crescerent in multa
milia populorum, pergens itinere suo, usquedum inveniret reginam[8]
Oswiu, nomine Eanfled, et per nobiles viros, quibus ante in domo
patris sui ministrabat[9], laudatus praesentatusque est reginae. Statim,
Deo adiuvante, *invenit gratiam in conspectu illius*‡. Erat enim decorus
aspectu et acutissimi ingenii, et concessit[10] ei quod petierat, ut sub
illius[11] consilio et munimine Deo serviret. Tunc quidam nobilis eo
tempore ex sodalibus regis, valde sibi amabilis et fidelis, nomine
Cudda, proponens[12] secularia desideria contempnere propter infirmitatem paralisin, coenobialemque vitam sub regulari disciplina in
Lindisfarne insula[13] arripere maluit; cui regina supradicta puerum
nuper ad se venientem diligenter commendavit, ut sibi ministraret et
Deo serviret. Iam enim ille secundum praeceptum reginae, accepta
diligenti ministratione, domino suo et omnibus senioribus in mona-
sterio quasi filius et coetaneis quasi frater statim in amore factus est,
pro eo quod omnem regularem vitam cum intimo cordis amore in
humilitate et obedientia adimplere nitebatur et omnem psalmorum
seriem memoraliter[14] et aliquantos libros didicit. Adhuc enim laicus
capite, corde vero a vitiis circumcisus, Deo serviebat et partem cum
Samuele[15] Heli sacerdoti ministrante benedictionis accipere meruit.

---

[1] *omit* F   [2] sunt F   [3] dona C   [4] inmittis F   [5] pueros F   [6] *omit* C
[7] *omit* F   [8] (*insert* regis C) regina F   [9] *insert* que C   [10] concedit C
[11] suo C   [12] pro nomen C   [13] Lindisfarna (*omit* insula) C
[14] memorialiter C   [15] Samuhele C

* James 1. 19.   † John 6. 45.   ‡ Esth. 2. 9.

ministered skilfully and humbly to all who came to his father's house, whether they were the king's companions or their slaves, even as the prophet says, "all shall be taught by the Lord." At last, however, when fourteen years of age, he meditated in his heart leaving his father's fields to seek the Kingdom of Heaven. For his step-mother (his own mother being dead) was harsh and cruel; but he obtained arms and horses and garments for himself and his servants in which he could fitly stand before the royal presence. So, when his father had blessed him as Isaac did Jacob, and Jacob his sons, in order that their seed might grow into many thousands of peoples, he made his way to Oswiu's queen, Eanfled by name, and, being recommended by nobles whom he had once ministered to in his father's house, he was presented to her. At once, by the help of God, he found grace in her sight. For he was comely in appearance and exceedingly sharp of wit; so that his request, that he might be allowed to serve God under her counsel and protection, was granted.

At that time there was a certain nobleman among the king's companions named Cudda, one of his truest friends, who resolved, owing to a paralytic infirmity, to despise worldly ambitions, preferring to take to the monastic life with its regular discipline, on the island of Lindisfarne. So this same queen earnestly commended the boy who had just come to her, to Cudda, to minister to him and to serve God. The boy fulfilled the task appointed by the queen with such earnest solicitude that his master and all the older monks loved him like a son and his equals like a brother, because with a loving heart he sought to live the full monastic life in all humility and obedience. He learned the whole Psalter by heart as well as several books. So, although his head was still untonsured, yet he served God in purity and circumcision of heart. He therefore deserved to receive a share of the blessing which Samuel received when he ministered to Eli the priest.

CHAPTER III

De eo, quod amaverit sancti Petri apostolorum principis[1] limina videre

Deinde post circulum annorum, suggerente spiritu sancto, apellare et videre sedem apostoli Petri et apostolorum principis, adhuc inattritam viam genti nostrae temptare in cor adolescentis[2] supradicti ascendit et[3] ab ea omnem nodum maculae solvendum sibi credens et beatitudinem benedictionis accipiendam. Hunc talem sensum domino suo enotuit; qui statim, ut erat sapiens, suggestum a Deo esse cognoscens, consensum dedit filio carissimo omnis boni caput accipere. Tunc autem cum consilio patris sui Eanflaed regina[4] ad suum proprium propinquum Erconberhtum regem Cantuariorum per nuntios diligenter commendatum[5] honorifice emisit[6], ut tamdiu esset cum eo, usque dum fideles socios itineris ad apostolicam sedem tendentes inveniret. Rex vero venientem servum Dei ad se videns, iuxta consuetudinem suam in orationibus et ieiuniis, in lectione et vigiliis semper occupatum, mirifice diligebat. Psalmos namque, quos prius secundum Hieronymi emendationem legerat, more Romanorum iuxta quintam editionem memoraliter transmetuit[7]. Anni vertente quoque die, rex secundum petitionem reginae languenti taedio ducem nobilem et admirabilis ingenii quendam nomine Biscop Baducing inveniens ad sedem apostolicam properantem, ut in suo comitatu esset, adquisivit. Pergens[8] igitur servus Dei cum benedictione parentum suorum ad peregrinationem sicut Iacob, benedictio[9] quae ei[10] demum in bonum contigit. Omnibus affabilis, mente sagax[11], corpore strenuus, pedibus velox, habilis[12] ad omne opus bonum, tristia ora numquam contraxit[13]; alacer et gaudens navigio secunde[14] Lugdunam[15] Galliae civitatem pervenit; ibique cum suis sociis aliquod spatium mansit, discedente ab eo austerae mentis duce, sicut a Paulo Barnabas propter Iohannem recessit, qui cognominabatur Marcus.

---

[1] apostoli C   [2] adholescentis F   [3] omit C   [4] ac Eonfledae regine C   [5] emendatum F   [6] commendatus et honorifice emissus est C   [7] memorialiter transmutavit C   [8] Perrexit C   [9] omit C   [10] eis peregrinantibus C   [11] sagaci F   [12] stabilis F   [13] omit F   [14] glossed id est prospere in C   [15] Lugduno C

CHAPTER III

How he longed to see the abode of St Peter the chief of the Apostles. [652?]

After the lapse of a few years, it came into the heart of this same young man, by the promptings of the Holy Spirit, to pay a visit to the see of the Apostle Peter, the chief of the Apostles, and to attempt a road hitherto untrodden by any of our race. By so doing he believed that he would cleanse himself from every blot and stain and receive the joy of the divine blessing. When he made this known to his master, the latter, who was a wise man, recognized that the plan was of God and gave his consent that his dear son should thus attain to the source of all good. Thereupon Queen Eanfled, on the advice of his father, sent him forth with all honour to her own kinsman, Erconberht, King of Kent, giving him the warmest commendations through her messengers, to the end that he might stay there until he found trustworthy fellow-travellers bound for the Apostolic See. When the king saw the servant of God approach, finding him continually occupied, as was his wont, in prayers and fastings, in reading and vigils, he loved him exceedingly. Now the Psalms which he had first of all read in Jerome's revision he committed to memory from the fifth edition, after the Roman use. After a year of weary waiting from day to day, the king, in accordance with the queen's request, found him a guide, a man of high rank and of remarkable understanding named Biscop Baducing, who was bound for the Apostolic See, and prevailed upon him to take the youth in his company. So the servant of God set out on his journey with the blessing of his kinsfolk, like Jacob; and that blessing did not fail him. He was friendly to all, wise of mind, strong in body, and swift of foot, ready for every good work, his face never clouded with sorrow. Glad of heart and rejoicing in his journey, he came at last in safety to Lyons, a city of Gaul; there he remained with his companions for a certain time, his stern guide having left him, just as Barnabas separated from Paul on account of John whose surname was Mark.

CHAPTER IV

De eo, quod Dalfinus episcopus sanctum Wilfrithum benigne acceperat

Benedictus Deus qui servos suos defendit et protegit et per bonorum auxilia adiuvabit! Nam in[1] supradicta civitate sanctae memoriae Dalfinus archiepiscopus erat, qui super servum Dei mitissimum Wilfrithum posuit oculos suos in bonum et benigne cum sociis[2] hospitio susceperat, videns in facie serena, quod benedictam mentem[3] gerebat. Ideoque omnia illis necessaria, quasi proprii sui essent, abundare[4] fecit et sibi illum in adoptivum filium eligere voluit dicens ad eum: "Si manseris mecum fiducialiter, dabo tibi bonam partem Galliarum ad regendam in saeculum virginemque filiam fratris mei[5] in uxorem et te ipsum adoptivum filium habebo[6] et tu me patrem, in omnibus fideliter adiuvantem." Et respondens sanctus Wilfrithus servus Dei sapienter, sicut erat edoctus, dixit: "Sunt vota mea Domino, quae reddam, relinquens ut Abraham[7] cognationem et domum patris mei, ut visitem sedem apostolicam et ecclesiasticae disciplinae regulas didicerim in augmentum gentis nostrae ad serviendum Deo, desiderans a Deo accipere[8] quod diligentibus se promisit, dicens: *Qui reliquerit patrem aut matrem* et reliqua, *centuplum accipiet et vitam aeternam possidebit**. Iam enim vita comite, Deo adiuvante, si vixero, iterum revertens videbo faciem tuam." Haec et alia audiens sanctus episcopus, veraciter servum Dei esse et a Spiritu sancto imbutum intellexit; praeparans sibi necessaria, in pace Christi secundum voluntatem eius cum ducibus et opibus[9] ad sedem apostolicam emisit.

CHAPTER V

De eo, quod ad sanctum Petrum apostolum benedicte pervenit

Servus igitur Dei Wilfrithus ad sedem olim optatam apostoli Petri et principis apostolorum gaudens et gratulans cum sociis suis prospere pervenit. Sicut doctor gentium excellentissimus pergens Hiero-

---

[1] *omit* F   [2] *insert* suis C   [3] benedicta mente F   [4] habundare C
[5] *after* uxorem *in* F   [6] habeo C   [7] Habraham F   [8] recipere C
[9] operibus F

* Matth. 19. 29.

CHAPTER IV

How Bishop Dalfinus received Saint Wilfrid kindly. [653]

Blessed be God who defends and protects His servants and is also wont to give help through the services of good men! Now in this same city was Archbishop Dalfinus of saintly memory, who was favourably impressed with Wilfrid the gentle servant of God, and received him and his companions with generous hospitality, seeing his saintly mind imaged in his peaceful countenance. For this reason he provided them bountifully with all the necessities of life as if they were his own kinsmen; he even wished to adopt Wilfrid as his own son. "If you will stay with me in all confidence," he said, "I will give you a good part of Gaul over which you shall be permanent governor, and you shall have for your wife a maiden who is my niece; I will adopt you as my son and you shall have me as a father to help you faithfully in all your affairs." But Saint Wilfrid the servant of God was wise in his reply, and answered as he had been taught, "My vows have been rendered to the Lord and I will fulfil them, leaving my kin and my father's house as Abraham did, to visit the Apostolic See, and to learn the rules of ecclesiastical discipline, so that our nation may grow in the service of God. My desire is to receive from God the reward He has promised to those who love Him, saying, 'Everyone that hath forsaken father or mother and so forth shall receive a hundredfold and shall inherit everlasting life.' But now if life abides with me, and God helps me, if I live, I say, I will return and see your face again."

When the holy bishop heard him say such things as these, he realized that Wilfrid was a true servant of God and filled with the Holy Spirit. So, when the bishop had provided him with what he required, he sent him forth to the Apostolic See according to his wish, in the peace of Christ, with guides and supplies for the journey.

CHAPTER V

How he prosperously reached the see of St Peter the Apostle. [654]

So, with joy and thankfulness, Wilfrid, the servant of God, and his companions safely reached their long-desired goal, the see of Peter the Apostle and the chief of the Apostles. Even as the most

solimam ad discipulos Domini *ne forte in vacuum curreret aut*[1]
cucurrisset★; ita et iste humillimus gentis nostrae igniculus, excitante
Deo *a finibus terrae audire sapientiam*† praesulum mundi Romam
venit et in oratorio sancto Andreae apostolo dedicato ante altare,
supra cuius summitatem IIII euangelia posita erant, humiliter
genuflectens, adiuravit in nomine Domini Dei apostolum[2], pro quo
passus est, ut pro sua intercessione Dominus ei legendi ingenium et
docendi in gentibus eloquentiam euangeliorum concedisset. Et sic
factum est, ut multorum testimonio comprobatur. Nam per multos
menses loca sanctorum omni die ad orationem circumiens, invenit
doctorem, sibi amicum per Deum et apostolum fidelem factum,
nomine Bonifacium archidiaconem[3] unum ex consiliariis sapientissimum; a quo quattuor euangelia Christi perfecte didicit et paschalem
rationem, quam scismatici Brittanniae et Hiberniae non cognoverunt
et alias multas ecclesiasticae disciplinae regulas Bonifacius archi-
diaconus quasi proprio[4] filio suo diligenter dictavit[5]. Nam postremo
praesentavit eum papae beatae memoriae et omnem causam itineris
adolescentuli servi Dei mirabiliter ostendit; qui ponens manum suam
benedictam super caput eius, cum oratione benedixit eum. Ille vero
servus Dei cum reliquiarum sanctarum quas illic invenit auxilio in
pace Christi profecturus, iterum ad patrem suum archiepiscopum
Lugdunae[6] Galliae civitatis commode pervenit.

CHAPTER VI

De eo, quod a Dalfino episcopo tonsurae Petri
apostoli formam accepit[7] et de martirio eiusdem Dalfini

Invento igitur Dalfino archiepiscopo sospite et sano, gratulabundus
filius[8] ad patrem ingreditur et per ordinem servus Dei Wilfrithus
beatitudinem ei itineris sui omnem narravit. Et episcopus gratias
agebat Deo, quod filium suum incolumem pergentem et iterum
revertentem[9] Dominus custodivit. Nam et[10] per tres annos simul cum
eo mansit et a doctoribus valde eruditis multa didicit; et[11] amor magis

---

[1] *omit* cur. aut C   [2] apostolorum F   [3] Bonifatium archidiaconum C
[4] propria F   [5] *insert* Et F   [6] Lugduno C   [7] acceperit F. *Rest of*
sentence omitted C   [8] *omit* C   [9] reverentem F   [10] *omit* C   [11] *omit* F

★ Cf. Gal. 2. 1, 2.   † Matth. 12. 42.

excellent teacher of the Gentiles wrote to the disciples of the Lord when he was making his way to Jerusalem, "lest by any means I should run or had run in vain"; so this lowly spark of fire, kindled in our race, was fanned to flame by God and came to Rome "from the ends of the earth to hear the wisdom" of the rulers of the world.

In the oratory dedicated to St Andrew the Apostle, he humbly knelt before the altar above which the four gospels had been placed, and besought the Apostle, in the name of the Lord God for whom he suffered, that the Lord, by his intercession, would grant him a ready mind both to read and to teach the words of the Gospels among the nations. And thus it came to pass as many bear witness. For, during the course of his daily visits to the shrines of the saints to pray, a custom which he observed for many months, he met a teacher whom God and the Apostle made his faithful friend. This was Boniface the archdeacon, one of the wisest of the counsellors, from whom he learned the four Gospels of Christ perfectly and the Easter rule, of which the British and Irish schismatics were ignorant, and many other rules of ecclesiastical discipline. These things Boniface the archdeacon taught him diligently as though he were his own son. Finally he presented him to the Pope of blessed memory and explained to him with singular clearness the whole reason for the journey of the young servant of God. The Pope placed his blessed hand on Wilfrid's head, prayed over him, and gave him his blessing. So the servant of God, with the aid of the holy relics which he found there, setting out in the peace of Christ, returned safely to his father, the Archbishop of Lyons (a city of Gaul).

CHAPTER VI

How he received from Bishop Dalfinus the Apostle Peter's form of tonsure, and how the same Dalfinus was martyred. [655–658]

So Wilfrid, the servant of God, finding the Archbishop Dalfinus safe and sound, went to offer his greetings as a son would do to a father and recounted to him in detail how his journey had been crowned with blessing. The bishop gave thanks to God because the Lord had preserved his son unharmed both as he set forth and as he returned again. Now for three years he remained with him, learning many things from the most learned teachers, and the love between

ac magis crescebat inter eos. Nam[1] servus Dei Wilfrithus desiderio concupiscens tonsurae Petri apostoli *formulam in modum coronae spineae caput Christi cingentis*★, a sancto Dalfino archiepiscopo libenter *suscepit*. Manus[2] sanctas super caput eius ponens, cogitabat in corde suo illum habere post se heredem, si sic Deus voluisset, aliquod autem[3] melius genti nostrae Deo providente. Nam illo tempore malivola regina nomine Baldhild[4] ecclesiam Dei persecuta est; sicut olim[5] pessima[6] regina Iezabel[7], quae prophetas Dei occidit, ita ista, exceptis sacerdotibus ac diaconibus, novem episcopos occidere iussit, ex quibus unus est iste Dalfinus episcopus, quem duces malignissime ad se venire iusserunt. Ille vero intrepida mente, sciens quid esset sibi futurum, ad agonis locum pervenit; simulque cum eo sanctus Wilfrithus servus Dei, episcopo tamen prohibente[8], gaudens dixit: "Nil melius est nobis, quam pater et filius simul mori et esse cum Christo." Iam enim sanctus episcopus martyrio coronatus est. At vero cum sanctus Wilfrithus spoliatus et paratus ad palmam martyrii intrepidus staret, duces interrogaverunt, dicentes: "Quis est iste iuvenis formosus, qui se praeparat ad mortem?" Dictumque est illis: "Transmarinus de Anglorum gente ex Britannia[9]." Iterumque dixerunt: "Parcite illi et nolite tangere eum." Ecce! iam sanctus Wilfrithus noster nunc[10] confessor factus est, sicut Iohannes apostolus et euangelista in dolio oleo fervente illaesus sedebat et venenum mortiferum bibebat et nihil ei nocuit. De quo et Iacobo Apostolo fratre eius Iesus dixit: "*Vos potestis calicem bibere, quem ego bibiturus sum?*"† et cetera.

CHAPTER VII

De eo, quod invitatus est ab Alhfritho[11] rege[12]

Tunc eo tempore sanctus Wilfrithus confessor, patre suo episcopo honorifice sepulto, cum multiplici benedictione et reliquiarum sanctarum auxilio navem ascendens, flante vento secundum desiderium nautarum, ad regionem suam prospere in portum salutis pervenerunt. Audiens autem Alchfrithus[13], qui cum Oswiu[14] patre suo regnabat, talem servum Dei cum suis sociis de apostolica sede

[1] Etenim C   [2] *insert* suas C   [3] aliquid enim C   [4] Brunechild C
[5] *omit* C   [6] impiissima C   [7] Gezabel F   [8] *insert* qui C   [9] Brittannia C
[10] *omit* C   [11] Aluchfrido C   [12] *omit* rege C   [13] Ealhfridus C   [14] Osuiu C

★ V. Cudbercti c. 12.   † Matth. 20. 22.

them grew greater and greater. Wilfrid, the servant of God, in accordance with his own desire, gladly received from the holy Archbishop Dalfinus the form of tonsure of the Apostle Peter in the shape of the crown of thorns which encircled the head of Christ. As he placed his holy hands upon Wilfrid's head he purposed in his heart to make the young man his heir if God so willed. But God had something better in view for our race. For at that time there was an evil-hearted queen named Baldhild who persecuted the church of God. Even as of old the wicked Queen Jezebel slew the prophets of God, so she, though sparing the priests and deacons, gave command to slay nine bishops, one of whom was this Bishop Dalfinus, whom the dukes with evil intent summoned to their presence. But he made his way with undaunted heart to the place of trial, knowing what lay before him. St Wilfrid the servant of God went with him, and though the bishop wished to prevent him, joyfully replied, "Nothing could be better for us than that father and son should die together and be with Christ." So the holy bishop won a martyr's crown; but when St Wilfrid, despoiled and ready for the prize of martyrdom, was standing by fearlessly, the dukes asked, "Who is that handsome young man who is preparing for death?" "A foreigner of the English race from Britain" they were told. Thereupon they said, "Spare him and do not touch him." So now our St Wilfrid has become a confessor like John the Apostle and Evangelist, who sat uninjured in a cauldron of boiling oil and drank deadly poison unharmed; it was of St John and his brother the Apostle James, that Jesus asked the question, "Can you drink the cup that I am about to drink?" and so forth.

CHAPTER VII

How he was welcomed by King Alhfrith. [658?]

At that time, St Wilfrid the confessor, after his father the bishop had been buried with due honour, embarked on a vessel with many blessings and with the aid of the holy relics, and when the wind blew as the sailors wished, they made a prosperous voyage towards their own land, to a harbour of safety. When Alhfrith, who was reigning with his father Oswiu, heard that so worthy a servant of God had come from the Apostolic See with his companions, preaching the

venisse et verum pascha praedicantem et sancti Petri apostoli
ecclesiae disciplinam multiplicem didicisse, quam maxime rex
diligebat, suadente sibi fideli amico Coenowalcho[1] Occidentalium
Saxonum rege; et ideo ad se venire iussit. Veniens ergo sanctus
Wilfrithus ad regem invitantem se[2], pacifice salutavit eum, dicens:
"Iesus Christus, filius Dei, praecepit discipulis suis et principi eorum
Petro apostolo: *Domum in quamcumque intraveritis, dicite: Pax huic
domui**. Huius pacis fundamenta primum inter corpus et animam
in nobis ponere debemus, ut doctor gentium praedicavit, dicens:
Pax Christi exultet[3] *in cordibus vestris*†. Deinde inter nos et proximos
pacem habere Iesus Christus praecepit, dicens: *Habete sal in vobis
et pacem habete inter vos*‡." Postquam autem finivit[4] praedicationis
verba, humiliter rex prosternens se ante pedes suscepit verba[5] servi
Dei electi et petivit ab eo benedictionem; videbatur enim ei, quasi
angelus Dei loqueretur. Deinde benedixit eum, et mutuo loqui
coeperunt. Interrogavit[6] eum prudenter, sicut erat sapiens, de
disciplina diversa Romanae ecclesiae et[7] institutionis[8]. Ille vero, ut
erat edoctus, sermone perspicuo scienter in omnibus respondit.
Postea rex adiuravit eum per Dominum et per sanctum Petrum
apostolum, ut esset cum eo, ut[9] sibi et omni populo, organo spiritali
de[10] se canente, verbum Dei praedicaret. Ille vero intellegens amorem
regis in eum, consensit ei esse cum eo. Tunc autem[11] mirifice anima
utriusque in alterum conglutinata est, sicut animam David et
Ionothae inter[12] alterutrum compaginatam legimus.

CHAPTER VIII

De eo, quod dedit ei Alhfrithus[13] *coenobium Inhripis*[14]

Deinde postquam de die in diem inter eos augebatur amor[15],
Alchfrithus[16] dedit primum sancto Wilfritho confessori terram decem[17]
tributariorum Aetstanforda et post paululum coenobium Inhrypis[18]
cum terra xxx mansionum pro animae suae remedio concessit ei,
et abbas ordinatus est. Iam autem[19], sicut ei saeculi huius lata ianua
per Dominum aperiebatur et per sanctum Petrum apostolum, ita large

[1] Coenualcho C   [2] *insert* et F   [3] exultat C   [4] finit C   [5] *omit* s.v. F
[6] interrogans C   [7] *omit* et C   [8] constitutionis C   [9] et C   [10] *omit* de C
[11] enim C   [12] in C   [13] Aluchfridus C   [14] Inhrypis C   [15] amor aug. C
[16] Alhfridus C   [17] x C   [18] Inripis C   [19] enim C

* Matth. 10. 12.   † Col. 3. 15.   ‡ Mark 9. 49.

true Easter rule and thoroughly conversant with the manifold discipline of the Church of St Peter the Apostle which the king greatly loved, he accepted the advice of his faithful friend, Coenwalh, King of the West Saxons, and ordered Wilfrid to come into his presence. St Wilfrid accepted the king's invitation and gave him a greeting of peace, saying, "Jesus Christ, the Son of God, taught His disciples and their chief the Apostle Peter, saying, 'Into whatsoever house ye enter, first say "Peace be to this house."'" The foundations of this peace ought to be first of all laid within us, between body and soul, as the teacher of the Gentiles declared when he said, 'Let the peace of Christ rule in your hearts.' Then Jesus Christ taught that we must keep peace between ourselves and our neighbours, saying, 'Have salt in yourselves and have peace with one another.'" When he had finished the words of his address, the king humbly prostrated himself before the feet of the chosen servant of God and asked for his blessing, for it seemed to him as though an angel of God were speaking. Then Wilfrid blessed him and they began to converse. The wise king skilfully questioned him about the varied discipline of the Roman Church order. Wilfrid, being well informed, answered in all things clearly and with knowledge. Afterwards the king adjured him, by the Lord and the holy Apostle Peter, to stay with him and preach the word to himself and to all the nation, the music of the Spirit sounding through him. Wilfrid realized the king's affection for him and consented to remain. Then the soul of each was joined to the other in a wondrous way, even as we read that the soul of David was knit together with the soul of Jonathan.

CHAPTER VIII

How Alhfrith gave him the monastery at Ripon. [660?]

As love grew between them from day to day, Alhfrith first gave St Wilfrid the confessor an estate of ten hides at *Stanforda*, and shortly afterwards, for the good of his own soul, he granted him the monastery at Ripon together with thirty hides of land, and he was ordained abbot. And now, even as the door of this world was being opened wide by the Lord and the holy Apostle Peter, so ever more

crescebat ei porta aperta elemosinarum[1] pro Domino in pauperes, pupillos ac viduas omnique languore infirmitatis colligatos, ostendens perspicue, quid animo gerebat in paupertate. Ecce! iam fratres, videte et ammiramini, quam magnum bonum Deus regi concedit[2] qui *invenit bonam margaritam et statim sine mora comparavit eam**. Non solum autem Alchfrithus[3] rex sanctum Wilfrithum abbatem diligebat, sed omnis populus, nobiles et ignobiles, eum habebant quasi prophetam Dei, ut erat.

CHAPTER IX

De eo, quod ab Aegilberhto episcopo presbiter ordinatus est

In illis autem diebus veniens Aegelberchtus[4] episcopus transmarinus ad regem Oswiu et ad[5] Alchfrithum[6], filium eius, visitavit eos, indicavitque ei Alchfrithus[7] rex de sancto Wilfritho abbate ab apostolica sede veniente[8], sicut illi nuntiatum est ab his, qui eum[9] noverant, dicentes[10] virum[11] esse humilem et quietum, in ieiuniis et orationibus occupatum, benignum, sobrium, modestum, misericordem, plenum auctoritatis[12] gratiae Dei, pudicum, prudentem, non vinolentum, docibilem et bene docentem, sermone puro et aperto. "Ideoque rogo te ut imponas[13] super eum presbiterii gradum, et sit[14] mihi comes individuus." Episcopus autem respondit ei prophetico spiritu: "Talis utique debet[15] episcopus fieri," et eum secundum praeceptum regis Inhripis[16] presbiterum ordinavit. Sicut autem[17] David puer electus a Domino est et, per Samuelem[18] unctus, dona prophetiae accipere post multas temptationes[19] meruit; ita[20] sanctus Wilfrithus presbiter post multas benedictiones sanctorum Dei[21] tam multiplices donationes coram Deo et hominibus, quam enumerare nullus potest, Deo concedente et in angustiis suis[22] custodiente, accepit.

---

[1] elimoysinis C   [2] concessit C   [3] Alhfridus C   [4] Aegilbehrtus C
[5] *omit* C   [6] Alhfridum C   [7] Alhfrid C   [8] venienti C   [9] *insert* bene C
[10] dicens C   [11] verum F   [12] *insert* et C   [13] inpones F   [14] sic F
[15] decet F   [16] Inrypis C   [17] enim C   [18] Samuhelem C   [19] tribulationes C   [20] ita meruit et C   [21] *insert* et C   [22] *omit* C

* Cf. Matth. 13. 46.

widely opened the door for the giving of alms in the Lord's name to the poor, the orphan and widow, and those who were afflicted by any kind of infirmity; thus he clearly proved what his intention had been in the days of his poverty.

Behold, brethren, see and wonder at the great benefit God bestows upon the king, who "found a goodly pearl and straightway bought it." Not only did King Alhfrith love St Wilfrid the abbot, but all the people both high and low looked upon him as a prophet of God, as indeed he was.

CHAPTER IX

How he was ordained priest by Bishop Agilberht. [663 or 4]

In those days came Agilberht, a foreign bishop, on a visit to King Oswiu and to Alhfrith his son. King Alhfrith told him about St Wilfrid the abbot who had come from the Apostolic See and what was reported to himself by those who knew him, namely that he was a humble and peaceable man, given to fastings and prayers, kind, sober, discreet, compassionate, full of the power and grace of God, modest, prudent, not given to wine, teachable and able to teach, in conversation pure and frank. "So," said he, "I ask you to bestow upon him the order of priesthood and that he may be my inseparable companion." Then the bishop answered him in the spirit of prophecy, "Such a man ought surely to become a bishop," and in accordance with the king's commands he ordained him priest at Ripon. And thus as David was chosen of God while a boy and anointed by Samuel and, after many tribulations, was judged worthy to receive the gift of prophecy, so St Wilfrid the priest, after many blessings from the saints of God, received so many gifts in the presence of God and men that no one can enumerate them. For God who upheld him in the days of his poverty was the giver of them.

CHAPTER X

De conflictu sancti[1] Wilfrithi presbiteri contra Colmanum[2] episcopum de ratione paschae[3]

Quodam tempore in diebus Colmani Eboracae civitatis episcopi metropolitani, regnantibus Oswiu et Alchfritho[4] filio eius, abbates et presbiteri omnesque ecclesiasticae disciplinae gradus simul in unum convenientes[5] in coenobio, quod Streuneshalgh[6] dicitur, praesente sanctimoniale matre piissima Hilde, praesentibus quoque regibus et duobus Colmano et Aegilberhto[7] episcopis, de paschali ratione conquirebant, quid esset rectissimum, utrum more Britonum[8] et Scottorum omnisque aquilonalis partis a XIIII luna, dominica die veniente, [usque ad XXII pascha agendum, an melius sit ratione sedis apostolicae a XV luna][9] usque in[10] XXI paschalem diem[11] dominicam celebrandam. Tempus datum est Colmano episcopo primum, ut dignum erat, audientibus cunctis, reddere rationem. Ille autem intrepida mente respondens dixit: "Patres nostri et antecessores eorum, manifeste spiritu sancto inspirati, ut erat Collumcillae[12], XIIII luna die dominica pascha celebrandum sanxerunt, exemplum tenentes Iohannis apostoli et evangelistae, *qui supra pectus Domini in coena recubuit**[*] et amator Domini dicebatur; ille XIIII luna pascha celebravit, et nos, sicut discipuli eius Policarpus et alii, ea fiducia celebramus; nec hoc audemus pro patribus nostris neque volumus mutare. Nostrae partis detuli sententiam[13], vos vestram dicite." Imperatum est ab Aegilberchto[14] episcopo transmarino et Agathone[15] presbitero suo[16], sancto Wilfritho presbitero et abbati suaviloqua eloquentia in sua lingua Romanae ecclesiae et apostolicae sedis dare rationem. Ipse vero, humiliter ut erat, respondit dicens[17]: "Hanc quaestionem olim iam[18] in Nicea Bithyniae[19] civitate patres nostri sanctissimi et sapientissimi trecenti decem et octo congregati in unum mirifice investigaverunt et statuerunt inter alia iudicia nono decimo anno circulum lunae in se revertentem, qui nunquam ostendit quod

---

[1] *omit* sancti C   [2] Colmannum C *and so throughout*   [3] *omit* d.r.p. C
[4] Alhfrido C   [5] conveniente F   [6] quae Streaneshel C   [7] Aegelberhto C
[8] Bryttonum C   [9] *omit words in brackets* F. *The figures* XXI *and* XXII *must have been transposed by scribal error in* C. *See note*   [10] *omit* C   [11] *omit* C
[12] Columcille C   [13] sententia F   [14] Aegelberto C   [15] *insert* papa C
[16] *omit* C suoque F   [17] d.r. C   [18] *omit* iam C   [19] Bithiniae C

* John 21. 20.

CHAPTER X

*Of the strife of St Wilfrid the priest with Bishop
Colman about the keeping of Easter.* [664]

On a certain occasion in the days of Colman, Bishop of York and
Metropolitan, while Oswiu and Alhfrith his son were reigning, the
abbots and priests and men of all ranks in the orders of the Church
gathered together in a monastery called Whitby, in the presence of
the holy mother and most pious nun Hild, as well as of the kings and
two bishops, namely Colman and Agilberht, to consider the question
of the proper date for the keeping of Easter—whether in accordance
with the British and Scottish manner and that of the whole of the
northern district, Easter should be kept on the Sunday between the
fourteenth day of the moon and the twenty-second, or whether the
plan of the Apostolic See was better, namely to celebrate Easter
Sunday between the fifteenth day of the moon and the twenty-first.
The opportunity was granted first of all to Bishop Colman, as was
proper, to state his case in the presence of all. He boldly spoke in
reply as follows: "Our fathers and their predecessors, plainly
inspired by the Holy Spirit as was Columba, ordained the celebration
of Easter on the fourteenth day of the moon, if it was a Sunday,
following the example of the Apostle and Evangelist John 'who
leaned on the breast of the Lord at supper' and was called the friend
of the Lord. He celebrated Easter on the fourteenth day of the moon
and we, like his disciples Polycarp and others, celebrate it on his
authority; we dare not change it, for our fathers' sake, nor do we
wish to do so. I have expressed the opinion of our party, do you
state yours."

Agilberht the foreign bishop and Agatho his priest bade St Wilfrid,
priest and abbot, with his persuasive eloquence explain in his own
tongue the system of the Roman Church and of the Apostolic See.
With his customary humility he answered in these words:

"This question has already been admirably investigated by the
three hundred and eighteen most holy and learned fathers gathered
together in Nicaea, a city of Bithynia. They fixed amongst other
decisions upon a lunar cycle which recurs every nineteen years. This
cycle never shows that Easter is to be kept on the fourteenth day

in[1] xIIII luna pascha faciendum sit[2]. Haec ratio disciplinae apostolicae sedis est[3] et paene totius mundi, et sic dixerunt patres nostri post multa iudicia: 'Homo qui unum ex his condempnaverit, anathema sit.'" Tunc Oswiu rex, tacente sancto Wilfritho presbitero, subridens interrogavit omnes, dicens: "Enuntiate mihi, utrum maior est Columcillae[4] an Petrus apostolus in regno coelorum?" Omnis synodus una voce et consensu respondit: "Hoc Dominus diiudicavit qui dixit: *Tu es Petrus et super hanc petram aedificabo ecclesiam meam et portae inferi non praevalebunt adversus eam. Et tibi dabo claves regni coelorum et quodcumque ligaveris super terram erit ligatum et in coelis*[5]. *Et quodcumque super terram erit solutum et in coelis.*"* Iterum rex sapienter dixit: "Ille est hostiarius et clavicularius, contra quem conluctationem controversiae non facio nec facientibus consentio et iudiciis eius in vita mea in nullo contradicam[6]." Colmanus vero episcopus audiens, quid esset faciendum, dum tonsuram et paschae rationem propter timorem patriae suae contempsit, ut secederet[7] et alii[8] meliori sedem suam occupandam relinqueret, et sic fecit.

CHAPTER XI

De electione Wilfrithi in episcopatum

Reges deinde consilium cum sapientibus suae gentis post spatium inierunt, quem eligerent in sedem vacantem, qui voluisset sedis apostolicae disciplinam sibi facere et alios docere et esset dignus moribus et Deo acceptabilis et hominibus amabilis. Responderunt omnes uno consensu: "Neminem habemus meliorem et digniorem nostrae gentis quam Wilfrithum presbiterum et abbatem, quia[9] in omnibus rebus sapientem agnovimus[10] et talem esse, qualem Paulus apostolus ad Titum scribens docuit: *Oportet episcopum sine crimine esse, ut Dei dispensatorem; non superbum, non iracundum, non vinolentum, non percussorem, non litigiosum, non turpe lucrum sectantem: sed hospitalem, benignum, sobrium, iustum, sanctum, continentem amplectentemque eum, qui secundum doctrinam est, fidelem sermonem*[11], *ut potens sit exhortari ad doctrinam et contradicentes revincere*†. Haec

---

[1] *omit* q.i. F   [2] *sit after full stop* F   [3] *omit* est F   [4] Columhcillae C
[5] *The quotation runs in* C "Tu es Petrus et cetera. Tibique trado claves regni celorum et quemcumque usque erit solutus et in coelo."   [6] controversiae et iudiciorum eius in vita mea non facio, nec facientibus consentio C
[7] recederet C   [8] alio F   [9] quem C   [10] cognovimus C   [11] eam quam secundum Deum est doctrinam fidelem in sermone C

* Matth. 16. 18, 19.   † Titus 1. 7–9. Cf. 1 Tim. 3. 3.

of the moon. This is the fixed rule of the Apostolic See and of almost
the whole world and our fathers; after many decrees had been made,
uttered these words: 'he who condemns any one of these let him be
accursed.'"

Then, after St Wilfrid the priest had finished his speech, King
Oswiu smilingly asked them all, "Tell me which is greater in the Kingdom of Heaven, Columba or the Apostle Peter?" The whole synod
answered with one voice and one consent, "The Lord settled this
when He declared: 'Thou art Peter and upon this rock I will build
my Church and the gates of Hell shall not prevail against it. And
I will give thee the keys of the Kingdom of Heaven; and whatsoever
thou shalt bind on earth shall be bound in Heaven; and whatsoever
thou shalt loose on earth shall be loosed in Heaven.'"

The king wisely replied, "He is the porter and keeps the keys.
With him I will have no differences nor will I agree with those who
have such, nor in any single particular will I gainsay his decisions
so long as I live."

So Bishop Colman was told what he must do, should he reject the
tonsure and the Easter rule for fear of his fellow-countrymen, namely,
he must retire and leave his see to be taken by another and a better
man. Thus indeed he did.

CHAPTER XI
How Wilfrid was elected to the bishopric. [664]

After an interval the kings had a consultation with the counsellors of
the realm as to whom they should elect to the vacant see, one willing to
accept the discipline of the Apostolic See and to teach it to others, a
man of high character, acceptable to God and beloved of men. They
all answered with one consent, "We consider that none of our fellow-
countrymen is better and more worthy than Wilfrid, priest and abbot,
for we have seen that he is wise in all matters and such a man as the
Apostle Paul writing to Titus described: 'For the bishop must be
blameless, as the steward of God, not self-willed, not soon angry,
not given to wine, no striker, not quarrelsome, not greedy of filthy
lucre, but a lover of hospitality, kind, sober, just, holy, temperate,
holding fast the faithful word as he hath been taught, that he may
be able, by sound doctrine, both to exhort and to convince gain-
sayers.' All these qualities according to the judgment of the Apostle

omnia secundum apostoli iudicium iste habet, et ideo eum eligimus in perfecta aetate ad legem Dei docendam." Erat autem[1] ita homo ille electus, sicut Iohannes praecursor Domini et Ezechiel propheta, xxx annorum aetatis. Tunc quoque consenserunt reges et omnis populus huic electioni, et sancto Wilfritho presbitero omnis conventus in nomine Domini accipere gradum episcopalem praecepit. Ille autem primo abnuens, non esse se dignum excusavit; postremo tamen oboediens factus est, noluitque[2] benedictionem Dei effugere. Qualem ergo illi tunc eum intellexerunt, talem et nos adhuc[3] viventes novimus. *Fuit enim sermo eius purus et apertus, plenus gravitatis et honestatis, plenus suavitatis et gratiae, tractans de misterio legis, de doctrina fidei, de virtute continentiae, de disciplina iustitiae; unumquemque diversa ammonens exhortatione secundum morum qualitatem: videlicet ut praenosceret, quid, cui, quando vel quomodo proferret*[4]. *Prae caeteris ei*[5] *speciale officium erat, ut ieiuniis et orationibus et vigiliis incumberet, scripturas legens—memoriam autem*[6] *miram in libris habuit—percurrens canones, exempla sanctorum imitatus, cum fratribus pacem implens, tenens quoque humilitatem*[7] *et illam supereminentem* omnibus donis *caritatem, sine qua omnis virtus nihil est, curam pauperum gerens, esurientes pascens, nudos vestiens, peregrinos suscipiens, captivos redimens, viduas ac pupillos tuens, ut mercedem vitae aeternae inter choros angelorum cum Domino nostro Iesu Christo accipere mereatur**.

CHAPTER XII

De eo, quod in Gallia ordinatus sit

Locutus est autem sanctus Wilfrithus electus, dicens: "O domini venerabiles reges, omnibus modis nobis necessarium est provide considerare, quomodo cum electione vestra sine accusatione catholicorum virorum ad gradum episcopalem cum Dei adiutorio venire valeam. Sunt enim hic in Britannia[8] multi episcopi quorum nullum meum est accusare, quamvis veraciter sciam quod[9] quattuordecimanni sunt ut Brittones[10] et Scotti; ab illis sunt ordinati, quos nec apostolica sedes in communionem recipit[11] neque eos qui scismaticis consentiunt; et ideo in mea humilitate a vobis posco, ut me mittatis

---

[1] enim C   [2] *omit* que C   [3] adh. et nos C   [4] propherret F   [5] *omit* ei C
[6] enim C   [7] humilitate F   [8] Bytannia C   [9] *insert* aut C   [10] Brytones C
[11] recepit C

* V. Cudbercti c. 30.

this man possesses. And so we elect him in the prime of his manhood to teach God's law."

Now this man was elected like John the forerunner of the Lord and the prophet Ezekiel, when thirty years of age. The kings and all the people agreed to this election and the whole gathering bade St Wilfrid the priest accept the rank of bishop in the name of the Lord. At first he refused, excusing himself on the plea of unworthiness, but at last he became obedient and did not desire to flee from the blessing of God.

Their opinion of him in those days did not differ from that of us who are still alive. His discourse was pure and frank, full of gravity and virtue, full of sweetness and grace, dealing with the mystery of the law, the teaching of faith, the virtue of temperance or the practice of righteousness. To each one he gave varied advice suitable to his character, because he always knew beforehand what advice to give to any man, and when and how it should be given. Before everything it was his special care to take part in fastings, prayers and vigils. He read the Scriptures and had a wonderful memory for their text. He studied the canons of the Church too and imitated the example of the saints, fulfilling the duty of peace towards his brethren: he practised humility and that charity which is greater than all gifts and without which every other virtue is nothing worth. He cared for the poor, fed the hungry, clothed the naked, took in strangers, redeemed captives and protected widows and orphans, that he might merit the reward of eternal life amid the choirs of angels in the presence of our Lord Jesus Christ.

CHAPTER XII

How he was consecrated in Gaul. [664]

On his election St Wilfrid said these words: "O lords and venerable kings, it is necessary for us in every way to take careful forethought so that I may attain to the rank of bishop by the help of God, in accordance with your election, without any criticism on the part of catholic men. Now there are here in Britain many bishops whom it is not for me to criticize, but I know for a fact that they are Quartodecimans like the Britons and Scots; by them were ordained men whom the Apostolic See does not receive into communion, nor does she even receive those who have fellowship with the schismatics. So, in all humility, I ask you to send me under your protection across

cum vestro praesidio trans mare ad Galliarum regionem, ubi catholici episcopi multi habentur, ut sine controversia apostolicae sedis, licet indignus, gradum episcopalem merear accipere." Tale iam consilium bene regibus complacuit, praeparantes ei navem et auxilia hominum et pecuniae multitudinem, ita ut valde honorifice ad Galliae regionem pervenerit[1]. Ibique statim conventio magna facta est non minus quam duodecim episcoporum catholicorum, e quibus unus erat Aegilberhtus[2] episcopus. Qui omnes[3] eum propter fidem suam indicatam gratanter et honorifice coram omni populo publice ordinaverunt et in sella aurea sedentem more eorum sursum elevaverunt, portantes manibus soli episcopi intra oratorium[4], nullo alio attingente, hymnos canticaque[5] in choro canentes; sicque[6] post spatium[7] temporis ad sedem episcopalem Eboracae civitatis hunc emiserunt et praeceperunt ei in nomine Domini in catholica fide permanere, sicut Paulus apostolus Timotheo filio suo custodire propositum suum praecepit, quod per manus impositionem[8] eius accepit.

CHAPTER XIII

Quomodo Dominus pontificem nostrum de mare et de manu paganorum cum suis liberavit

Navigantibus quoque eis de Gallia Britannicum[9] mare cum beatae memoriae Wilfritho episcopo, canentibus clericis et psallentibus laudem Dei pro celeumate in choro, in medio mari validissima tempestas exorta est, et venti contrarii, sicut discipulis Iesu in[10] mare Galileae[11] erant. Flante namque vento euroaustro dure, albescentia undarum culmina in regionem[12] Australium Saxonum, quam non noverant, proiecerunt eos. Mare quoque navem et homines relinquens, terras fugiens, litoraque[13] detegens, et[14] in abyssi matricem recessit. Gentiles autem cum ingenti exercitu venientes, navem[15] arripere, praedam sibi pecuniae dividere, captivos subiugatos deducere resistentesque gladio occidere incunctanter proposuerunt. Quibus sanctus pontifex[16] noster copiosam pecuniam promittens, animas redimere cupiens leniter pacificeque loquebatur. Illi vero feroces et indurato corde cum Pharaone populum Dei dimittere nolentes et

---

[1] pervenire C [2] Aegilberchtus C [3] *omit* omnes C [4] inter oratoria C
[5] himnosque et cantica C [6] *omit* C [7] *insert* namque C [8] inpositione C
and F [9] Brytannicum C [10] *omit* F [11] Gallieae F [12] regione F
[13] *omit* que C [14] *omit* et C [15] navim F [16] praesul C

the sea to the land of the Gauls where there are many bishops who are considered catholic, so that, without any objection on the part of the Apostolic See, I may, though unworthy, deserve to receive the rank of bishop."

This plan met with the cordial approval of the kings. They prepared him a ship and a force of men as well as a large sum of money, so as to enable him to enter Gaul in great state. Here at once there took place a large meeting consisting of no less than twelve catholic bishops, one of whom was Bishop Agilberht. When they heard the testimony to his faith they all joyfully consecrated him publicly before all the people with great state, and raising him aloft in accordance with their custom as he sat in the golden chair, the bishops unaided and alone carried him with their own hands into the oratory, chanting hymns and songs in chorus. And so, after a time, they sent him back to the see of York, bidding him, in the name of the Lord, abide in the catholic faith, just as the Apostle Paul bade Timothy his son keep what had been committed to him, which he had received through the laying on of his hands.

CHAPTER XIII

How the Lord rescued our bishop and his companions from the sea and from the hands of the pagans. [666]

While they were crossing the British sea on their return from Gaul with Bishop Wilfrid of blessed memory, and the priests were praising God with psalms and hymns, giving the time to the oarsmen, a violent storm arose in mid-ocean and the winds were contrary, just as they were to the disciples of Jesus on the sea of Galilee. The wind blew hard from the south-east and the foam-crested waves hurled them on to the land of the South Saxons which they did not know. Then the sea left ship and men high and dry, fled from the land, and, laying the shores bare, withdrew into the depth of the abyss. Forthwith a huge army of pagans arrived intending to seize the ship, to divide the money as booty for themselves, carry off the captives whom they vanquished and incontinently put to the sword all who resisted them. The holy bishop spoke to them soothingly and peaceably, and sought to purchase the lives of his companions by the promise of a large sum of money. The enemy however were fierce, and, hardening their hearts like Pharaoh, were unwilling to let the people of God

dicentes superbe, sua esse omnia quasi propria, quae mare ad terras proiecit. Stans quoque princeps sacerdotum idolatriae coram paganis in tumulo excelso, sicut Balaam, maledicere populum Dei et suis magicis artibus manus eorum alligare nitebatur. Tunc vero unus ex sodalibus pontificis nostri lapidem ab omni populo Dei benedictum[1] more Davidico de funda emittens, fronte perforata[2] usque ad cerebrum magi exprobrantis illisit; quem, retrorsum exanimato cadavere cadente, sicut Goliad in harenosis locis mors incerta praevenit. Ad bellum ergo se praeparantes pagani, aciem frustra in populum Dei direxerunt. Dominus enim pro paucis pugnavit; sicut iam Gedeon Domini iussu cum CCC viris[3] bellatorum[4] Madianitum CXX milia uno impetu occidit, ita et isti sodales sancti pontificis[5] nostri bene armati, viriles animo, pauci numero—erant enim CXX viri in numero Mosaicae[6] aetatis—inito consilio et pacto, ut nullus ab alio in fugam terga verteret, sed aut mortem cum laude aut vitam cum triumpho, quod Deo utrumque facile est, habere mererentur[7]. Igitur sanctus Wilfrithus episcopus cum clero suo, flexis poplitibus genuum et iterum elevatis manibus ad coelum, Domini auxilium perpetravit[8]. Sicut enim Moyses, Hur et Aaron sustentantibus manus[9] eius, Iesu Nave cum populo Dei adversum Amalech pugnante, frequenter Domini protectionem implorans triumphavit, ita et hic isti pauci christiani feroces et indomitos paganos tribus vicibus in fugam versos strage non modica obruerunt, quinque tantum viris, quod mirum dictu[10] est, ex sua parte occisis, orante sacerdote magno ad Dominum Deum suum, qui statim iussit ante horam plenam, priusquam consuerat, mare venire. Praeparantibus autem paganis cum rege veniente totis viribus ad quartum proelium, tunc mare redundans fluctibus tota litora implevit, elevataque[11] nave[12], cimba processit in altum. Gloriose autem a Deo honorificati, gratias ei agentes, vento flante ab affrico, prospere in portum Sandwicae[13] salutis[14] pervenerunt.

---

[1] benedicto C *and* F   [2] fronti perforatae C   [3] viros F   [4] bellatoribus C
[5] praesulis C   [6] moysaicae C   [7] merentur   [8] perperravit F vel imperpetravit C   [9] manibus F   [10] dictum C   [11] *omit* que F   [12] *omit* C
[13] Sonduic C   [14] *omit* salutis *insert* atque suaviter C

depart, proudly declaring that they treated as their own possessions all that the sea cast upon the land. The chief priest of their idolatrous worship also took up his stand in front of the pagans, on a high mound, and like Balaam, attempted to curse the people of God, and to bind their hands by means of his magical arts. Thereupon one of the companions of our bishop took a stone which had been blessed by all the people of God and hurled it from his sling after the manner of David. It pierced the wizard's forehead and penetrated to his brain as he stood cursing; death took him unawares as it did Goliath, and his lifeless body fell backwards on to the sand. The pagans then got ready for battle, but in vain did they draw up their array against the people of God. For the Lord fought for the few, even as when Gideon with his 300 warriors at the bidding of the Lord slew 120,000 Midianite warriors at one onslaught. In the same way these companions of our holy bishop being well-armed and brave in heart though but few in number (there were 120 of them, equal in number to the years of the age of Moses), formed a plan and made a compact that none should turn his back upon another in flight, but that they would either win death with honour or life with victory, God being able with equal ease to bring either event to pass. So St Wilfrid the bishop and his clergy on bended knees lifted their hands again to heaven and gained the help of the Lord. For as Moses continually called upon the Lord for help, Hur and Aaron raising his hands, while Joshua the son of Nun was fighting against Amalek with the people of God, so this little band of Christians overthrew the fierce and untamed heathen host, three times putting them to flight with no little slaughter, though, marvellous to relate, only five of the Christians were slain. Then the great bishop prayed to the Lord his God, who straightway bade the tide return before its usual hour and, while the pagans, on the coming of their king, were preparing with all their strength for a fourth battle, the sea came flowing back and covered all the shore, so that the ship was floated and made its way into the deep. They returned thanks to God for the glorious way He had honoured them, and with a south-west wind they prosperously reached a port of safety at Sandwich.

CHAPTER XIV

De eo, quod interim ordinatus est
Ceadda in sedem eius[1]

Quodam igitur tempore, adhuc sancto Wilfritho episcopo trans mare non veniente, Oswi[2] rex, male suadente invidia, hostis antiqui instinctu alium praearripere inordinate sedem suam edoctus consensit ab his, qui quartamdecimanam[3] partem contra apostolicae sedis regulam sibi elegerunt; ordinantes servum Dei religiosissimum et admirabilem doctorem, de Hibernia insula venientem, nomine Ceadda[4], adhuc eo ignorante, in sedem episcopalem Eboracae[5] civitatis indocte contra canones constituerunt. Veniente vero sancto Wilfritho episcopo, res, ut erat male acta, non latuit; revertens quippe ad sedem coenobialem abbatis, humiliter Inhripis III annis resedit, nisi quod frequenter a Wlfario rege Merciorum ad officia diversa episcopalia in regione sua cum vera dilectione invitatus est. Suscitavit enim Dominus sibi regem hunc mitissimum, qui inter alia bona in diversis locis multa spatia terrarum pro animae suae remedio episcopo nostro[6] concessit, in quibus mox monasteria servorum Dei constituit. Ecgberhtus[7] quoque rex Cantwariorum[8] religiosus pontificem nostrum ad se accersivit, et illic presbiteros multos, ex quibus unus erat Putta, qui postea episcopatum accepit, et non paucos diacones ordinavit. Deusdedit enim episcopus post Honorium[9] archiepiscopum diem obiit[10]. Ideo autem venerabiliter vivens, omnibus carus, episcopalia officia per plura spatia agens, cum cantoribus[11] Aedde et Eonan[12] et caementariis omnisque paene artis institoribus[13] regionem suam rediens, cum regula sancti[14] Benedicti instituta ecclesiarum Dei[15] bene meliorabat[16]. Tunc ergo in illis regionibus sancto episcopo, sicut Paulo apostolo, magnum ostium[17] fidei, Deo adiuvante, apertum est.

---

[1] suam F [2] Osuiu C [3] quartam decimam F XIIII manam C [4] Caeodda C
[5] Euroicae C [6] *omit* C [7] Ecberhtus C [8] Cantuariorum C [9] bonorum C [10] *omit* d.o. F [11] cantatoribus C [12] Aeona C [13] institutoribus C
[14] *omit* C [15] *omit* C [16] melioravit C [17] hostium C *and* F

CHAPTER XIV

How Chad had meanwhile been consecrated to Wilfrid's see. [665?]

After a lapse of time, when Saint Wilfrid the bishop did not arrive from across the sea, King Oswiu, moved by envy and at the instigation of the ancient foe, consented to allow another to forestall him in his see in an irregular manner; for he was instructed by those who adhered to the Quartodeciman party in opposition to the rule of the Apostolic See; they consecrated to the See of York a deeply pious servant of God and admirable teacher named Chad, who came from Ireland, but they did it ignorantly and in defiance of canon law. Meanwhile St Wilfrid himself knew nothing of it; but when he arrived it became obvious that a wrong deed had been done. He, however, returned to his post of abbot of the monastery and humbly dwelt once more in Ripon for three years, except for the frequent occasions when Wulfhere, King of the Mercians, out of sincere affection for him, invited him into his realm to fulfil various episcopal duties. The Lord raised up for himself this most kindly monarch, who, amongst his other good deeds, for the benefit of his soul, granted our bishop many pieces of land in various places, on which he forthwith founded monasteries for the servants of God. Egbert too, the pious King of Kent, summoned our bishop to his presence, and there he ordained many priests (one of whom was Putta who afterwards became a bishop), and not a few deacons. For Deusdedit, who had been appointed bishop after the death of Archbishop Honorius, was dead.

So he lived in honour, dear to all men, and, after fulfilling episcopal duties in various places, returned to his own land with the singers Aedde and Aeona, and with masons and artisans of almost every kind, and there, by introducing the rule of St Benedict, he greatly improved the ordinances of the churches of God. At that time therefore, by the help of God, a great door of faith was opened in those parts to our holy bishop, as it was to the Apostle Paul.

CHAPTER XV

*De eo, quod iterum in sedem suam
constitutus est*

Postquam ergo, tribus annis transactis, Theodorus[1] archiepiscopus de regione Cantuaria veniens ad regem Deyrorum[2] et Berniciorum[3], statuta iudicia apostolicae sedis, unde emissus venerat, secum deportans, primoque ingressu regionis illius rem contra canones male gestam a veris testibus audivit, quod praedonis more episcopus alterius episcopi sedem praeeripere ausus sit; indigneque ferens, Ceaddam[4] episcopum de sede aliena iussit deponi. Ille vero servus Dei[5] verus et mitissimus tunc peccatum ordinandi a quattuordecimannis in sedem alterius plene intelligens, poenitentia[6] humili secundum iudicium[7] episcoporum confessus, emendavit et cum consensu eius in propriam sedem Eboracae[8] civitatis sanctum Wilfrithum episcopum constituit. Tunc sanctus pontifex noster secundum praeceptum Domini non malum pro malo, sed bonum, ut David Saulo[9], pro malo reddens, qui dixit: *Non mittam manum meam in christum Domini**, sciebat sub Wlfario rege Merciorum, fidelissimo amico suo, locum donatum sibi Onlicitfelda[10] et ad episcopalem sedem aut sibimetipsi aut alio, cuicumque voluisset dare, paratum; ideoque pacifice inito consilio[11] cum vero servo Dei Ceaddan, in omnibus rebus episcopis oboediens, per omnes gradus ecclesiasticos ad sedem praedictam plene eum ordinaverunt et, honorifice rege suscipiente eum, in locum praedictum constituerunt; ibique benedicte in vita sua multa bona perficiens, tempore opportuno in viam patrum exiit[12], expectans diem Domini in iudicio venturo, ut credimus, sibi mitissimum, sicut dignum est.

CHAPTER XVI

De renovatione basilicae in Euroica civitate

Igitur supradicto rege regnante, beatae memoriae Wilfritho episcopo metropolitano Eboracae civitatis constituto, basilicae oratorii Dei, in ea civitate a sancto Paulino episcopo in diebus olim Eadwini chris-

[1] Thedorus C   [2] Derorum C   [3] Bernicorum C   [4] Caedda C   [5] D.s. C
[6] paenitentia C   [7] *omit* F   [8] Euboriae C   [9] Sauli C   [10] Anliccitfelda C
[11] *At this point two leaves are missing in C. There is a marginal note in a seventeenth century hand* Multa hic desiderantur   [12] Levison. exigit F

* 1 Kings 24. 7.

CHAPTER XV

How he was restored to his see. [669]

So, after the lapse of three years, Archbishop Theodore came from Kent to the King of Deira and Bernicia, bringing with him the decrees of the Apostolic See from which he had been sent. As soon as he had reached that land he heard from the lips of true witnesses the story of the offence against the canon law and how one bishop had dared, like a thief, to snatch another bishop's see. He indignantly ordered that Bishop Chad should be deposed from the see of another man.

Chad, being a true and meek servant of God and fully understanding then the wrongdoing implied in his ordination to another's see by the Quartodecimans, with humble penance confessed his fault in accordance with the decision of the bishops: whereupon Theodore, with Chad's consent, installed St Wilfrid as bishop in his own see of York. Then our holy bishop, in accordance with the command of the Lord, returned good for evil, not evil for evil, just as David did to Saul when he said, "I will not stretch forth my hand against the Lord's anointed." He knew of a place in the kingdom of Wulfhere, King of the Mercians, his faithful friend, which had been granted to him at Lichfield and was suitable as an episcopal see either for himself or for any other to whom he might wish to give it. So a friendly arrangement was made with that true servant of God, Chad, who in all things obeyed the bishops: they thereupon consecrated him fully to the said see through all the ecclesiastical degrees. The king received him in an honourable manner and the bishops installed him in the said place. There he performed many good and pious deeds during his life, and at the fitting time he passed to his fathers, awaiting the day when the Lord shall come in judgment, a day which we believe will rightly have no terrors for him.

CHAPTER XVI

How the church at York was restored. [669–671]

Now during the reign of the above-mentioned king, after Wilfrid of blessed memory had been appointed metropolitan bishop of the city of York, the stone buildings of the church in that city were obviously in a ruinous condition. This church of God had been first founded by the holy Paulinus the bishop and dedicated to God in

tianissimi regis primo fundatae et dedicatae Deo, officia semiruta lapidea eminebant. Nam culmina antiquata tecti distillantia fenestraeque apertae, avibus nidificantibus intro et foras volitantibus, et parietes incultae omni spurcitia imbrium et avium horribiles manebant. Videns itaque haec omnia sanctus pontifex noster, secundum Danielem horruit spiritus eius in eo, quod domus Dei et orationis[1] quasi speluncam latronum factam agnovit, et mox iuxta voluntatem Dei emendare excogitavit. Primum culmina corrupta tecti renovans, artificiose plumbo puro detegens, per fenestras introitum avium et imbrium vitro prohibuit, per quod tamen intro lumen radiabat. Parietes quoque lavans, secundum prophetam *super nivem*★ dealbavit. Iam enim non solum domum Dei et altare in varia supellectili vasorum intus ornavit[2], verum etiam, deforis multa territoria pro Deo adeptus, terrenis opibus paupertatem auferens, copiose ditavit. Tunc sententia Dei de Samuhele et omnibus sanctis in eo implebatur: *Qui*, inquit, *me honorificat, honorificabo eum*†; erat enim Deo et omni populo carus et honorabilis.

CHAPTER XVII

De aedificatione basilicae Inhripis et dedicatione eius

Crescebat ergo cum seculari sumptu, Deo donante, pontifici nostro, amico sponsi aeternalis, magis ac magis ardentissimus amor sponsae virginis[3], uni viro desponsatae, de matre omnium bonorum caritate[4] progenitae; quam disciplinae moribus quasi floribus virtutum, castam et pudicam, continentem et modestam, circumamictam varietate, subiectam pulchre adornavit. Secundum prophetam *omnis gloria filiae regis ab intus*‡. Sicut enim Moyses tabernaculum seculare manu factum ad exemplar in monte monstratum[5] a Deo ad concitandam Israhelitico populo culturae Dei fidem distinctis variis coloribus aedificavit, ita vero beatissimus Wilfrithus episcopus thalamum veri sponsi et sponsae in conspectu populorum, corde credentium et fide confitentium, auro et argento purpuraque varia mirifice decoravit.

---

[1] *insert* prophetas F   [2] oravit F   [3] virginae F
[4] caritatis F   [5] *insert* est F

★ Psa. 50. 9.   † 1 Kings 2. 30.   ‡ Cf. Psa. 44. 14 (Vulg.).

the days of Edwin, that most Christian king. But now the ridge of the roof owing to its age let the water through, the windows were unglazed and the birds flew in and out, building their nests, while the neglected walls were disgusting to behold owing to all the filth caused by the rain and the birds. When our holy bishop saw all this his spirit was vexed within him, as Daniel's was, because he saw that the house of God and the house of prayer had become like a den of thieves; so, forthwith, in accordance with the will of God, he made a plan to restore it. First of all he renewed the ruined roof ridges, skilfully covering them with pure lead; by putting glass in the windows he prevented the birds or the rain from getting in, although it did not keep out the rays of light. He also washed the walls, and, in the words of the prophet, made them "whiter than snow." Furthermore, not only did he adorn the inside of the house of God and the altar with various kinds of vessels and furniture, but outside he richly endowed the church with many estates which he had acquired for God, thus removing its poverty by endowing it with lands. Then the word of the Lord concerning Samuel and all saints was fulfilled in him: "Them that honour me," He said, "I will honour"; for he was beloved and honoured both by God and by the whole nation.

CHAPTER XVII

Concerning the building of the church at Ripon and its dedication. [671–678]

So, amid the worldly prosperity which God gave him, there grew up in our bishop, the friend of the eternal Bridegroom, a love which ever increased in ardour for the virgin Bride espoused to one husband and born of charity the mother of all goodness. He adorned her fairly with the rules of discipline as with the flowers of virtue, making her chaste and modest, continent, temperate and submissive, and clothed her in garments of many hues. In the words of the prophet, "The king's daughter is all glorious within." For as Moses built an earthly tabernacle made with hands, of divers varied colours according to the pattern shown by God in the mount, to stir up the faith of the people of Israel for the worship of God, so the blessed Bishop Wilfrid wondrously adorned the bridal chamber of the true Bridegroom and Bride with gold and silver and varied purples, in the sight of the multitudes who believed in their hearts and made confession

Nam Inhrypis basilicam polito lapide a fundamentis in terra usque ad summum aedificatam, variis columnis et porticibus suffultam, in altum erexit et consummavit. Iam postea, perfecta domu, ad diem dicationis eius, invitatis regibus christianissimis et piissimis Ecgfritho et Aelwino, duobus fratribus, cum abbatibus praefectisque et subregulis, totiusque dignitatis personae simul in unum convenerunt: consecrantes secundum sapientissimum Salomonem domum, Domino in honorem sancti Petri apostolorum principis dicatam precesque in ea populorum suffragantem, altare[1] quoque cum bassibus suis Domino dedicantes purpuraque auro texta induentes populique communicantes, omnia canonice compleverunt. Stans itaque sanctus Wilfrithus episcopus ante altare conversus ad populum, coram regibus enumerans regiones, quas ante reges pro animabus suis et tunc in illa die cum consensu et subscriptione episcoporum et omnium principum[2] illi dederunt, lucide enuntiavit necnon et ea loca sancta in diversis regionibus quae clerus Bryttannus, aciem gladii hostilis manu gentis nostrae fugiens, deseruit. Erat quippe Deo placabile donum, quod religiosi reges tam multas terras Deo ad serviendum pontifici nostro conscripserunt, et haec sunt nomina regionum: iuxta Rippel et Ingaedyne et in regione Dunutinga et Incaetlaevum in caeterisque locis. Deinde, consummato sermone, magnum convivium trium dierum et noctium reges, cum omni populo laetificantes, magnanimes in hostes, humiles cum servis Dei inierunt. Addens quoque sanctus pontifex noster inter alia bona ad decorem domus Dei inauditum ante seculis nostris quoddam miraculum. Nam quattuor evangelia de auro purissimo in membranis depurpuratis, coloratis, pro animae suae remedio scribere iussit: necnon et bibliothecam librorum eorum, omnem de auro purissimo et gemmis pretiosissimis fabrefactam, compaginare inclusores gemmarum praecepit; quae omnia et alia nonnulla in testimonium beatae memoriae eius in ecclesia nostra usque hodie reconduntur, ubi reliquiae illius requiescunt, et sine intermissione cotidie in orationibus nominis eius recordantur.

---

[1] adlatere F   [2] *insert* qui F

of their faith. For in Ripon he built and completed from the foundations in the earth up to the roof, a church of dressed stone, supported
by various columns and side aisles.

Afterwards, when the building had been finished, he invited to
the day of its dedication the two most Christian kings and brothers,
Ecgfrith and Aelfwini, together with the abbots, the reeves and the
sub-kings; dignitaries of every kind gathered together; like Solomon
the wise, they consecrated the house and dedicated it to the Lord in
honour of St Peter the chief of the Apostles, to assist the prayers of
the people in it. The altar also with its bases they dedicated to the
Lord and vested it in purple woven with gold; the people shared
in the work, and thus all was completed in a canonical manner.

Then St Wilfrid the bishop stood in front of the altar, and, turning
to the people, in the presence of the kings, read out clearly a list of
the lands which the kings, for the good of their souls, had previously,
and on that very day as well, presented to him, with the agreement
and over the signatures of the bishops and all the chief men,
and also a list of the consecrated places in various parts which the
British clergy had deserted when fleeing from the hostile sword
wielded by the warriors of our own nation. It was truly a gift well
pleasing to God that the pious kings had assigned so many lands to
our bishop for the service of God; these are the names of the regions:
round Ribble and Yeadon and the region of Dent and Catlow and
other places. Then, when the sermon was over, the kings started
upon a great feast lasting for three days and three nights, rejoicing
amid all their people, showing magnanimity towards their enemies
and humility towards the servants of God. Our holy bishop also
provided for the adornment of the house of God, among other
treasures, a marvel of beauty hitherto unheard of in our times. For
he had ordered, for the good of his soul, the four gospels to be written
out in letters of purest gold on purpled parchment and illuminated.
He also ordered jewellers to construct for the books a case all made of
purest gold and set with most precious gems; all these things and
others besides are preserved in our church until these times as a
witness to his blessed memory; here too his remains rest, and daily,
without any intermission, his name is remembered in prayer.

CHAPTER XVIII

De eo, quod infantem resuscitavit

*Mirabilis est Deus in sanctis suis** et clarificatus in virtutibus eorum! Olim iam in veteri lege servos Dei varias virtutes per Deum fecisse legimus; sicut Helias et Heliseus servi Dei [mortuos][1] suscitaverunt, ita et apostoli Christi, magistri exemplum sequentes, secundum promissum eius omnes varios languores in nomine eius depulerunt, et nunc eodem modo a subsecutoribus illorum, quibus unus est sanctus pontifex noster, ad Dei gloriam infirmitate prostrati sanantur. Nam quadam die sancto Wilfritho episcopo equitanti et pergenti ad varia officia episcopatus sui, baptizandi utique et cum manus impositione confirmandi populos; inter quos quaedam mulier in villa quae dicitur Ontiddanufri inventa est, amaro animo, susurrans maerore et onere fatigata; habens enim infantem primogenitum suum mortuum sub sinu, pannis involutum, latitantem, cuius cadaveris mortui faciem inter alios ad confirmandam episcopo revolvit, volens sic posse vivificare. Ille vero sanctus episcopus noster statim, ut vere mortuum esse intellexit, aliquantulum tamen moratus, quid de eo esset agendum: at illa mater coram facie[2] agnoscentis cecidit in terram, flens amare; adiuravit eum audacter[3], ut in nomine Domini Dei sui cum sua sanctitate filium suum suscitaret et baptizaret, de oreque leonis liberaret. His et aliis verbis magis ac magis non cessavit adiurare per omnes sanctitates episcoporum[4], genuflectens et pedes eius amplectens, deosculavit[5] lacrimisque amarissimis irrigavit dicens: "O sanctissime, noli fidem orbatae mulieris extinguere; sed credulitatem meam adiuva†; suscita eum et baptiza; tibi enim et Deo vivit: in virtute Christi ne dubites!" Tunc ille sanctus pontifex[6] indubitata Christi virtute, et fidem eius secundum Syrophenissam[7] mulierem audiens, oratione facta, manum ponens super cadaver mortui, et[8] statim respiravit et spiritum vitae recepit. Resuscitatum itaque et baptizatum matri infantem reddidit, praecipiensque[9] ei in nomine Domini, ut sibi filium suum in septima[10] annorum aetate Deo ad serviendum redderet. Quod mulier, malivolo[11] suadente marito,*

---

[1] *omit* mortuos F   [2] *At this word* C *begins again after the break*   [3] audaciter C   [4] episcopi C   [5] deosculabatur C   [6] vir C   [7] Syrofenissam C   [8] *omit* C   [9] *omit* que C   [10] septimo C   [11] malivola C

* Psa. 67. 36 (Vulg.).   † Mark 9. 23

CHAPTER XVIII

How he restored a child to life

"God is wondrous in His saints" and glorified in their miracles. In the Old Law we read that once the servants of God performed various miracles by His help. Even as Elijah and Elisha the servants of God raised the dead, so the Apostles of Christ, following the example of their Master, according to His promise, drove out all kinds of diseases in His name; and now in a similar manner those afflicted by infirmities are healed to the glory of God by their successors, one of whom is our holy bishop. It happened that St Wilfrid was out riding on a certain day, going to fulfil the various duties of his bishopric, baptizing and also confirming the people with the laying on of hands; among these there was a certain woman in a town called "*On Tiddanufri*," sad at heart, moaning with grief and wearied with her load. For she held in her bosom the body of her first-born child, wrapped in rags and hidden from sight; she uncovered the face of the corpse for the bishop to confirm it amongst the rest, hoping thus to be able to bring it back to life. Now our holy bishop, as soon as he perceived that it was dead, hesitated a little as to what he ought to do. But the mother fell to the earth before the face of the bishop on his perceiving what she had done, and, weeping bitterly, she boldly adjured him, in the name of the Lord his God, by virtue of his holiness to raise her son, to baptize him and free him from the mouth of the lion. With such words she never ceased to adjure him again and again, by all the holiness of bishops, kneeling and kissing his feet, embracing and bedewing them with bitter tears, and saying, "Most holy man, do not destroy the faith of a bereaved mother but help thou my (un)belief, raise him up and baptize him and he will live to God and to you. By the power of Christ, do not hesitate!"

Then the holy bishop, not doubting the power of Christ, and hearing her faith like that of the Syro-Phoenician woman, uttered a prayer, and when he had placed his hand on the dead body it breathed again forthwith, receiving the spirit of life. So he baptized the child which had been brought to life again and gave it into the charge of the mother, bidding her, in the name of the Lord, give back her child to himself at the age of seven, for the service of God. The mother, however,

videns elegantem puerum, contempsit, fugiens de terra[1] sua. Quem praefectus episcopi nomine Hocca latentem sub aliis Bryttonum[2] quaesitum invenit et coacte abstraxit, ad episcopumque contulit. Erat autem puer cognomine Eodwald et agnomine[3] Filius Episcopi, vivens in Dei servitio Inhripis[4], usquedum in mortalitate magna diem obiit. O quam magna et mirabilis misericordia Dei! qui per famulum suum venerandae mentionis infantulum defunctum et non baptizatum ideo in hanc vitam revocavit, ut baptizatus vitae perenni viveret futurae beatitudinis[5].

CHAPTER XIX

De victoria regis in feroces Pictos

In diebus autem illis Ecfrithus[6] rex religiosus cum beatissima regina Aethiltrythae[7], cuius corpus vivens ante impollutum[8] post mortem incorruptum manens adhuc demonstrat, simul in unum Wilfritho[9] episcopo in omnibus oboedientes facti, pax et gaudium in populis et anni frugiferi victoriaeque in hostes, Deo adiuvante, subsecutae sunt[10]. Sicut enim iuvenis Ioas[11] rex Iuda, Ioada[12] sacerdote magno vivente adhuc, Deo placuit et in hostes triumphavit: mortuo vero sacerdote, Deo displicuit et regnum minuit, ita, Ecfritho[13] rege in concordia pontificis nostri vivente, secundum multorum testimonium[14] regnum undique per victorias triumphales augebatur: concordia vero inter eos sopita[15] et regina supradicta ab eo separata et Deo dicata[16], triumphus[17] in diebus regis desinit. Nam in primis annis eius tenero adhuc regno populi bestiales Pictorum feroci animo subiectionem Saxonum despiciebant et iugum servitutis proicere a se minabant; congregantes undique de utribus et folliculis aquilonis innumeras[18] gentes, quasi formicarum greges in aestate de tumulis verrentes[19] aggerem contra domum cadentem muniebant[20]. Nam, quo audito, rex Ecgfrithus[21], humilis in populis suis, magnanimus in hostes, statim equitatui exercitu praeparato, tarda[22] molimina nesciens, sicut Iudas Machabeus in Deum confidens, parva manu populi Dei

---

[1] dextera C   [2] Brytonum F   [3] *omit* E. et ag. F   [4] Inhrypis C   [5] *All last sentence* O quam...beatitudinis *omitted in* F   [6] Ecgfridus C
[7] Aetheldritha C   [8] inpullutum F   [9] Uilfrydo C   [10] *At this point there is a marginal note in a seventeenth century hand* legis in Thoma Elyensi in V. Etheldredae. Non nominat Heddium   [11] Iosias F   [12] Ioiada C
[13] Ecfrido C   [14] t.m. C   [15] posita C   [16] dedicata C   [17] triumphum C *and* F
[18] innumeros C   [19] ferventes C   [20] minuebant F   [21] Ecfridus C
[22] tarde C

when she saw how handsome the boy was, listened to the evil counsel of her husband, made light of her promise, and fled from her country.

The bishop's reeve, named Hocca, having sought and found him hidden among others of the British race, took him away by force and carried him off to the bishop. The boy's Christian name was Eodwald and his surname was Bishop's Son: he lived in Ripon serving God until he died during the great plague. O how great and wonderful is God's mercy, Who, by His servant of honoured memory, called back to life a little child who was dead and unbaptized, so that, being baptized, he might live to inherit an eternal life of future blessedness.

CHAPTER XIX

Of the king's victory over the warlike Picts. [671–673]

Now in those days, the pious King Ecgfrith, and his most blessed Queen Aethilthryth (whose body, still remaining uncorrupted after death, shows that it was unstained before, while alive) were both obedient to Bishop Wilfrid in all things, and there ensued, by the aid of God, peace and joy among the people, fruitful years and victory over their foes. For as when Joash, the King of Judah, was young, so long as Jehoiada the great high priest was alive, he pleased God and triumphed over his enemies; but when the priest was dead, he displeased God and diminished his kingdom; so when King Ecgfrith lived in peace with our bishop, the kingdom, as many bear witness, was increased on every hand by his glorious victories; but when the agreement between them was destroyed, and his queen had separated from him and dedicated herself to God, the king's triumph came to an end during his own lifetime. For in his early years, while the kingdom was still weak, the bestial tribes of the Picts had a fierce contempt for subjection to the Saxon and threatened to throw off from themselves the yoke of slavery; they gathered together innumerable tribes from every nook and corner in the north, and as a swarm of ants in the summer sweeping from their hills heap up a mound to protect their tottering house. When King Ecgfrith heard this, lowly as he was among his own people and magnanimous towards his enemies, he forthwith got together a troop of horsemen, for he was no lover of belated operations; and trusting in God like Judas Maccabaeus and assisted by the

contra inormem et supra invisibilem hostem cum Beornheth[1] audaci subregulo invasit stragemque immensam populi subruit, duo flumina cadaveribus mortuorum replentes, ita, quod mirum dictu[2] est, ut supra siccis pedibus ambulantes, fugientium turbam occidentes persequebantur: et in servitutem redacti, populi usque ad diem occisionis regis captivitatis iugo subiecti[3] iacebant.

CHAPTER XX

De victoria adversum regem Merciorum

Deinde post hanc victoriam rex Ecgfrithus[4] cum pontifice[5] Dei iustus et sanctus regensque populos et validus sicut David in contritione hostium, humilis tamen in conspectu Dei apparens et colla tumentium[6] populorum et ferocium regum, audacior a Deo factus, confringens, semper in omnibus Deo gratias agebat. Nam Wlfharius[7], rex Merciorum, superbo animo et insatiabili corde[8] omnes australes populos adversus regnum[9] nostrum concitans, non tam ad bellandum[10] quam ad redigendum sub tributo servili animo, non regente Deo, proponebat. Ecgfrithus[11] vero rex Derorum et Bernicorum, animo rigido, mente fideli, consilio senum patriam custodire, ecclesias Dei defendere, episcopo docente, in Deum confisus, sicut Barach et Dabora[12], cum parili manu hostem superbum invadens, Deo adiuvante, cum parvo exercitu prostravit et, occisis innumeris, regem fugavit regnumque eius sub tributo distribuit, et eo postea quacumque ex causa moriente, plenius aliquod spatium pacifice imperavit.

CHAPTER XXI

De bonitate pontificis nostri[13]

Sicut ergo Ecgfritho[14] rege religiosissimo[15] regnum ad aquilonem et austrum per triumphos augebatur, ita beatae memoriae Wilfritho episcopo ad austrum super Saxones et ad aquilonem super Brittones[16] et Scottos[17] Pictosque regnum ecclesiarum multiplicabatur. Omnibus[18]

---

[1] Bernhaeth C   [2] dictum C   [3] s.i.c. C   [4] Ecfridus C   [5] supradicto servo C   [6] tum Merciorum C   [7] Uulfarius C   [8] animo F   [9] regem C   [10] debellandum C   [11] Ecfridus C   [12] Barac et Daeborra C   [13] *There is no chapter heading in F. The heading is from C*   [14] Ecfrido C   [15] religioso C   [16] Bryttones C   [17] Scotthos C   [18] *insert* que C

brave sub-king, Beornhaeth, he attacked with his little band of God's people an enemy host which was vast and moreover concealed. He slew an enormous number of the people, filling two rivers with corpses, so that, marvellous to relate, the slayers, passing over the rivers dry foot, pursued and slew the crowd of fugitives; the tribes were reduced to slavery and remained subject under the yoke of captivity until the time when the king was slain.

CHAPTER XX

Of his victory over the King of the Mercians. [673–675]

Thereupon after this victory King Ecgfrith, ruling the people with the bishop of God, in righteousness and holiness, strong like David in crushing his enemies yet lowly in the sight of God, breaking the necks of the tumultuous tribes and their warlike kings, emboldened as he was by the help of God, in all things always gave thanks to God. Now Wulfhere, King of the Mercians, proud of heart and insatiable in spirit, roused all the southern nations against our kingdom, intent not merely on fighting but on compelling them to pay tribute in a slavish spirit. But he was not guided by God. So Ecgfrith, King of Deira and Bernicia, unwavering in spirit and true-hearted, on the advice of his counsellors trusted God, like Barak and Deborah, to guard his land and defend the churches of God even as the bishop taught him to do, and with a band of men no greater than theirs attacked a proud enemy, and by the help of God overthrew them with his tiny force. Countless numbers were slain, the king was put to flight and his kingdom laid under tribute, and afterwards, when Wulfhere died through some cause, Ecgfrith ruled in peace over a wider realm.

CHAPTER XXI

Concerning the goodness of our bishop

Thus that most pious king, Ecgfrith, found his kingdom extending both north and south by his triumphs, while at the same time the ecclesiastical kingdom of St Wilfrid of blessed memory increased to the south among the Saxons and to the north among the British, the Picts, and the Scots. Beloved and dear to all people, he diligently

gentibus carus et amabilis ecclesiastica officia diligenter persolvebat: in omnibus locis presbiteros et diacones[1] sibi adiuvantes abundanter ordinavit: inter secularesque[2] undas fluctuantes moderate navem ecclesiae gubernat. Sicut enim eum unda convivii non demersit, ita et abstinentiae[3] in superbiam non proiecit, quia in conviviis tam abstinenter vivebat, ut numquam solus, quamvis parvissima fiala esset, potu consumpsisset, aut pro calore solis in aestate sitienti aut pro frigore hiemis fatigato, ut multorum testimonio comprobatur; in vigiliis et orationibus, in lectione et ieiuniis quis similis ei inveniebatur[4]? Corpus quoque ab utero matris suae integrum, sicut coram fidelibus testatus est, sine pollutione[5] custodivit, quod in aqua benedicta et sanctificata nocturnis horis indesinenter aestate et hieme consuetudinarie lavavit, usquedum papa Iohannes beatae memoriae et apostolicae sedis[6] pro aetate sua huius laboris resolutionem habere praecepit. Ideo namque paene omnes abbates et abbatissae coenobiorum, aut sub suo nomine secum substantias custodientes aut post obitum suum haeredem illum habere optantes, voto voverunt. Principes quoque seculares, viri nobiles, filios suos ad erudiendum sibi dederunt, ut aut Deo servirent[7], si eligerent, aut adultos, si maluissent, regi armatos commendaret. Haec autem omnia facem[8] invidiae et odii in pectoribus multorum, flante diabolo, accenderunt[9]. Sanctus tamen pontifex noster secundum egregium doctorem[10] *arma a dextris et a sinistris*** in prosperis et in[11] adversis aequali lance patienter portabat, dans semper tam spiritalibus[12] quam secularibus dona et munera tam large, ut nullus ei aequalis inveniebatur.

CHAPTER XXII

De aedificatione domus Dei Inhaegustaldesei[13]

Adhaerebat igitur secundum psalmistam† indesinenter Domino, ponens in eo[14] spem suam reddensque Domino vota sua[15] dulcissima, qui ei omnia concedit. Nam Inaegustaldesae[16], adepta regione[17, 18] a regina sancta Aethelthrithae[19] Deo dicata[20], domum Domino in hono-

---

[1] diaconos C   [2] spiculares C   [3] abstinentia C   [4] inveniatur C
[5] pullutione F   [6] Iohannes *after* sedis *in* C   [7] servientem F   [8] Mabillon.
a facie F faciem C   [9] accederunt F   [10] praedicatorem C   [11] *omit* C
[12] spiritali C   [13] Inhagustaldensae C   [14] eum C   [15] *omit* vota, suo *for* sua C   [16] Inhagustaldaesae C   [17] regionem F   [18] *insert* et commutata F
[19] Aethilthrythe C   [20] dedicatae C

* 2 Cor. 6. 7.   † Cf. Psa. 72. 28.

accomplished his ecclesiastical duties; in every part he ordained numbers of priests and deacons to help him, and thus he steered the ship of the Church carefully amid the tossing billows of the world. For no wave of feasting submerged him, nor did the waves of fasting toss him on to the rocks of pride. For even amid feasting he lived so abstemiously that he never by himself drank to the dregs though it were but the smallest cup, either when he was thirsty owing to the heat of the sun, or when wearied by the cold of winter, as many witnesses can prove. In watching and prayers, in fastings and study, who was to be found like him? He kept his body, as he testified before the faithful, pure from his mother's womb, and unspotted, for he made it his custom to wash it during the night hours, winter and summer alike, with blessed and holy water, until Pope John of the Apostolic See and of blessed memory advised him to put an end to this rigour, out of consideration for his age. Almost all the abbots and abbesses of the monasteries dedicated their substance to him by vow, either keeping it themselves in his name or intending him to be their heir after their death. Secular chief men too, men of noble birth, gave him their sons to be instructed, so that, if they chose, they might devote themselves to the service of God; or that, if they preferred, he might give them into the king's charge as warriors when they were grown up. Now all these things kindled the flame of envy and hatred in the breasts of many, and the devil fanned it. Nevertheless our holy bishop, in the words of the great teacher, patiently bore his "armour, on the right hand and on the left," in prosperity and in adversity alike, always making gifts to the clergy as well as to the laity with such munificence that his equal could not be found.

CHAPTER XXII

Concerning the building of the house of God at Hexham. [672–678]

So continually, in the words of the Psalmist, he drew near to God, placing in Him his hope and rendering to the Lord who had given him all things, his dearest vows. For in Hexham, having obtained an estate from the queen, St Aethilthryth, the dedicated to God, he founded and built a house to the Lord in honour of St

rem sancti[1] Andreae apostoli fabrefactam fundavit: cuius profundi-
tatem in terra cum domibus mire[2] politis lapidibus fundatam et super
terram multiplicem domum columnis variis et porticibus multis
suffultam mirabileque[3] longitudine et altitudine murorum ornatam
et liniarum variis[4] anfractibus[5] viarum, aliquando sursum, aliquando
deorsum per cocleas circumductam, non est meae parvitatis hoc
sermone explicare, quod sanctus pontifex noster[6], a spiritu Dei
doctus, opera[7] facere excogitavit, neque enim[8] ullam domum aliam
citra Alpes montes talem aedificatam audivimus. Porro beatae
memoriae adhuc vivens gratia Dei Acca episcopus, quae magnalia
ornamenta huius multiplicis domus de auro et argento lapidibusque
pretiosis et quomodo altaria purpura et serico induta decoravit, quis
ad explanandum sufficere potest? Redeamus ad proposita.

CHAPTER XXIII

De sanato puero semivivo

Dum[9] aedificantes namque caementarii murorum huius domus
altitudines, quidam iuvenis ex servis Dei, de pinna inhormae pro-
ceritatis elapsus ad terram, deorsum cadens in pavimentum lapideum,
elisus cecidit; confracta sunt crura et brachia, omnibusque[10] membris
desolutis[11], ultima spiramina trahens iacebat. Quem cito caementarii
secundum praeceptum pontificis sancti[12], lacrimantis in oratione, in
feretro foras portabant, mortuum putantes; statimque, facto signo,
tota familia simul in unum conveniens, et stans pontifex[13] noster[14] in
medio fratrum, dixit: "Petamus[15] omnes unanimiter Deum plena
fide ut animam huius pueri in corpus emittat, et vivat, sicut Paulo
apostolo concessit[16]." Orantes ergo Deum, ut ne illusor omnis boni[17]
in hoc aedificio gaudium victoriae haberet, et flectentes genua,
secundum Heliam et Heliseum oratione facta a sancto episcopo
nostro et benedictione, spiritum vitae recepit, et alligantes medici
panibus ossa confracta, de die in diem melioratus[18], adhuc vivit[19],
nomenque eius[20] est Bothelm[21], gratias agens Deo.

---

[1] beati C   [2] mirifice C   [3] minacieque F   [4] v.l. C   [5] ac fractibus F
[6] ipse presul animarum C   [7] opere C   [8] omit C   [9] cum C
[10] insert in F   [11] desolutus F   [12] s.p. C   [13], [14] homo Dei C   [15] petemus F
[16] concedit C   [17] bonis C   [18] insert est C   [19] omit adhuc vivit insert
et multo tempore vixit C   [20] omit eius C   [21] Boðhelm C

Andrew the Apostle. My feeble tongue will not permit me to enlarge here upon the depth of the foundations in the earth, and its crypts of wonderfully dressed stone, and the manifold building above ground, supported by various columns and many side aisles, and adorned with walls of notable length and height, surrounded by various winding passages with spiral stairs leading up and down; for our holy bishop, being taught by the Spirit of God, thought out how to construct these buildings; nor have we heard of any other house on this side of the Alps built on such a scale. Further, Bishop Acca of blessed memory, who by the grace of God is still alive, provided for this manifold building splendid ornaments of gold, silver, and precious stones; but of these and of the way he decorated the altars with purple and silk, who is sufficient to tell? Let us return to our subject.

CHAPTER XXIII

Of the boy who was healed when at the point of death

Now while the masons were constructing the highest part of the walls of this building, a certain young man among the servants of God slipped from a pinnacle of enormous height, fell to the ground and was dashed upon a stone pavement. His arms and legs were broken, all his limbs were out of joint and he lay breathing his last; the masons, thinking he was dead, quickly carried him outside on a bier in obedience to the commands of the holy bishop who was tearfully praying. Forthwith, at a signal, the whole brotherhood gathered together, and our bishop stood in the midst of the brethren and said, "Let us all with one accord seek God in full confidence, that He may send the soul of the lad back into his body and that he may live, even as was granted to the Apostle Paul." So they prayed God that he who scoffs at all good might not have the joy of victory in this building; and while they bent their knees, our holy bishop, after the manner of Elijah and Elisha, prayed and gave his blessing, and the boy recovered the breath of life. The physicians bound the broken limbs with bandages and he grew better gradually from day to day. He is still alive and gives thanks to God. His name is Bothelm.

CHAPTER XXIV

De invidia excitata contra pontificem nostrum et de sede sua expulso

Insidiator *quasi leo rugiens** secundum Petrum apostolum circumiit ovile Dei, quaerens introitum, die noctuque vigilans semper, primum militem fortissimum vincere concupiscens, ut timidi facilius[1] superentur. Consueta arma arripiens, vasa fragilia muliebria quaesivit, per quae totum mundum maculavit frequenter. Nam regis Ecfrithi[2] regina nomine Iurmenburg[3], suadente diabolo, invidia tunc temporis torquebatur. Nam de lupa post occisionem regis agna Dei et perfecta abbatissa materque familias optima[4] commutata[5] est[6]. Iamiamque de faretra sua venenatas sagittas venifica[7] in cor regis, quasi impiissima Gezabel[8] prophetas Dei occidens et Heliam persequens, per auditum verborum emisit, enumerans ei eloquenter sancti Wilfrithi episcopi omnem gloriam eius secularem et divitias necnon coenobiorum multitudinem et aedificiorum magnitudinem innumerumque exercitum sodalium regalibus vestimentis et armis ornatum. Talibus itaque iaculis cor regis vulneratum, ambo callide quaerentes sanctum caput ecclesiae[9] in suum interitum contempnere donaque regum pro Deo a se audaciter fraudare, ad auxilium suae vesaniae archiepiscopum Theodorum cum muneribus, quae excaecant etiam sapientium oculos, quasi Balah[10] Balaam contra Dei voluntatem invitaverunt. Veniente vero archiepiscopo ad eos, quid mente agerent in contemptu eius, patentes, et sine aliquo culpandi piaculo inique dampnare,—quod absit—consensit. Nam tres episcopos aliunde inventos et non de subiectis illius parrochiae in absentia pontificis nostri in sua propria loca episcopatus sui noviter inordinate solus ordinavit. Quo audito, sanctus pontifex noster regem[11] et archiepiscopum[12] adiit, interrogans, quid causae esset ut sine aliquo delicti peccato suis substantiis a regibus pro Deo donatis praedonum more defraudarent. Illi responderunt famosum verbum pontifici nostro coram omni populo, dicentes: "Nullam criminis culpam in aliquo

---

[1] facile F   [2] Ecfridi C   [3] Irminburh C   [4] obtima C *and* F   [5] commotata F   [6] *omit* est C   [7] venenifica F   [8] Iesabel C   [9] ecclesiarum C   [10] Balac C   [11] regi F   [12] archiepiscopus C

* I Pet. 5. 8.

CHAPTER XXIV

How hatred was aroused against our bishop and how
he was driven from his see. [678]

The tempter, "like a roaring lion," according to the Apostle Peter, prowled round the sheepfold of God, seeking an entrance, always on the watch by day and by night and eagerly desiring to overthrow the bravest soldier first, in order that the fearful ones may be more easily overcome. So, taking his usual weapons he sought the weaker vessel, the woman, by whom he has constantly defiled the whole world. For Ecgfrith's queen, named Iurminburg, was at that time tortured with envy owing to the persuasions of the devil, although, after the death of the king, from being a she-wolf she was changed into a lamb of God, a perfect abbess and an excellent mother of the community. Forthwith this sorceress shot poisoned arrows of speech from her quiver into the heart of the king, as the wicked Jezebel did when she slew the prophets of the Lord and persecuted Elijah. She eloquently described to him all the temporal glories of St Wilfrid, his riches, the number of his monasteries, the greatness of his buildings, his countless army of followers arrayed in royal vestments and arms. With such shafts as these the king's heart was wounded. They both sought skilfully to humiliate the holy head of the Church to their own destruction and boldly to defraud him of the gifts which the kings had given him for God's sake. Contrary to the will of God and as Balak summoned Balaam, they summoned the Archbishop Theodore with the aid of bribes to help them in their madness; for bribes blind the eyes even of wise men.

When the archbishop had come, they explained to him what they intended to do to bring about Wilfrid's humiliation and he consented to condemn him unjustly—(Heaven save the mark!)—for no crime whatever. So in the absence of our bishop he consecrated, by himself, over parts of Wilfrid's own diocese, irregularly and contrary to all precedent, three bishops who had been picked up elsewhere and were not subjects of this diocese.

When our holy bishop heard this, he went to see the king and the archbishop and asked for what reason, without any wrong-doing on his part, they, like robbers, should defraud him of the possessions with which the kings, for God's sake, had endowed him. They made our bishop a scandalous reply before all the people:

nocendi tibi ascribimus, sed tamen statuta de te iudicia non muta-
mus." Ille vero episcopus noster tali iudicio fraudabili non[1] con-
tentus, cum consilio coepiscoporum suorum iudicium apostolicae
sedis magis elegit, sicut Paulus apostolus, sine causa dampnatus a
Iudaeis, Caesarem apellavit.   Deinde autem sanctus pontifex,
conversus a tribunali regali, adulatoribus cum risu gaudentibus
dixit: "Hoc anniversario die, qui nunc ridetis in meam pro invidia[2]
condempnationem, tunc in vestram confusionem[3] amare flebitis."
Et sic secundum prophetiam sancti evenit. Nam eo die anniversario
Aelfwini[4] regis occisi cadaver in Eboracam[5] delatum est; omnes
populi amare lacrimantes vestimenta et capitis comam lacerabant,
et frater[6] superstes usque ad mortem sine victoria regnabat.

CHAPTER XXV

Quomodo Winfrithus[7] episcopus[8] spoliatus sit

Beatae memoriae Wilfrithus episcopus praeparans cum suis
sodalibus et clero naves ascendere, multa milia monachorum suorum
sub manu episcoporum noviter ordinatorum relinquens, maerentes
et flentes Deumque[9] indesinenter deprecantes, ut suum iter in voluntatem eius dirigeret. Inimici vero praesulis nostri[10] malorum suorum
memores, putantes in austrum ad Qwoentawic[11], navigantem, ea[12] via
rectissima ad sedem apostolicam pergentem, praemiserunt nuntios
suos cum muneribus ad Theodericum regem Francorum et ad
Eadefyrwine[13] impium ducem, ut aut exilio maiori dampnarent aut,
occisis sociis, omni substantia sua spoliarent. Dominus enim[14] de
manu inimicorum, quasi de manu Herodis, liberavit eum. Nam eo[15]
tempore sanctus Winfrithus[16] episcopus, de Licitfelda[17] expulsus, ea
via pergens venit in manus supradictorum inimicorum, quasi in
fauces leonis; captus statim est[18] et omni pecunia spoliatus, multisque
ex sociis suis occisis, misere[19] ad extremum[20] sanctum episcopum
nudum dereliquerunt. Putabant enim, ut non erat, illum esse
sanctum Wilfrithum episcopum, errore bono unius syllabae seducti.

---

[1] *omit* F   [2] providia F   [3] confusione C   [4] Elfwini C   [5] Euroicam C
[6] *insert* eius C   [7] Levison. Wilfri F Wilfrithus C   [8] *omit* C
[9] Dominumque C   [10] n.p. C   [11] Quoentavic C   [12] et C   [13] Efruinum C
[14] *omit* F   [15] *omit* F   [16] Wilfridus C   [17] Lyccitfelda C   [18] *omit* C
[19] miseri F   [20] extremo C

"We do not," they said, "ascribe to you any criminal offence in any injurious act, but we will not change our established decrees respecting you."

But our bishop was not content with so fraudulent a judgment, and, on the advice of his brother-bishops, he sought the judgment of the Apostolic See, as the Apostle Paul, when he had been condemned by the Jews without cause, appealed to Caesar. Then the holy bishop, turning away from the royal tribunal, amid the mirthful laughter of the king's flatterers, said, "On this day twelvemonth you who now laugh at my condemnation through malice, shall then weep bitterly over your own confusion." And so it happened, in accordance with the prophecy of the saint. For on that day twelvemonth the body of the slain King Aelfwini was carried into York and all the people with bitter tears tore their garments and their hair, while his brother who survived him reigned, but gained no victory until the day of his death.

CHAPTER XXV

How Bishop Winfrid was robbed. [678]

Bishop Wilfrid of blessed memory now prepared to embark with his companions and clergy, while many thousands of his monks were left, mourning and weeping, in the power of the newly ordained bishops, and praying God without ceasing to direct Wilfrid's journey in accordance with His will. But the enemies of our prelate, mindful of their misdeeds, believed that he would be sailing south to Etaples and making his way by the most direct route to the Holy See, and so they sent ahead their messengers with bribes to Theodoric, King of the Franks, and to Ebroin, a wicked duke, to persuade them to condemn him to the greater exile, or to slay his comrades and rob him of all his substance. But the Lord freed him from the hands of his enemies, as though from the hands of Herod. For at that time the holy Winfrid the bishop, who had been driven out of Lichfield, was making his way by the same route and fell into the hands of these same enemies, as though into the jaws of a lion. He was immediately captured and robbed of all his money. Many of his companions were slain and the holy bishop was left naked and in the utmost straits of misery. They thought that he was the holy Bishop Wilfrid, which was not the case, being misled by a fortunate mistake in one syllable.

CHAPTER XXVI

Quomodo in Freis navigio pervenit

Nam e contrario sanctus pontifex noster, secundum desiderium eius flante zefiro[1] vento ab occidente temperanter, versis navium rostris ad orientem, usque dum in Freis prospere cum omnibus pervenit: ibique gentilium copiis inventis, ab Aldgislo[2] rege eorum honorifice est susceptus[3]. Tunc statim sanctus pontifex noster cum licentia regis verbum Dei gentibus[4] cotidie praedicavit, enuntians eis verum Deum patrem omnipotentem et Iesum Christum, filium eius unicum, et Spiritum sanctum sibi coaeternum, et baptismum unum in remissionem peccatorum et vitam aeternam post mortem in resurrectione manifeste docuit. Et doctrinam[5] eius omnem[6] secundum paganos bene adiuvabat[7]; erat enim in adventu eorum eo tempore solito amplius in piscatione et in omnibus frugifer annus et[8] ad Domini gloriam reputantes, quem sanctus vir Dei praedicavit. Deinde eo anno, accepta praedicatione, omnes principes, exceptis paucis, et multa milia vulgi in nomine Domini baptizabat[9]; et primum ibi secundum apostolum[10] fundamentum fidei posuit, quod adhuc superaedificat filius eius, Inhripis nutritus, gratia Dei Wilbrordus episcopus, multo labore desudans, cuius merces manet[11] in aeternum.

CHAPTER XXVII

De eo, quod pretium appretiati rex renuit

Eodem quoque tempore Eferwine[12] dux Theoderici regis Francorum misit nuntios suos cum litteris ad Aldgislum[13] regem Fresis[14], salutans eum verbis pacificis promittensque ei[15] sub iureiurando modium plenum solidorum aureorum dare, pretium utique sceleste[16], si Wilfrithum episcopum aut vivum deductum aut caput eius occisi sibi emisisset[17]. Statimque rex, praesentibus nobis et nuntiis coram populo suo in palatio epulantibus omnibus[18] audientibus, legi[19] litteras iussit. Post lectionem[20] vero cartam, accipiens inter manus suas, cunctis videntibus discerpens dissipavit et in ignem coram se

---

[1] omit C   [2] Aldgiso C   [3] susceptus est C   [4] gentilibus F   [5] doctrina C
[6] omit C   [7] adiuvavit C   [8] omit C   [9] baptizavit C   [10] apostolorum F
[11] omit F   [12] Efyruinus C   [13] Aldgelsum C   [14] Freis C   [15] eis F
[16] celeste F   [17] emisit F   [18] omnibusque C   [19] omit F   [20] lectam C

CHAPTER XXVI

How he came to Friesland in his voyage. [678]

On the contrary, however, our holy bishop, with a west wind blowing gently according to his wish, and with the vessels heading eastward, came after a prosperous voyage to Friesland with all his companions. There he found great crowds of heathen and was honourably received by Aldgisl their king. Immediately our holy prelate, with the consent of the king, preached the word of God daily to the people, telling them of the true God, the Almighty Father, Jesus Christ His only Son, and the Holy Spirit coeternal with them, and of one baptism for the remission of sins; he also taught them clearly about life everlasting after death in the resurrection. And he greatly confirmed all his teaching in the eyes of the pagans, for, at the time of their coming, the catch of fish was unusually large and the year was more than usually fruitful in every kind of produce. They attributed all this to the glory of the Lord whom the holy man of God had been preaching to them. So that year they accepted his teaching and with a few exceptions all the chiefs were baptized by him in the name of the Lord, as well as many thousands of common people. Like the Apostle he first laid the foundation of the faith there, and his son who was brought up at Ripon, Willibrord, bishop by the grace of God, is still building upon it, toiling very laboriously, and his reward awaits him in eternity.

CHAPTER XXVII

How the king refused the price when a price was set upon him

At the same time Ebroin, duke of Theodoric, King of the Franks, sent messengers with letters to Aldgisl, King of the Frisians, saluting him with words of peace and promising under oath to give him a bushel full of gold solidi, a reward of crime indeed, if he would either send him Bishop Wilfrid taken alive or else slay him and send his head. The king at once ordered the letter to be read for all to hear, while we were present and while the messengers were feasting in the palace with his people. After the reading he took the missive in his hands, tore it up in the sight of all and threw it into the fire which was burning

ardentem proiecit[1], dicens portitoribus: "Enuntiate domino vestro[2]
hoc modo me dicentem: Sic rerum creator regnum et vitam in Deo
suo periurantis pactumque initum non custodientis scindens destruat
et consumens in favillam devellat!" Deinde autem nuntii cum confusione a rege, non consentiente piaculo, ad dominum[3] suum, unde
venerunt, redierunt.

CHAPTER XXVIII

Quomodo Daegberht[4] et Berhthere[5]
reges duo susceperunt eum

Postquam Deo amabilis pontifex noster in Fresis[6] hiemaverat,
populum multum Domino lucratus, verno tempore adveniente,
coeptum iter, Deo adiuvante, ad sedem apostolicam cum comitanti-
bus[7] carpebat, veniens ad Francorum regem nomine Daegberht qui
eum cum honore mansuetissime pro meritis eius anteactis in eum
suscepit. Nam supradictus rex in iuventute sua ab inimicis regnantibus in exilium perditionis pulsus, navigando ad Hiberniam insulam,
Deo adiuvante[8] pervenit. Post annorum circulum amici et proximi[9]
eius, viventem et in perfecta aetate florentem a navigantibus audientes,
miserunt nuntios suos ad beatum Wilfrithum episcopum, petentes
ut[10] eum de Scottia[11] et Hibernia ad se invitasset et sibi ad regem
emisisset. Et sic sanctus pontifex noster perfecit[12], suscipiens eum de
Hibernia venientem, per arma[13] ditatum et viribus sociorum elevatum
magnifice ad suam regionem emisit[14]. Et nunc rex beneficiorum
eius memoratus, diligenter poscens[15] ut in suo regno episcopatum
maximum ad civitatem Streithbyrg[16] pertinentem susciperet; et eum
nolentem accipere cum muneribus et donis magnis et cum Deodato
episcopo suo duce ad apostolicam sedem emisit. Pergentes itaque
sancti episcopi, viam Domino dirigente, pervenerunt ad Berhtherum
regem Campaniae, virum humilem et quietum[17] et trementem ser-
mones Dei; qui peregrinos secundum praeceptum Domini benigne
suscipiens, sancto pontifici nostro enuntiavit, dicens: "De Brittannia[18] inimici tui nuntios ad me mittentes, suis sermonibus salu-

[1] proicit F   [2] nostro F   [3] Deum F   [4] Daegbereht C   [5] Berehtere C
[6] Freis C   [7] comitatibus C   [8] iuvante C   [9] propinqui C   [10] omit F
[11] Scottica F   [12] perficit F   [13] omnia C   [14] Mabillon. emisisset F and C
[15] poposcens F and C   [16] Streitburg C   [17] equitum F   [18] Bryttannia C

in front of him, saying to the bearers of the document, "Tell your master what I now say: Thus let the Creator of all things rend and destroy the realm and life of him who perjures himself before God and does not keep the covenant he has made; thus may he tear him up and consume him to ashes." Then the ambassadors in confusion returned from the presence of a king who would not consent to commit a crime, to their own master whence they had come.

CHAPTER XXVIII
How Dagobert and Perctarit, two kings, received him. [679]

After our bishop the beloved of God had spent the winter among the Frisians winning much people for the Lord, when spring came, with God's help he continued the journey he had undertaken with his companions to the Apostolic See. He came to the King of the Franks called Dagobert who received him with great kindness and with all honour for the service which Wilfrid had once rendered him. For this King Dagobert when he was a young man had been driven into exile and ruin by his enemies who were then reigning, and sailing away, came to Ireland by God's help. In the course of years his friends and kinsmen heard from some travellers that he was alive and flourishing in the prime of manhood. So they sent messengers to the blessed Bishop Wilfrid asking him to invite Dagobert across from Scotland and Ireland and to send him out to them as king: this our holy bishop did and, receiving him as he came from Ireland, he sent him forth to his own country in great state, well supplied with weapons and supported by the strength of his companions. Now the king mindful of these kindnesses strongly urged him to undertake the chief bishopric in his own kingdom which belonged to the city of Strassburg. But when Wilfrid refused he sent him to the Apostolic See with gifts and rich presents making his bishop, Deodatus, the guide.

As the holy bishops proceeded on their journey under the guidance of God, they came to Perctarit, King of Campania, a humble and peaceful man who feared the words of God. He received the pilgrims kindly according to the bidding of the Lord and then addressed our holy bishop with these words: "Some enemies of yours have sent me messengers from Britain, offering me their salutations and pro-

tantes me et dona mihi maxima promittentes, si te subterfugientem, ut dixerunt, episcopum[1] angarizarem et ad apostolicam sedem tendentem retinerem. Quibus tam nefariam rem renuens, dixi: 'Fui aliquando in diebus[2] iuventutis meae exul de patria pulsus[3], sub pagano quodam rege Hunorum degens, qui iniit mecum foedus in deo suo idolo, ut numquam me inimicis meis prodidisset[4] aut[5] dedisset. Et post spatium temporis venerunt ad regem paganum sermone inimicorum meorum nuntii, promittentes sibi dare sub iureiurando solidorum aureorum modium plenum, si me illis[6] ad internicionem dedisset. Quibus non consentiens dixit: "Sine dubio dii vitam meam succidant, si hoc piaculum facio, irritans pactum deorum meorum." Ego[7] quanto magis, qui Deum verum scio, animam meam pro totius mundi lucro in perditionem non dabo.'" Tunc itaque sanctum pontificem nostrum et suos socios cum honore et ducibus, sicut eum Dominus ubique in peregrinatione protegens magnificavit, ad apostolicam sedem olim optatam in gratiarum emisit actione[8].

CHAPTER XXIX

Quomodo beatissimus[9] Agatho apostolicae sedis papa[10] cum sancta[11] synodo[12] pontificis[13] nostri[14] scripta receperit[15]

Perveniente igitur Deo amabili Wilfritho episcopo prospere cum omnibus ad sedem praedictam, causa[16] adventus eius praelata ubi[17] enotuit, quod[18] eo tempore Cenowald[19] religiosus monachus a sancto Theodoro archiepiscopo cum suis litteris emissus Romam venit, et beatissimum Agathonem sedis apostolicae papam rerum dissensio non latuit. Tunc vero congregantibus sanctissimis[20] episcopis et presbiteris plus quam .L. in basilicam salvatoris Domini nostri Iesu Christi quae apellatur[21] Constantiniana, Agatho autem sanctissimus ac ter beatissimus episcopus sanctae catholicae atque apostolicae ecclesiae urbis Romae consedentibus dixit: "Non credo latere vestram sanctam fraternitatem, quamobrem ad hunc venerabilem conventum eam ascriberim. Cognoscere quippe vestram cupio reverentiam mecumque tractare,

[1] episcopi F   [2] die C   [3] expulsus C   [4] prodisset F *and* C   [5] vel C
[6] ullis F   [7] *insert* vero C   [8] a.e. C   [9] beatissimo F beatissa C
[10] papae C   [11] sancto F   [12] sinodi F   [13] Mabillon. pontifici F *and* C
[14] nostro C   [15] reciperit F *and* C   [16] causam F   [17] urbe C   [18] quia C
[19] Coenvald C   [20] sancti-sanctissimis C   [21] apellatus F

mising me very great rewards if I would lay hands on you who are a bishop fleeing secretly, as they declared, and would hold you back as you make your way to the Apostolic See. I refused to do so wicked a thing and answered them thus: 'I was once an exile in the days of my youth, driven from my fatherland, dwelling with a certain pagan King of the Huns who entered into a covenant with me before the idol that was his god, to the effect that he would never betray me nor hand me over to my enemies. After some time some messengers came to the heathen king with word from my enemies, promising under oath to give him a bushel full of gold solidi if he would hand me over to be slain. He would not come to an agreement with them, "For," said he, "doubtless the gods would cut off my life if I were to commit this crime and break the pledge made before them." How much more shall I, who know the true God, refuse to give my soul over to destruction for the wealth of the whole world!'" Then in truth the king with thanksgiving sent our holy bishop and his companions to the Apostolic See which they had so long desired to behold, giving him honourable treatment and providing him with guides; in such ways the Lord glorified him by His protecting care throughout his journey.

CHAPTER XXIX

How the most blessed Agatho, Pope of the Apostolic See, together with the holy synod, received the letters of our bishop. [679]

When therefore Bishop Wilfrid, beloved of God, reached the before mentioned see in safety with all his companions, the cause of his coming had preceded him and had become known there, for at that time Coenwald, a religious monk, had been sent by the holy Archbishop Theodore with letters from him and had reached Rome; and the quarrel was not hidden from the most blessed Agatho, Pope of the Apostolic See. Then indeed, when the most holy bishops and priests had gathered together to the number of over fifty in the church of our Lord and Saviour Jesus Christ which is called the Constantinian, Agatho the most holy and thrice-blessed Bishop of the Holy Catholic and Apostolic Church in the city of Rome said to those who sat in council, "I do not think that it is hidden from your holy brotherhood why I have summoned you to this venerable gathering. I desire this reverend body to learn and to discuss with me the dissension which

qualis in ecclesiis Brittanniae insulae, per Dei gratiam ubi fidelium
multitudo concrevit, nuper est[1] exorta dissensio, quae ad nos tam per
relationem exinde huc venientium quam per scriptorum seriem
perlata est." Andreas reverentissimus episcopus Ostiensis et
Iohannes episcopus Portuensis dixerunt: "Omnium quidem ecclesiarum ordinatio in vestrae apostolicae auctoritatis pendet arbitrio,
qui vicem beati Petri apostoli principis geritis, cui claves ligandi
solvendique[2] conditor ac redemptor omnium Christus Dominus
contulit. Verum erga quod nobis est iniunctum ab apostolica vestra
censura, ante hos dies, consedentibus nobis[3] una cum nostris
coepiscopis atque confamulis, relegimus singula scripta, quae de
Brittannia insula directi apostolico vestro pontificatui detulerunt tam
ea[4], quae ex persona Theodori reverentissimi[5] archiepiscopi, illuc[6]
ab apostolica sede olim directi, missa sunt, aliorumve cum eisdem
scriptis relationes[7] adversus quendam episcopum subterfugientem,
ut asserunt, quem huc venisse arbitrati sunt: quamque ea, quae a
Wilfritho Deo amabili episcopo sanctae Eboracae[8] ecclesiae oblata
sunt, qui de sua sede eiectus a praenominato sanctissimo apostolicam
sedem apellans huc usque pervenit; in quibus cum multas questiones
insererent, neque[9] sanctorum canonum subtilitate[10] convictum[11] eum
de aliquibus facinoribus et ideo non canonice deiectum repperimus,
neque quaelibet facinora eum perpetrasse dictis propriis accusatores
eius comprobare valuerunt, pro quorum flagitiis degradari debuisset.
Potius autem et modestiam hunc tenuisse perpendimus, quod non
seditiosis quibusdam decertationibus seipsum implicuit. Sed postquam de sua sede repulsus est, coepiscopis suis facti meritum in-
notescens, memoratus Deo amabilis Wilfrithus episcopus exinde ad
hanc apostolicam sedem accurrit, in qua summi sacerdotii princi-
patum fundavit, qui suo sanguine sanctam ecclesiam redemit,
omnipotens Christus Dominus et principis apostolorum auctoritatem
firmavit. Vestri denique apostolatus auctoritati concessum est, quid
in hoc ordinare praecipiatis." Agatho sanctissimus ac ter beatissimus
episcopus sanctae ecclesiae catholicae[12] urbis Romae dixit: "Wilfrithus
Deo amabilis episcopus sanctae Eboraicae[13] ecclesiae prae foribus
nostri secretarii esse narratus[14] est[15]; ad nostrum secretarium iuxta

---

[1] *omit* C   [2] atque solvendi C   [3] *omit* F   [4] eo F eorum C   [5] reveren-
tissima F   [6] illic C   [7] relationibus F   [8] Euroycae C   [9] ne quis C
[10] subtilitatem C   [11] Mabillon. convinctum C *and* F   [12] *insert* atque
apostolicae C   [13] Euroicae C   [14] Raine. narratum C *and* F   [15] *omit* C

has of late arisen in the churches of the island of Britain, where the company of the faithful has increased through the grace of God; accounts have been brought by the narratives of those who have come hither from thence, and by a succession of letters."

Andrew, the most reverend Bishop of Ostia, and John, Bishop of Porto, then spoke: "The regulation of all the churches rests on the decisions of your Apostolic authority who fill the place of the blessed Peter, chief of the Apostles, to whom the Lord Christ, the Creator and Redeemer of all men, gave the keys for binding and loosing. But in accordance with what was enjoined upon us lately by your Apostolic judgment, meeting together in company with our brother-bishops and fellow-servants, we have re-read the several letters which envoys have brought from the island of Britain to your Apostolic See. We have read those which have been despatched from the person of the most reverend Archbishop Theodore, who was formerly sent thither by the Apostolic See, with the reports of others in addition to those same writings, against a certain bishop who, as they assert, is supposed to have come hither in secret flight; and we have also read those writings which have been presented by Wilfrid, beloved of God, the Bishop of the holy church of York, who has been ejected from his see by the most holy man before mentioned and has come all the way to appeal to the Holy See. In these letters, though they introduce many doubtful points, we find that he has not been convicted of any crimes in accordance with the plain sense of the sacred canons, and therefore his ejection is not canonical, nor have his accusers been able to prove by their own statements that he had been guilty of any crimes whatsoever, the scandal of which would justify his degradation. But on the contrary we consider that it was moderation which kept him from mixing himself up in certain seditious strife. But, after he was driven from his see, the aforesaid Bishop Wilfrid, beloved of God, informed his fellow-bishops of the merits of his case and forthwith hastened to this Apostolic See in which He who redeemed the Holy Church by His blood, Christ the Almighty Lord, founded the primacy of the chief priesthood and established the authority of the chief of the Apostles. Finally the matter has been submitted to your Apostolic authority to learn what you enjoin to be done in this case."

Agatho, the most holy and thrice-blessed bishop of the Holy Catholic Church in the city of Rome, said, "Wilfrid the beloved of

suam postulationem cum petitione quam[1] secum afferre dictus est, ammittatur." Wilfrithus Deo amabilis episcopus, dum venerabile secretarium ingrederetur, dixit: "Deprecor vestram pontificalem beatitudinem ut meae humilitatis petitionem excipi coramque relegi praecipiatis." Agatho sanctissimus episcopus dixit: "Wilfrithi Deo amabilis episcopi[2] petitio suscepta coram omnibus relegatur." Et accipiens Iohannes notarius relegit sancto[3] apostolico concilio.

CHAPTER XXX

Haec est petitio Wilfrithi episcopi

"Wilfrithus humilis et indignus episcopus Saxoniae ad hoc[4] apostolicum fastigium tamquam ad locum munitum turremque fortitudinis gressus cordis, Deo[5] praeviante, perduxi[6], quia unde normam sacrorum canonum in omnes Christi ecclesias per totum orbem diffusas emanare cognosco, praedicatione[7] apostolica traditas et plena fide susceptas, ex eo meae humilitatis iustitiae censuram confidenter praestolor conservari. Cognovisse quippe non ambigo vestrum pontificale fastigium tam[8] meae parvitatis suggestionem[9] quam quae viva voce presentialiter[10] intimavi. Et per satisfactionem petitionis scriptis narrantibus obtuli, eius apostolicis obtutibus in ipso mei adventus exordio presentatus, quod, nullam[11] in me supplici canonicam culpam repperientes, quidam mei episcopatus invasores illicita praesumptione contra sacrorum canonum normas ac definitiones[12] in conventu Theodori sanctissimi archiepiscopi Cantuariorum ecclesiae aliorumque tunc temporis cum eo convenientium antistitum sedem, quam per decem et eo amplius annos cum Dei clementia dispensabam, raptorum more invadere atque eripere moliti sunt et in eadem sede subsedere[13]; et non solum unum, sed tres in mea ecclesia sese promoverunt episcopos, licet canonica eorum non sit promotio. Quid autem acciderit, ut Theodorus sanctissimus archiepiscopus me superstite in sedem, quam licet indignus dispensabam, absque consensu cuiuslibet episcopi tres sua auctoritate, mea[14]

---

[1] qua F   [2] insert eius C   [3] insert et C   [4] adhuc F   [5] omit F
[6] perduxit C   [7] per...predicatione omit F   [8] insert ex C   [9] suggestione C
[10] prentialiter F   [11] Mabillon. nulla C and F   [12] diffinitionis F
[13] subsere F   [14] me F

God and bishop of the holy church of York is said to be at the doors of our secretarium; let him be admitted to our secretarium in accordance with his request, with the petition which he is said to be bringing with him."

As Bishop Wilfrid the beloved of God entered the hallowed secretarium, he said, "I pray your Pontifical Holiness that you will command that my humble petition be received and read in your presence."

The most holy Bishop Agatho answered, "Let the petition of Bishop Wilfrid the beloved of God be received and read before the whole assembly." So John the secretary took it and read it to the holy Apostolic Council.

CHAPTER XXX
This is the petition of Bishop Wilfrid

"I, Wilfrid, a humble and unworthy bishop of England, have ordered the goings of my heart, by the guidance of God, to this, the Apostolic Eminence, as though to a fortress or a strong tower; for I confidently expect that in the place whence I know the rules of the sacred canons go forth to all the churches of Christ spread throughout the whole world, handed down through the preaching of the Apostles and received in full assurance, in that place a righteous judgment upon me, humble as I am, will be maintained. I have no doubt but that your Pontifical Eminence has taken knowledge not only of the case I have put before you in my weakness, but also what I have declared to you in your presence face to face; and in support of my petition as set forth in written documents, I alleged at the very beginning of my visit, on my introduction to the Apostolic presence, that, though discovering no canonical offence in me your suppliant, certain invaders of my bishopric, unlawfully presuming against the laws and declarations of the sacred canons, at the synod of Theodore the most holy Archbishop of Canterbury, and of other bishops at that time assembling with him, have attempted like brigands to assail the see which, by God's mercy, I had been controlling for more than ten years, to rob me of it, and to plant themselves in the same see; and they have preferred themselves to be bishops in my church, not merely one but three of them, though their preferment is not canonical. How comes it then that the most holy Archbishop Theodore, while I am still alive, should consecrate three bishops

humilitate non acquiescente, ordinaret episcopos, omittere magis
quam flagitare pro eiusdem viri reverentia condecet; quem quidem
eo, quod ab hac apostolicae summitatis sede directus est, accusare
non audeo. Verum si claruit, quod contra ius[1] regularium sanc-
tionum de dispensatione[2] ecclesiae, cui licet indignus praeeram, ab
infestis[3] propulsus sum sine convictione cuiuspiam criminis et
absque culpa facinoris, citra ullius delicti piaculum, quod canonica
percellit severitas, et neque de pristina sede pulsus tumultuosus
cuiquam apparui neque seditionis quaestionem[4] succensi neque
ambitiosus[5] contentionibus obstiti, sed confestim huius sacrosanctae
sedis appellavi subsidium; confamulos atque consacerdotes meos
earundem provinciarum episcopos tantummodo protestatus, abscessi.
Si quidem praevidet[6] vestra apostolica summitas una[7] cum consedentibus[8] sanctissimis episcopis, privatum me esse, qui pro nulla
culpa convictus sum, humili devotione quae[9] censentur amplector.
Si autem et pristinum episcopatum percipere, sequor totisque viribus
veneror[10] ab apostolica sede prolatam sententiam, tantum ut invasores
de pristinis parrochiis ecclesiae, cui ego indignus vester famulus
praefui, vestra synodali sanctione pellantur. Et si rursus in eadem
parrochia, cui praefui, praesules adhibere praeviderit, saltem tales
iubeat praevidere[11] promovendos, cum quibus possim, pacifica atque
tranquilla inter nos concordia obtinente[12], Deo unanimiter deservire,
ut videlicet unusquisque nostrum concessa[13] ecclesiae iura cognoscat
et vigilantiam sibi commissis impertiat[14] ut, si ita placuerit archiepiscopo et coepiscopis meis, ut augeatur numerus episcoporum,
tales eligant de ipso clero ecclesiae, quales in synodo placet[15] congregatis episcopis, ut ne a foris et ab alienis damnetur ecclesia. Quicquid
enim confusum et indiscretum est, inextricabiles atque inexplebiles
dissensiones exaggerat, nec valebit a quoquam[16] pacifice ullatenus,
de quo contenditur, dispensari. Confido enim, quod omnem devotae
oboedientiae obsequelam statutis apostolicis exhibeo[17], ad cuius
aequitatem omnibus abiectis cum tota mentis confidentia properavi[18]."

---

[1] iu su C   [2] (*omit* de) dispensationi F   [3] infectis C   [4] questione C
[5] ambitiosis C   [6] Mabillon. praevidit C *and* F   [7] unam F   [8] sedentibus
F   [9] *omit* F   [10] venerari C   [11] providere C   [12] optinente C *and* F
[13] concessae C *and* F   [14] impertierat F   [15] placeat C   [16] quodam C
[17] exhibebo C   [18] preparavit C

by his own authority to the see, which, though unworthy, I had been controlling; and that without the consent of any bishop and in spite of my humble opposition; for the reverence due to the archbishop I will pass over this question and not demand a reason for it; indeed I dare not accuse him because he has been despatched by this the Apostolic and the Principal See. But even if it has been made clear that I have been driven by my enemies from the control of the church over which, though unworthy, I was presiding, against the law of the canonical rules, without being convicted of any crime, and without any wrongful act falling short of any misdemeanour which the stern canonical law punishes, yet I can assure you I was not known as a stirrer up of strife when I was driven from my former see, nor did I kindle any dispute, nor did I ostentatiously take a stand against their attacks; but forthwith I appealed to this most Holy See for help; and without doing more than make a protest to my fellow-servants and my fellow-bishops in these same provinces, I departed. If indeed your Apostolic Eminence, together with the most holy bishops who sit with you, decides that I have been deprived, though guilty of no fault, I accept your decision with humble devotion. If however I am to get back my former bishopric, then I accept and venerate the decision promulgated by the Apostolic See with all my heart, provided only that the usurpers are driven out by the sanction of your synod from my old sees in the church over which I, your unworthy servant, have been ruling. But if again it has been decided to appoint bishops in the same see over which I have been ruling, at any rate let your Eminence order that it be decided that only such be preferred with whom I can serve God in unity, so that a peaceful and unbroken agreement obtain amongst us; to wit that each one of us may recognise the established laws of the Church and may each watch diligently over what has been committed to him. So, if it please the archbishop and my fellow-bishops to increase the number of bishops, let them choose such from our own clergy as the bishops gathered together in synod may decide upon, so that the Church may not be harmed from outside and by strangers; for whatever is done irregularly and unadvisedly increases unappeasable and implacable quarrels and no one will avail at all to bring the matter in dispute to a peaceful conclusion in any respect whatever. For I am sure that I show the absolute compliance of devoted obedience to the Apostolic laws to whose justice I have hastened, casting everything else aside with absolute confidence of heart."

CHAPTER XXXI
De responsione Agathonis Papae[1]

Agatho sanctissimus ac ter beatissimus episcopus sanctae catholicae atque apostolicae ecclesiae urbis Romae dixit: "Non mediocriter audientibus satisfacit petitionis series, quam Wilfrithus Deo amabilis episcopus obtulit, in hoc, quod, cum[2] se indigne de episcopali sede eiectum agnoscat[3], non contumaciter obstitit ambientibus nec cui vim repellere saeculariter maluit, sed humiliter sentiens, auctoris nostri beati Petri apostoli principis canonicum expedivit[4] subsidium; supplici praestolatione, quae super eo censenda sunt, prompte se suscepturum pollicetur[5] nec ambigit de prolatione sententiae, sed quae terminantur amplectitur, integra fide suscepturum se perhibens, quod nostro ore auctor noster beatus Petrus apostolus, cuius ministerio fungimur, statuendum praeviderit[6]."

CHAPTER XXXII
De responsione synodus[7]

Universa synodus, quae una cum sanctissimo atque ter beatissimo Agathone apostolico papa convenit, regulariter inter caetera diffiniens dixit: "Statuimus atque decernimus, ut Deo amabilis Wilfrithus episcopus episcopatum, quem nuper habuerat, recipiat, salva definitione superius ordinata[8]; et quos cum consensu concilii[9] ibidem congregandi elegerit sibi adiutores episcopos, cum quibus debeat pacifice conversari, secundum regulam superius constitutam a sanctissimo archiepiscopo promoti ordinentur episcopi[10], expulsis procul dubio eis, qui in[11] eius[12] absentia in episcopatum inormiter missi sunt. Si quis proinde contra horum statutorum synodalium decreta ausu[13] temerario obsistere temptaverit vel non oboedienter susceperit vel post quodlibet temporis spatium, quiqui sint vel fuerint, infringere ea in totum vel in partem[14] temptaverit, ex auctoritate beati Petri apostolorum principis eum hac[15] sanctione percel-

[1] omit C   [2] omit F   [3] agnoscet F   [4] expetivit C   [5] pollicitur C   [6] p.s. C
[7] sinodis C   [8] ordinater F   [9] consilii C   [10] episcopis C   [11] omit F
[12] eis F   [13] ausa F   [14] partes C   [15] ac F

CHAPTER XXXI
Of Pope Agatho's answer

The most holy and thrice-blessed Agatho, Bishop of the Holy Catholic and Apostolic Church of the city of Rome, made reply: "It gives no small satisfaction to those of us who have listened to the course of the petition which Bishop Wilfrid, beloved of God, has offered, that, though he believes himself to be unworthily driven from the episcopal see, he did not contumaciously oppose his rivals, nor did he choose to repel force with force in a worldly manner, but, with humble mind, he procured the canonical aid of our blessed founder, Peter the chief Apostle. With humble expectation he promises to acknowledge immediately that which is decreed concerning him, nor does he cavil about the pronouncement of our opinion; but he accepts the conclusions, whatever they may be, declaring that he will with unshaken loyalty accept whatever our founder, the blessed Apostle Peter, whose ministry we fulfil, shall decide by our mouth."

CHAPTER XXXII
Of the synod's answer

The whole synod which met together with the most holy and thrice-blessed Apostolic Father Agatho made the following declaration amongst others, according to rule:

"We decide and decree that Bishop Wilfrid, beloved of God, shall receive back the bishopric which he had of late, within the limits previously defined; and those whom he shall choose as fellow-bishops with the consent of the council there to be assembled, men with whom he may live peaceably, according to the rule previously laid down, shall be preferred and consecrated as bishops by the most holy archbishop; and those must most decidedly be driven out, who in his absence have been unlawfully placed in the episcopal see. If anyone therefore attempts with rash daring to withstand the decrees of these synodal statutes or does not obediently accept them, or if any, whoever they be or shall be, after whatsoever lapse of time, shall attempt to break them, either wholly or in part, we declare by the authority of the blessed Peter the chief of the Apostles that he shall be punished by

lendum censemus: ut, siquidem episcopus est, qui hanc piam dispositionem temerare temptaverit, sit ab episcopali[1] ordine destitutus et aeterni anathematis reus; similiter, si presbiter aut diaconus fuerint vel inferioris gradus ecclesiae; si vero clericus, monachus vel laicus cuiusvelibet dicionis vel rex, extraneus efficiatur a salvatoris corpore et sanguine Domini nostri Iesu Christi nec terribilem eius adventum dignus appareat conspicere. Si quis vero haec, quae a nobis statuta vel diffinita[2] sunt, cum sincera devotione et perfecta satisfactione susceperit, tenuerit[3], perfecerit, ad perficiendum concursum praebuerit[4], videat *bona Domini in regione vivorum*★ consorsque dextrae partis existat, aeternam beatitudinem possideat et illam beatificam vocem mereatur audire cum omnibus sanctis, qui divino conspectui placuerunt et aeternam gloriam possederunt[5], audiens et ipse pro oboedientia, quod Deus prae[6] omnibus sacrificiis diligit, ab ipso iudice omnium, Deo[7] nostro Iesu Christo: *Venite, benedicti patris mei, percipite regnum, quod vobis paratum est ab origine mundi*†."

CHAPTER XXXIII
De reditu pontificis nostri

Transactis itaque ibi multis diebus, secundum apostolicum imperium et totius sanctae synodus iussum[8] patriam remeare, iudicia apostolicae sedis scripta secum portare et sancto archiepiscopo Theodoro et regi Ecgfritho[9] ostendere Deo amabili Wilfritho episcopo praeceperunt. Ille vero sanctus pontifex noster indubitata fide praeceptus apostolicae sedis, sicut promiserat, in omnibus humiliter oboediens, circumiens loca sanctorum ad orationem per plures dies et reliquiarum sanctarum ab electis viris plurimum ad consolationem ecclesiarum Brittanniae adeptus, nomina singulorum scribens, quae cuiusque sancti essent reliquiae, multaque alia bona, quae nunc longum est enumerare, ad ornamentum domus Dei more suo lucratus, cum apostolicae sedis et universa sanctae[10] synodus benedictione, cum omnibus laetus et gaudens ad regionem suam redire et ad patriam pervenire, Deo adiuvante, incipiebat. Pergente ergo sancto pontifice[11] nostro ab apostolica sede cum triumphali

---

[1] episcopale C   [2] difinita C   [3] tenuere F   [4] ad per. con. prae. *omit* C
[5] et...possederunt *omit* F   [6] pro C   [7] domino C   [8] iussu C
[9] Ecfrido C   [10] sancta F   [11] praesule C

★ Psa. 26. 13 (Vulg.).   † Matth. 25. 34.

this decree; so that if he be a bishop who attempts to flout this pious ordinance, let him be deprived of episcopal rank and be the object of an eternal curse; likewise if he be a priest, a deacon, or of lower rank in the church, indeed whether he be a cleric, a monk, or a layman of whatever degree, even a king, let him be cut off from the body of our Saviour and the blood of our Lord Jesus Christ; nor let him be accounted worthy to gaze upon His dread appearing. He however who receives these decisions, laid down or defined by us, with true devotion and complete satisfaction—keeps them, carries them out, or helps to carry them out—may he see the 'goodness of the Lord in the land of the living,' may he have his part with those on the right hand, may he possess eternal bliss and deserve to hear that beatific voice, together with all the saints who have won favour in the sight of God and have inherited eternal glory, hearing as a reward for that obedience, which God loves beyond all sacrifices, the words of the Judge of all, our Lord Jesus Christ, 'Come ye blessed of my Father, inherit the kingdom prepared for you from the foundation of the world.'"

CHAPTER XXXIII

Of our bishop's return. [680]

So after Bishop Wilfrid, the beloved of God, had spent many days there, he was bidden by the Apostolic authority and the command of all the holy synod to return to his country, to carry with him the commands of the Apostolic See in writing, to show them to the holy Archbishop Theodore and also to King Ecgfrith. So our holy bishop, humbly obeying with unwavering loyalty the commands of the Apostolic See in all things, as he had promised, spent several days going round the shrines of the saints to pray there; he also obtained from chosen men a great many holy relics, for the edification of the churches of Britain, writing down what each of the relics was and to which saint it belonged; and many other possessions he acquired which it is tedious to enumerate now, for the adornment of the house of God, in accordance with his custom. So, with the blessing of the Apostolic See and all the holy synod, he began his journey homewards to his own land with all his train, rejoicing and glad, God being his helper.

So when our holy bishop, triumphantly bearing the decision, had made his way from the Apostolic See through Campania and had

iudicio per Campaniam et montana transcendens[1], in regionem
Francorum pervenit, ibique nuper amico suo fideli Degberthto[2] rege
per dolum ducum et consensum[3] episcoporum—quod absit!—
insidiose occiso; ex quibus unus cum ingenti exercitu obviavit,
cogitans impie in corde suo, nisi Deus restitisset ei, sodales suos
omnes spoliatos[4] aut in servitutem redigere aut vendere sub corona
seu rebellantes occidere atque sanctum pontificem[5] nostrum anxiatum
in custodia atque[6] ad Yverwini[7] ducis iudicium reservare. Inter-
rogavitque eum[8], dicens, qua fiducia tam temere[9] per Francorum
regionem pergisset[10]: "Qui dignus es morte, quod[11] nobis regem
subsidio tuo factum de[12] exilio emisisti, dissipator[13] urbium, consilia
seniorum despiciens, populos ut Roboam filius Salomonis tributo
humilians, ecclesias Dei cum praesulibus contempnens; quorum
malorum poenas luens occisus, cadaver eius humatum iacet."
Sanctus vero pontifex noster humiliter respondit episcopo: "*Veritatem dico in Christo* Iesu et per sanctum Petrum apostolum *non
mentior**, quod[14] talem virum exulantem[15] et in peregrinatione de-
gentem secundum praeceptum Dei populo Israhelitico[16], qui accola
fuit in terra aliena, auxiliatus enutrivi et exaltavi in bonum et non
in malum vestrum, ut aedificator urbium, consolator[17] civium, con-
siliator senum, defensor Dei ecclesiarum[18] in nomine Domini secundum eius promissum[19] esset. O rectissime episcope, quid aliud
habuisti facere, si exul de genere nostro ex semine regio ad sanctitatem tuam perveniret quam quod ego in Domino feci?" Respondit
episcopus "*Dominus custodiat introitum tuum*†[20]" et reliqua: et "Vae
mihi peccatori, da indulgentiam, quod[21] secundum Iudam patriarcham
video te multo iustiorem me esse. Sit Dominus vobiscum et sanctus
Petrus apostolus in auxilio vestro."

---

[1] transcendenti C   [2] Deegberhto C   [3] consensu C   [4] spoliaturos F
[5] pastorem C   [6] usque C   [7] Yfiruini C   [8] *insert* episcopus C   [9] tenere F
temerarie C   [10] pergeret C   [11] quia C   [12] *omit* C   [13] dissipatorem C
[14] quia C   [15] exsulantem C   [16] Israelitico C   [17] consulator F   [18] e.D. C
[19] p.e. C   [20] *omit* C   [21] quia C

* I Tim. 2. 7.   † Psa. 120. 8 (Vulg.).

crossed the mountains, he came into the land of the Franks. But there his faithful friend Dagobert had been lately killed by treachery through the guile of certain dukes and with the consent of the bishops—(Heaven save the mark!). One of these bishops met him with a great army, plotting impious schemes in his heart and intending, if God had not hindered, to rob all his comrades and reduce them to serfdom, or to sell them as slaves, or to slay them if they resisted, and also to imprison our holy bishop and to reserve him for the judgment of Ebroin the duke.

He questioned him thus: "What gives you confidence to go through the land of the Franks so boldly, you who are worthy of death, seeing that you sent forth to us from exile one made king by your help; he wasted our cities and despised the counsels of the elders; like Rehoboam the son of Solomon, he humiliated the people with tribute and despised the churches of God and their rulers; he was slain to atone for these his sins and his body lies in the grave."

Then our holy prelate humbly made reply to the bishop: "I speak the truth in Christ Jesus and by the Apostle Saint Peter I lie not, that in accordance with the command of God to the people of Israel which dwelt a stranger in a strange land, I helped and nourished such a man living as an exile and a sojourner and I raised him up for your good and not for your harm that he might be the builder of your cities, the comforter of your citizens, the counsellor of your elders, the defender of the churches of God in the name of the Lord, even as he had promised. O most righteous bishop, what else would you have to do if an exile of our race and of royal descent should come to your holiness, other than what I did in the name of the Lord?"

The bishop answered, " 'The Lord preserve your coming in' " and so forth, and, "Woe is me a sinner: grant me indulgence because like Judah the patriarch I see that you are much juster than I am. The Lord be with you and Saint Peter the Apostle be your aid."

CHAPTER XXXIV

De eo, quod rex contempsit iudicia apostolicae sedis

Deinde longa[1] spatia terrarum peragrans, Dei adiutorio in navigio maris magnitudinem superans, illaesus cum omnibus evasit ad regionem propriam, in subditorum suorum taedio languentium et ad Dominum[2] cum lacrimis clamantium maximum gaudium[3] vita comite veniens, vexillum victoriae ferens, hoc est apostolicae sedis iudicium secum deportans, pacifice salutans regem adiit, regique humiliter scripta apostolicae sedis iudicia cum totius synodus consensu et subscriptione ostendens, cum bullis et sigillis signatis reddidit, deinde omnibus principibus ibidem habitantibus necnon servis Dei, in locum synodalem accersitis ad audienda salutifera consilia, ab apostolica sede causa pacis ecclesiarum transmissa. Postquam vero quaedam difficilia sibi et suae voluntati contraria lecta audierunt, contumaciter quidam ex eis respuerunt. Insuper—quod execrabilius est—defamaverunt[4] in animarum suarum[5] perniciem, ut pretio dicerent[6] redempta esse[7] scripta, quae ad salutem observantium ab apostolica sede destinata sunt. Tum vero iussione regis et eius consiliatorum[8] cum consensu episcoporum, qui eius episcopatum tenebant, in custodiam ducere et novem menses sine ullo honore custodire censuerunt. Iamiamque rex, ut diximus, scriptis apostolicae sedis apertis et recitatis, quod dictu horribile est, Petri apostoli et apostolorum[9] principis qui habet a Deo solvendi ligandique potestatem, cum adulatoribus[10] suis iratus iudicia contempnens, et sanctum pontificem nostrum[11] spoliatum seorsum in custodia in solo suo[12] vestimento custodire et omnes subiectos eius dispersos per competa viarum nullumque ad se ex amicis eius adire per salutem suam iurans austere praecepit. Regina vero eius olim suprafata[13] chrismarium hominis Dei sanctis reliquiis repletum,—quod me enarrantem horruit—de se absolutum, aut[14] in thalamo suo manens aut in curru pergens, iuxta se pependit. Quod reginae, sicut Philisteis, fugato populo Israhelitico[15] arcamque Dei captantes et sancta sanctorum per civitates suas reducentes, omnino in malum accidit.

---

[1] longe C   [2] Deum C   [3] g.m. C   [4] diffamaverunt F   [5] suam C   [6] omit F
[7] esset F   [8] consiliatoribus C   [9] apostolum C   [10] adolatoribus C adiutatoribus F   [11] famulum Dei C   [12] suo solo C   [13] suprafacta F   [14] omit C
[15] Israelitico C

CHAPTER XXXIV
How the king despised the judgments of the Apostolic See. [680]

Then, having traversed many lands, and with the help of God having passed over a great tract of sea by ship, he reached his own land unharmed, together with all his companions, to the great joy of his subjects who were languishing with weariness, and crying out to the Lord with tears. He came back alive, bearing the standard of victory, that is to say, bringing with him the judgment of the Apostolic See, and peaceably presented himself before the king saluting him. With all humility he showed the king the written judgment of the Apostolic See with the consent and subscription of the whole synod, and delivered it to him with its bulls and stamped seals. Then he summoned all the chief men who lived there as well as the servants of God to the synod's meeting place to hear the wholesome counsels sent from the Apostolic See for the sake of the peace of the churches. After they had heard matters read which were difficult for them and contrary to their will, some of them contumaciously rejected the judgment. Besides this—a fact more execrable—they defamed it, to the peril of their souls, by saying that the writings had been bought for a price, these writings which had been intended by the Apostolic See for the benefit of those that obeyed them.

Then, at the command of the king and his counsellors, with the consent of the bishops who held his bishopric, they decided to put him in prison and keep him there nine months without any token of respect. And forthwith, as we have said, after the writings of the Apostolic See had been opened and read, the king—horrible to tell—enraged, and abetted by his flatterers, despised the judgment of Peter the Apostle and chief of the Apostles who has the power from God to loose and to bind; then taking oath by his soul's salvation he sternly ordered that our holy bishop, despoiled of all save his garments, should be kept in solitary confinement, that all his subjects should be scattered far and wide, and that none of his friends should be allowed to visit him. His queen moreover, whom we have mentioned before, took away the reliquary of the man of God which was filled with holy relics, and (I tremble to say it) she wore it as an ornament both in her chamber at home and when riding abroad in her chariot. But this brought nothing but evil upon her, as it did to the Philistines, when, after routing the people of Israel, they captured the ark of God and brought the holy of holies through their cities.

CHAPTER XXXV

De hortatione sociorum

Locutusque est Deo amabilis Wilfrithus episcopus sociis suis, dicens: "Habete in mente et fratribus meis dicite dies antiquos, quomodo legimus in veteri lege patriarchas Deo amabiles et Israel primogenitum eius per quadringentos annos et amplius *de gente in gentem*[1] *et de regno ad populum alterum*★ expectantes[2] repromissionem et non desperantes *pertransierunt*: necnon Moyses et Aaron et omnes prophetae[3] Dei[4] ab hominibus persecutiones sperantes in Domino perpessi sunt. Legimus quoque in novo Testamento pastorem magnum ovium et totius ecclesiae caput Iesum Christum a Iudaeis crucifixum et discipulos suos dispersos et postea per totum mundum cum suis subsecutoribus in variis temptationibus coronatos, non obliviscentes *consolationis, quae nobis tamquam filiis loquitur, dicens: 'Fili mi, noli neglegere disciplinam Domini neque fatigeris, dum ab eo argueris; quem enim Dominus diligit*[5] *castigat, flagellat autem omnem filium quem recipit*†.' *Ideo* enim, fratres et adiutores mei in Christo, secundum egregium doctorem *nos tantam habentes impositam nubem testium, per patientiam curramus ad propositum nobis certamen*‡."

CHAPTER XXXVI

De domo illuminata a Deo

Finito igitur sermone consolationis, duces regis tenentes sanctum pontificem nostrum[6] et ducentes quasi *ovem ad occisionem* qui *non aperuit os suum*§ ad praefectum nomine Osfrith, qui praeerat Inbroninis urbi regis, ante eum statuerunt, praecipientes ei sermone regis, ut pontificem sanctum[7], eum, qui tunc ob maxima fidei merita lumen Brittanniae dici potuit[8], in absconditis[9] locis, tetra caligine obscuratis, nullo amicorum sciente[10], diligenter custodiret. Comes autem supradictus regi fidelis, iussu eius urgente, in latebrosis locis, ubi raro sol per diem illuxit, et lampas in honorem noctu non accenditur, cum custodibus servabat. Custodes vero iugiter psalmodiam sancti

---

[1] gente F [2] expeccantes F [3] Raine. prophetas C *and* F [4] *insert* varias C
[5] dil. Dom. C   [6] iustum doctorem disciplinae Dei C   [7] nostrum C
[8] eum...potuit *after* custodiret C [9] *omit* C [10] scientie F

★ Psa. 104. 13 (Vulg.).   † Heb. 12. 5, 6.   ‡ ib. 12. 1.   § Isa. 53. 7.

CHAPTER XXXV

How [*Wilfrid*] encouraged his comrades

Then Bishop Wilfrid the beloved of God spoke to his comrades and said, "Bear in mind and tell my brethren about the olden days, how we read in the Old Law that the patriarchs, beloved of God, and Israel His first-born, for four hundred years and more, went "from one nation to another, and from one kingdom to another," looking for His promise and not despairing. Moses and Aaron too and all the prophets of God endured the persecution of man, trusting in the Lord. We read also in the New Testament that the great Shepherd of the sheep and Head of the whole Church, Jesus Christ, was crucified by the Jews and His disciples scattered. Afterwards, throughout the whole world, they and their followers after various temptations received their crown, yet not forgetting the words of consolation which are addressed to us, as though to sons, saying, 'My son, despise not thou the chastening of the Lord, nor faint when thou art rebuked of Him: for whom the Lord loveth He chasteneth, and scourgeth every son whom He receiveth.' So, my friends and helpers in Christ, in the words of the excellent teacher, 'Seeing that we have so great a cloud of witnesses set about us, let us run with patience the race which is set before us.'"

CHAPTER XXXVI

Of the house illuminated by God

When he had finished his words of consolation, the king's officers took our holy bishop and, "as a lamb led to the slaughter, which opened not his mouth," so they led him to a man named Osfrith, the reeve of the royal borough of *Broninis*, and placed their prisoner before him, bidding him, in accordance with the king's word, guard diligently in dungeons darkened by foul mist, without the knowledge of any of his friends, the holy bishop who might well have been called at this time the light of Britain, considering the great merits of his faith. This same thegn was faithful to the king, and on his urgent bidding kept the bishop under guard in hidden dungeons, where the sun rarely shone by day and where no lamp is lit to give brightness by night. His guardians, however, when they heard the holy

hominis Dei audientes et videntes in obscura[1] nocte domum intus lucentem quasi per diem, omnibus sanctitatem eius narrantes, timorem[2] stupefacti incutierunt. O lumen aeternum, Christe, qui nunquam deseris confitentes te, sed qui *lux vera* crederis et *illuminans omnem hominem venientem in hunc mundum**! Qui in primordio nativitatis futuri famuli tui horam[3], qua de vulva matris egrediebatur, igneo splendore consignabas, nunc in antro nimiae obscuritatis oranti lucem angelicae visitationis adhibere dignatus es, sicut Petro apostolo tuo, ab Herode impio rege catenato in carcere, *angelus Domini adstitit et lumen refulsit in habitaculo*†; sit tibi gloria et gratiarum actio! In ipso[4] temporis spatio, quo eum detentum in custodia sine aliquo honore rex habuit, episcopatum ex parte, quem prius possidebat, et dona alia non mediocriter promittebat, si iussionibus et censuris eius adquiescere[5] voluisset et statuta canonica, quae ab apostolica sede missa sunt, eligeret[6] denegare esse vera[7]. Ille ad haec humiliter et tamen cum fiducia apostolicae auctoritatis respondit, prius se capite truncandum esse quam id umquam confiteri velle. Ecce! bona voluntas, quae Deum novit, immutari non potest.

CHAPTER XXXVII

De sanata muliere

Manente itaque sancto pontifice nostro patienter in custodia carceris, sic Dei virtutibus declaratus est, sicut Iohannes apostolus et evangelista, in Pathmos insula a Caesare religatus, vidit magnalia Dei. Nam eo tempore, ut diximus, anxiato sancto pontifice nostro, mulier praefecti huius urbis extimplo alligata languore, totis membris dissolutis[8] rigida, frigido corpore, clausis oculis spumantique ore ultima spiramina vitae de pectore insensata trahebat. Vir vero eius videns statim morientem mulierem, festinanter cucurrit ad sanctum pontificem nostrum, sicut centurio ad Dominum; genuflectens et peccata sua deplorans et regis in eum commissa confitens, adiuravit eum in nomine Domini, ut sibi non merenti et mulieri morienti subveniret. Sanctus autem pontifex noster immemor malorum, sicut

---

[1] obscuro C   [2] timore C   [3] hora F   [4] *insert* ergo C   [5] inquiescere C
[6] elegeret F   [7] v.e. C   [3] desolutis C

* John 1. 9.   † Acts 12. 7.

man of God perpetually singing psalms, and saw the place in the darkness of the night all lit up within as if it were day, spoke to all of his holiness, and, being amazed themselves, filled others with terror.

O Christ, eternal Light Who dost never desert those who acknowledge Thee, Who art held to be the "true light" and dost illumine "every man that cometh into the world," Who in the beginning didst mark by fiery splendour the hour of the nativity of Thy future servant when he came forth from his mother's womb: now Thou didst deign to bring the light of an angelic visitation into the deep obscurity of the dungeon as he prayed, just as when thine Apostle Peter was chained in the prison by the impious King Herod, "the angel of the Lord stood by him and a light shined in the cell"; to Thee be glory and thanksgiving.

During this time when the king had him in custody without any token of honour, he promised him part of the bishopric which he had formerly owned and other gifts, by no means small, if Wilfrid would be willing to acquiesce in his commands and decisions, and would choose to deny that the canonical statutes which had been sent from the Apostolic See were genuine. To this he made humble reply, yet with confidence in the Apostolic authority, that he would rather lose his head than ever make such an acknowledgment. So we see that a good will, based on a knowledge of God, cannot be moved.

CHAPTER XXXVII

How a woman was healed

And so, while our holy bishop waited patiently in the prison, he was manifested by the power of God, as John the Apostle and Evangelist was, when, being confined to the island of Patmos by Caesar, he saw the mighty works of God. For at that time, as we have said, when our holy bishop was in distress, the wife of the reeve of this town was suddenly overtaken by a palsy; all her limbs became nerveless, she was rigid, her body grew cold, her eyes closed, her mouth foamed, and she was just breathing from her breast the last breath of life in an unconscious condition. But her husband, as soon as he saw his wife on the point of death, quickly ran to our holy bishop, as the centurion ran to the Lord: he knelt before him and, bewailing his sins and acknowledging the king's misdeeds against him, he adjured him, in the name of the Lord, to help him, unworthy as he

Ioseph[1] ductus[2] de carcere, miserantem adiit, stans super eam, aqua
benedicta faciem aspergens, et oratione facta, Dei auxilium deplorans,
os eius guttatim aqua benedicta madefactum irrigavit; deinde autem
oscitante[3] et longa spiramina[4] trahente, apertis oculis sensum vitae
et intelligentiae recepit, et post paululum calefactis membris, capite
elevato, lingua movente[5], loquebatur, gratias agens Deo[6]: sicut
socrus Petri sanata sancto pontifici[7] nostro honorifice ministrabat[8];
et adhuc vivens illa, nunc sanctimonialis materfamilias nomine Aebbe,
cum lacrimis hoc narrare consuevit.

CHAPTER XXXVIII
De eo, quod vincula de se cadebant

Praefectus namque suprafatus sanctum praesulem nostrum in
honore habere propter timorem regis diutius non morari ausus est,
et propter sanctitatem eius Dei iram timens, in nullam contumeliam
ponere maluit, nuntios misit[9] ad regem, dicens: "Adiuro te per vitam
meam et salutem tuam ut ne me cogas hunc sanctum pontificem[10] et
innocentem in perditionem meam diutius punire, quia magis eligo
mori quam eum innoxium flagellare." Quo audito, rex iratus iussit
duci in urbem suam Dynbaer[11] ad praefectum nomine Tydlin quasi
ferociorem, praecipiensque ei ut hunc talem virum et tantum
pontificem, in compedibus et manicis alligatum, seorsum ab hominibus separatum custodiret. Ille vero, praecepto regis coactus, vincula
ferrea fabros facere iussit, qui sine causa opus diligenter[12] membra
sancti confessoris nostri metientes[13] facere inchoabant, Deo enim
resistente. Nam semper aut coangusta et anxiata vincula circum-
amplectere membra non poterant aut tam dilata et laxata, ut de[14]
pedibus evangelizantis et de manibus baptizantis resoluta cadebant[15];
et ideo timidi facti, sine vinculis hominem Dei, semper psallentem
et Deo gratias agentem,—secundum apostolum ad Ebreos[16] dicentem
magnum certamen sustinens passionum, in opprobriis spectaculum
factus et rapinam omnium bonorum suorum suscipiens*, et his a
contribulibus[17] suis illatis,—usque ad tempus a Deo difinitum[18] inviti
seorsum custodiebant.

[1] omit F　　[2] doctus F　　[3] eructuante C　　[4] suspiria C　　[5] monente C
[6] Domino C　　　[7] pontifice C　　　　[8] Petri...ministrabat omit F
[9] mittens C　　[10] episcopum C　　[11] Dyunbaer C　　[12] insert in C　　[13] men-
tientes F　　[14] omit F　　[15] caderent C　　[16] Hebreos C　　[17] contribulis C
[18] divinitum F

* Cf. Heb. 10. 32, 33.

was, and his dying wife. Then our holy bishop, being forgetful of his wrongs, like Joseph led forth from the prison, came to the wretched woman, and, standing over her, he sprinkled her face with holy water, imploring the help of God in prayer: then, drop by drop, he bedewed her face till it was wet with the holy water. Then she opened her mouth, drew in long breaths, unclosed her eyes, recovered consciousness and understanding, and shortly afterwards her limbs became warm; she raised her head and moved her tongue to speak, and thanked God. Like Peter's wife's mother, she ministered to our holy bishop in all honour; she is still living and is now a holy abbess named Aebbe, and is wont to tell this story with tears.

CHAPTER XXXVIII
How the chains fell off him

Now this same reeve did not dare to continue his honourable treatment of our holy bishop any longer, for fear of the king, yet, dreading the anger of God on account of Wilfrid's holiness, he preferred not to put him to any shame; so he sent messengers to the king, saying, "I adjure you by my life and your salvation not to compel me to punish this holy and innocent bishop to my perdition any longer, because I choose rather to die than to scourge him for no fault."

When the king heard this message he angrily ordered the holy bishop to be sent to his town of Dunbar, to the reeve named Tydlin, whom he considered to be a more cruel man: he ordered that he should be kept, though so good a man and so great a bishop, bound hands and feet with fetters, in solitary confinement. So in accordance with the king's command the reeve ordered the smiths to make iron fetters. The smiths, though they had no reason for doing so, entered upon their task with energy, measuring the limbs of our holy confessor. But God was opposing them. For the chains were always too small and narrow to go round his limbs or else they were so wide and loose that they fell free from the feet of the evangelist, the hands of the baptist. They were so terrified that they left the man of God unbound. He continued meanwhile to sing psalms and to give thanks to God, as the Apostle says to the Hebrews, "Enduring a great fight of afflictions, being made a gazing-stock by reproaches, and suffering the spoiling of all his goods," and such sufferings had been inflicted by his fellow-countrymen. Thus they kept him in confinement against their will until the time appointed by God.

CHAPTER XXXIX
De regina flagellata et sanata

Nam[1] interim rex cum regina sua per civitates et castellas[2] vicosque cotidie gaudentes et epulantes in pompa saeculari circumeuntes, tempore quodam[3] ad coenobium, quod Colodaesburg dicitur, pervenerunt, cui praesidebat sanctissima materfamilias nomine Aebbae, soror Oswiu[4] regis sapientissima. Illic enim regina illa[5] nocte arrepta a[6] daemone, sicut uxor Pilati multis flagellis fatigata, vix diem vivens expectavit. Crastina die vero[7] illucescente, mox sapientissima materfamilias veniens ad reginam, contractis membris simul in unum stricte alligatam et sine dubio morientem videns, regem adiit regique memorat lacrimabili voce, unde hoc miserabile malum secundum suam intelligentiam ei evenisset, dicens audacter[8]: "Ego scio et vere scio, quod Deo amabilem Wilfrithum episcopum sine alicuius sceleris piaculo de sede episcopatus abiecisti, et in[9] exilium[10] expulsus sedem apostolicam adiit, et inde reversurum cum scriptis apostolicae sedis, quae habet cum[11] sancto Petro apostolo potestatem ligandi et solvendi, insipienter contempnens spoliasti eum, et mala malis addens, in carcerem sanctum conclusisti. Et nunc, fili mi, secundum consilium matris tuae fac, disrumpe vincula eius et sanctas reliquias, quas regina de collo spoliati abstraxit et in perniciem sui, sicut arca Dei per civitates ducens, per fidelem nuntium emitte ei, et si nolueris, quod optimum est, illum in episcopatu habere, dimitte[12] eum liberum, et[13] de regno tuo cum suis, quocumque voluerit, abscedat. Tunc secundum meam fidem vita vives, et regina non morietur; sin vero hoc renueris, Deo teste, non eritis impuniti." Iam enim rex oboediens matri castissimae factus est et sanctissimum sacerdotem nostrum resolutum cum suis[14] reliquiis et cum[15] suis sociis congregatis a se libere discedere concessit, et regina sanabatur.

[1] *The first six words of the chapter are repeated within the capital* N *of the first word* C   [2] castella C   [3] q.t. C   [4] Levison. *omit* F Oswini C   [5] ea C   [6] *omit* F   [7] v.d. C   [8] audaciter C   [9] *omit* C   [10] exilio C   [11] quicumque F   [12] dimittere F   [13] ut C   [14] sanctis C   [15] *omit* C

CHAPTER XXXIX

How the queen was scourged and healed. [681]

Meanwhile the king and queen, who had been making their progress with worldly pomp and daily rejoicings and feasts, through cities, fortresses, and villages, came upon a certain occasion to a nunnery called Coldingham, over which presided a very holy and discreet abbess called Aebbe, the sister of King Oswiu. At this place the queen became possessed with a devil that same night, and like Pilate's wife was so plagued and scourged that she scarcely expected to live till day. On the next day however, as soon as dawn appeared, the discreet abbess came to the queen and saw that her limbs were all contracted and tightly bound together and that she was manifestly dying; Aebbe went to the king and with tearful voice reminded him of the reason why, in her opinion, that wretched calamity had happened to him, boldly declaring: "I know, and know for a fact, that you drove Bishop Wilfrid the beloved of God from his episcopal see for no crime whatever; that he was driven into exile and went to the Apostolic See; when he intended to return thence with the writings of the Apostolic See which has, in company with St Peter the Apostle, the power of binding and loosing, you foolishly despised them and despoiled him, and then adding evil to evil, you shut the saint up in prison. And now, my son, obey the instructions of your mother; break his bonds, send back to him by a faithful messenger those holy relics of which he has been robbed, which the queen took from his neck and carried about from town to town like the ark of God, to her own destruction. And, if you will not have him back as bishop (which would be best of all), then at least send him away free and let him depart with his friends and go wherever he will, away from your kingdom. Then, according to my belief, you will remain alive and the queen will recover, but if you refuse to do this, God is my witness that you will not be unpunished." Thereupon the king obeyed the chaste matron, released our most holy bishop and allowed him to depart freely with his relics, in company with all his friends; and the queen was healed.

CHAPTER XL

De eo quod Birhtwald[1] suscepit sanctum[2] episcopum[3]

Proficiscente ergo Deo amabili Wilfritho episcopo cum suis sodalibus, patria rura deserens, australia regna in exilio quaerens, Dominus, qui sanctis suis in temptationibus adest, praefectum[4] virum nobili genere et nomine Bergtwald[5], filium fratris Aethelredi regis Merciorum, mitissimo[6] animo in obviam emisit, et statim ut vidit tam honorabiles homines et causas peregrinationis, sancto doctore nostro revelante, audivit, adiurans in nomine Domini manere secum et partem territorii sui ad habitandum in eo servos Dei cum omni diligentia poposcit. Sanctus vero praevius noster, gratias agens Deo, quod aliquod solacium requiei dedisset, et[7] statim in eo territorio pro Deo donato monasteriolum fundavit, quod adhuc usque hodie monachi eius possident. Deinde, vigilante antiqui hostis invidia, Aethelredus[8] rex et regina sua, soror Ecgfrithi[9] regis, audientes hominem Dei de patria expulsum et illic manentem et modicum quiescentem, praefecto[10] viro Berehtwaldo[11] in sua salute interdicunt, ut sub eo unius diei spatium esset, pro adulatione Ecfrithi[12] regis. Deinde cum odio pontifex noster expulsus, manentibus tamen illic monachis suis, regem Occidentalium Saxonum[13] adiit nomine Centwine[14], per parvumque spatium pro subsequa persecutione ibi manebat. Nam illic regina, soror Irminburgae[15] reginae, odio oderat eum, uti propter amicitiam regum supradictorum trium dehinc fugatus abscessit.

CHAPTER XLI

Quomodo in Selaesiae[16] paganos convertit ad Deum

Quid igitur magis moror in verbis? Relaxata custodia, de propria provincia expulsus erat, ita ut nec in aliena regione ultra vel citra mare, ubi potestas Ecgfrithi[17] praevaluit, requiem habere permiserit: sed sine intermissione persecutionem, quam in eum exercuit, in unaquaque regione, in qua disponebat manere, iugiter commovere

---

[1] Beorhtuald C   [2] *omit* sanctum C   [3] eum C   [4] perfectum C   [5] Berhtwald C   [6] mittissime F   [7] *omit* C   [8] Ethilredus C   [9] Ecfridi C [10] perfecto C   [11] Berhtwaldo C   [12] Ecfridi C   [13] Westsexna C [14] Centwini C   [15] Irmenburge C   [16] se F   [17] Ecfridi C

CHAPTER XL

How Berhtwald received the holy bishop. [681]

So Wilfrid the bishop, the beloved of God, set out with his companions, and, leaving his fatherland, he sought the southern kingdoms as an exile. But the Lord, who is with His saints when they are tried, sent a man of noble race and kind heart to meet him, a reeve called Berhtwald, nephew of Aethilred, King of the Mercians. As soon as he saw such honourable men and heard the reason of their wanderings, as our holy teacher described them, he begged them, in the name of the Lord, to stay with him, and with all earnestness he requested the servants of God to dwell in some part of his estate. Our holy bishop gave thanks to God, because he had granted him some solace and rest, and forthwith he founded a little monastery on that land which had been given for God's sake, and his monks possess it to this day. But the hatred of the ancient enemy was ever on the alert; when King Aethilred and his queen, the sister of King Ecgfrith, heard that the man of God had been driven from his land and was staying there and was at peace for a little while, they forbade the reeve Berhtwald, if he valued his own safety, to remain for a single day under his direction. This they did to flatter King Ecgfrith. Then, when our bishop had been driven out by hatred, though his monks were left behind, he made his way to the King of the West Saxons named Centwini. There he remained but a short time owing to the persecution that followed him. For Centwini's queen was the sister of Queen Iurminburg and hated him greatly, so that on account of the friendship of the three kings we have spoken of, he was driven away and departed thence.

CHAPTER XLI

How he converted to God the pagans in Selsey.
[681–686]

Why should I linger in telling my story? On his release from prison he was driven from his own province in such a way that no rest was allowed him even in the land of strangers on either side of the sea, wherever the power of Ecgfrith prevailed. For he never ceased to stir up perpetual persecution, which he brought to bear upon him in whatever land he was disposed to remain. There was,

non cessavit. Tum[1] vero gentis nostrae quaedam provincia gentilis usque ad illud tempus perseverans vixit, quae pro rupium multitudine et silvarum densitate aliis provinciis inexpugnabilis restitit, et ad illos paganos Australios Saxones[2], Deo dirigente viam et humano auxilio cessante, sanctus episcopus noster confugit. Invento itaque rege eorum, cuius nomen erat Aethelwalch[3], totius exilii sui austeritatem per ordinem enarravit. Cui statim rex sub foedere pacis talem amicitiam promisit, ut nullus inimicorum eius aut minaci hostis gladio belligerantis sibi terrorem incuteret aut munerum[4] et donorum magnitudine pactum initum foederis secum irritaret. Sanctus vero homo Dei, gavisus in verbis consolationis, gratias agens Deo, primum regi et[5] reginae verbum Dei et regni eius beatitudinem et magnitudinem leniter suadens, quasi lac sine dolo dedisset, praedicare coepit; deinde[6] cum consensu regis, Deo concedente, et exortatione sancti pontificis nostri gentes, quibus ante praedicatum non erat, et numquam verbum Dei audierunt, congregatae sunt. Stans itaque sanctus Wilfrithus episcopus noster in medio gentilium, secundum exemplum Domini nostri Iesu Christi et praecursoris eius dixit: *Poenitentiam agite, appropinquabit enim regnum coelorum**: et *baptizetur unusquisque vestrum in nomine Dei Patris et Filii et Spiritus sancti*†, et cetera. Quae per[7] plures menses, longo ambitu verborum ab exordio mundi omnipotentis Dei facturam in contemptum idolatriae eleganter enumerans usque ad diem iudicii, ubi aeterna poena[8] peccatoribus et electis Dei vita perpetua praeparabitur, suaviloqua eloquentia omnia mirabiliter per ordinem praedicavit praedicator evangelicus. Tunc quippe sanctus pontifex noster, a Deo missus, invenit gratiam in conspectu regis, et ostium magnum fidei‡ secundum apostolum apertum est ei, et paganorum utriusque sexus, quidam voluntarie, alii vero coacti regis imperio, idolatriam[9] deserentes, Deum omnipotentem confitentes, sicut per beatum Petrum apostolum, in una die multa milia baptizati sunt. Rex namque mitis et pius per Deum[10] factus, villam suam propriam, in qua manebat, ad episcopalem sedem cum territoriis postea additis LXXXVII mansionum in Seolesiae[11] sancto novoque[12] evangelistae et baptistae[13], qui sibi suisque cunctis vitae

---

[1] tunc C   [2] In Suthsexun C   [3] Ethelwalhc C   [4] numerum C   [5] *omit* F
[6] *insert* postea C   [7] *omit* F   [8] p.ae. C   [9] idolatria C   [10] Dominum C
[11] Soelaesiae C   [12] nono C   [13] euuangelista et baptista F

* Matth. 3. 2.   † Acts 2. 38.   ‡ cf. Acts 14. 26 (27) and 1 Cor. 16. 9

however, a certain province of our race which had remained per-
sistently heathen up to this time, and on account of its rocky coast
and thick forests could not be conquered by the other kingdoms.
And to these pagans, the people of Sussex, our holy bishop fled, for
God directed his way when human aid had ceased.

When he had found their king, whose name was Aethilwalh, he
told him the whole story of his sufferings and exile. Forthwith the
king made a treaty of peace with him and promised such friendship
that none of his enemies should strike terror into him by the threatening sword of any warlike foe, or make void the treaty thus inaugurated
between them by the offer of rewards and gifts, however great.

Then the holy man of God rejoiced at these words of consolation,
and, giving thanks to God, he began, first of all, to proclaim the word
of God to the king and queen and to describe the blessedness and
greatness of His Kingdom, gently persuading them, giving them,
as it were, milk without guile. Then, with our king's consent
and by divine permission, at the exhortation of our holy bishop,
the people who had never been evangelized before, nor had heard
the word of God, were gathered together. Then our holy Bishop
Wilfrid stood in the midst of the heathen, after the example of our
Lord Jesus Christ and of His forerunner, and said, "Repent ye, for
the Kingdom of God is at hand, and let each one of you be baptized
in the name of God the Father and of the Son and of the Holy
Ghost, etc." All these matters the evangelist preached in order with
sweet and marvellous eloquence for many months. He elaborately
described with great fulness of words the works of Almighty God
to confound idolatry, from the beginning of the world down to
the day of judgment, when eternal punishment will be prepared for
sinners and everlasting life for the elect of God. Then our holy
bishop, who had been sent by God, found favour in the eyes of the
king, and in the words of the Apostle, a great door of faith was opened
to him; and many thousands of pagans of both sexes were baptized
in one day, as once they were by the blessed Apostle Peter. They
deserted idolatry and made confession of faith in Almighty God,
some of them willingly and some being compelled by the king's
command. The king, who had been made gentle and pious by God,
gave his own estate, in which he lived, to be an episcopal see, adding
to it afterwards 87 hides in Selsey. This he granted to the new and
holy evangelist and baptist who had opened for him and for all his

perpetuae viam aperuit, concedit, ibique, fratribus suis congregatis, coenobium ad requiem fundavit, quod usque hodie subiecti eius possident.

CHAPTER XLII

De Ceadwalla[1] rege facto

In diebus quoque illis per pontificem nostrum populus ecclesiae Dei copiose de die in diem crescens et nominis eius gloria magnifice clarescens, venit quidam exul nobili genere de desertis Ciltine et Ondred nomine Cedwalla[2]. Sancti parentis nostri amicitiam diligenter poscens, ut ei esset in doctrina et auxilio pater fidelis et ille ei filius oboediens, voto vovens promisit; quo pacto inito, teste Deo, veraciter compleverunt. Nam sanctus antistes Christi in nonnullis auxiliis et adiumentis[3] saepe anxiatum exulem adiuvavit et confirmavit, usquedum corroboratus, spernens inimicos, regnum adeptus[4] est. Quippe, regnante Caedwalla [5]occisis et superatis inimicis eius totam Westsexna[6] [7] regionis monarchiam[8] tenens, statim sanctum Wilfrithum episcopum nostrum, gentilem populum in Suthsexum bene ad Deum convertentem et nomen Domini per se magnifice glorificantem, patrem suum venerabilem et super omnes carissimum ad se venire humiliter accersivit. Iamiamque sancto ac venerabili patre nostro veniente, rex Caedwalla in omni regno suo excelsum consiliarium mox illum composuit, sicut Pharao[9] rex Egypti Ioseph de carcere educto secundum prophetam dicentem: *Constituit eum dominum domus suae* usque *prudentiam doceret**. Tunc vero rex Caedwalla triumphalis, sancto pontifici nostro per Deum elevato et, innumeris terrarum partibus et muneribus donorum secundum desiderium animae suae pro Deo donatis, magnifice patre suo honorificato, regnum suum, aut[10] acie gladii victor aut foedere indultor[11] pacis, illaesum audaci animo tuebatur.

---

[1] Ceadvala C   [2] Ceduala C *and throughout*   [3] iumentis F   [4] *omit* F
[5-6] *omit* F   [7] *insert* occidentalium Saxonum F   [8] monachiam F   [9] *omit* F
[10] *insert* ut C   [11] indulgentor F

* Psa. 104. 21, 22 (Vulg.).

people the way to everlasting life, and there the bishop gathered his brethren and founded a cloister and retreat, which his followers possess up to this day.

CHAPTER XLII

How Ceadwalla became King. [686]

Now in those days, when by the labours of our bishop the Church of God was increasing abundantly from day to day and the glory of His name was growing wondrously, there came a certain exile of noble descent from the desert places of Chiltern and the Weald whose name was Ceadwalla. He earnestly asked for the friendship of our holy father, praying Wilfrid to be his true father, to teach and help him, while he, on his side, promised him with a vow that he would be an obedient son. This compact, which they undertook with God as their witness, was faithfully fulfilled. For the holy bishop of Christ helped the exile, who was often in difficulties, assisting and supporting him in various ways, and strengthened him until he was powerful enough to overcome his enemies and to get the kingdom. When Ceadwalla had come to the throne and, after slaying or subduing his foes, was reigning over all the land of the West Saxons, he immediately, in all humility, summoned St Wilfrid our bishop to come to him; for Wilfrid, who was converting the heathen population of Sussex to God, and through his efforts wondrously glorifying the name of the Lord, was his venerable father and dearest of all to him. As soon as our holy and venerable father had arrived, King Ceadwalla made him supreme counsellor over the whole kingdom, just as the King of Egypt, when Joseph had been taken from prison, made him, in the words of the prophet, "lord of his house... to teach wisdom." Then was our holy bishop uplifted by God, and King Ceadwalla in his victory rewarded him with innumerable pieces of land and other gifts out of the love of his heart and for God's sake, and honoured his father exceedingly. His kingdom he courageously kept safe either by the edge of his sword as a victor in battle or by treaty as a supporter of peace.

CHAPTER XLIII

De pace pontificis nostri et Theodori archiepiscopi

Eodem quoque tempore Theodorus gratia Dei archiepiscopus, auctoritatem apostolicae sedis, a qua missus est, metu agitante, honorificans, cum Wilfritho beato[1], episcopo nostro, diu exule spoliato, vere amicitiam inire diutius moratus non distulit. Nam cum Theodorus archiepiscopus in senecta uberi frequenti infirmitate anxiatus[2] est, ad Lundoniam civitatem Wilfrithum et Erconwaldum[3] sanctos episcopos ad se invitavit. Venientibus autem[4] illis archiepiscopus sapienter totius vitae suae cursum cum confessione coram Domino pure revelavit, dicens: "Et hoc maxime scrupulum me premit, quod in te, sanctissime episcope, commisi, consentiens regibus, sine causa peccati propriis substantiis spoliantibus te et, moerentibus subiectis tuis, in longum exilium exterminantes—heu pro dolor!—omnis mali, et nunc confiteor Domino et[5] sancto Petro apostolo. Et vos, coepiscopi[6] mei, testes estote, et[7] cunctos amicos meos regales et principes eorum ubique ad amicitiam tuam pro remissione[8] peccati mei per omnem modum volentes nolentesque constringens attraho. Scio enim post hunc annum appropinquantem vitae meae terminum secundum Domini revelationem, et ideo te adiuro[9] per Deum et sanctum Petrum mihi consentire, ut in sedem meam archiepiscopalem superstitem et haeredem vivens te con- stituam[10], quia veraciter in omni sapientia et in iudiciis Romanorum eruditissimum te vestrae gentis agnovi." Tunc sanctus Wilfrithus episcopus dixit: "Det tibi Dominus et sanctus Petrus apostolus[11] remissionem omnis controversiae in me commissae, et ero pro tua confessione orans pro te amicus in perpetuum. Et modo primum mitte nuntios cum litteris ubique ad amicos tuos, ut nostram re- conciliationem in Domino et me olim innoxium exspoliatum agnos- cant et mihi per tuam[12] adiurationem in Domino secundumque praeceptum apostolicae sedis partem aliquam substantiae meae restituant, et postea, Deo volente, quis dignus sit sedem episcopalem post te accipere, cum consensu tuo in maiori concilio consiliemur[13]." Deinde archiepiscopus post pactum verae pacis initum[14] ad Ald- frithum[15] regem Aquilonalium misit litteras, per quas adiuravit eum,

---

[1] b.W. C [2] auxiliatus C [3] Ercenvoldum C [4] *omit* F [5] *omit* F [6] episcopi C [7] ut C [8] pro missione C [9] a.t. C [10] constituem F [11] *omit* C [12] perpetuam F [13] conciliemur C [14] initium F [15] Alfridum C

CHAPTER XLIII

How peace was made between our bishop
and Archbishop Theodore. [686–687]

At this time also, Theodore, archbishop by the grace of God, being troubled by fears, honoured the authority of the Apostolic See by which he had been appointed, and did not delay, though he had waited so long, to make friends with the blessed Wilfrid, our bishop, who had long been an impoverished exile. For when the Archbishop Theodore, in the fulness of his years, began to be troubled by recurrent infirmity, he summoned to London the holy bishops Wilfrid and Erconwald. When they had come, the archbishop prudently and frankly revealed to them the whole course of his life, making confession before God and saying, "And this troubles me most, what I did to your hurt, most holy bishop, when I consented to the kings who robbed you of your property for no fault and drove you into long and grievous exile to the grief of your own people; woe is me! And now I make confession to God and to the holy Apostle Peter. And you, my fellow-bishops, be witnesses: for the remission of my sin I will unite all my royal friends and their chief men in friendship with you, Wilfrid, constraining them by every means, whether they be willing or not. For I know that after this year the end of my life draws near, in accordance with the revelation of the Lord. And I adjure you, by God and St Peter, to agree to my appointing you while I am still alive to my archiepiscopal see as my successor and heir. For indeed I have recognized you to be the most learned of your race in all manner of wisdom and in the statutes of the Romans."

Then the holy Bishop Wilfrid said, "May God and St Peter the Apostle grant you remission for all the controversy you have aroused against me, and, as you have made confession, I will ever be your friend and pray for you. Only first send messengers with letters, in all directions, to your friends, that they may know of our reconciliation in the Lord and that I was formerly, without guilt of mine, deprived of my possessions and that thay may restore to me some part of my substance by your adjuration in the Lord and in accordance with the orders of the Apostolic See, and afterwards, if God will, let us consider in a greater council who is worthy, with your consent, to receive the episcopal see after you."

Then, when the archbishop had made a pact of real peace, he sent letters to Aldfrith, King of the North, in which he begged him, for

ut propter timorem Domini praeceptisque apostolicae sedis praesulum et pro redemptione animae Ecfrithi[1] regis, qui primus[2]
episcopum nostrum, privatis omnibus, de patria innocentem exter-
minavit, reconciliare[3] sub foedere pacis ad multorum salutem cum eo
dignatus sit. Non solum autem hunc regem archiepiscopus ad concordiam excitavit, sed sibi ubique amicos, quasi prius inimicos,
facere diligenter excogitavit. Nam ad Aelflaedam[4] sanctam virginem
et abbatissam suas litteras emittens, in quibus commendans secundum
auctoritatem apostolicae sedis, ut pacem cum sancto Wilfritho
episcopo sine dubio iniret; necnon Aethelredum[5] regem Mirciorum[6] adiurans in sua et Christi caritate, secundum quod prius in
mente habebat, suscipere eum his sequentibus dictis praecepit:
"Gloriosissimo et excellentissimo Aethelredo[7] regi Myrciorum[8]
Theodorus gratia Dei archiepiscopus in Domino perennem salutem.
Cognoscat itaque, fili[9] dilectissime, tua miranda sanctitas, pacem me
in Christo habere cum venerando episcopo Wilfritho. Et idcirco te,
carissime, paterna dilectione ammoneo et in Christi caritate tibi
praecipio, ut eius sanctae devotioni[10], quantum vires adiuvant,
praestante Deo, patrocinium, sicut semper fecisti, quamdiu vivas,
impendas, quia longo tempore, propriis orbatus substantiis, inter
paganos in Domino multum laboravit. Et idcirco ego Theodorus
humilis episcopus decrepita aetate hoc tuae beatitudini[11] suggero,
quia apostolica hoc, velut scis[12], commendat auctoritas, et vir ille
supranominatus sanctissimus in patientia sua, sicut dicit scriptura*,
possedit animam suam, et iniuriarum sibi iniuste irrogatarum,
humilis et mitis caput suum Dominum salvatorem sequens[13], medici-
nam expectans: et *si inveni gratiam in conspectu tuo*†, licet tibi pro
longinquitate itineris durum esse videatur, oculi mei faciem tuam
iocundam videant *et benedicat tibi anima mea antequam moriar*‡.
Age ergo, fili mi, taliter de illo suprafato viro sanctissimo, sicut te
deprecatus sum, quia, si patri tuo non longe de hoc saeculo
recessuro oboedieris, multum tibi proficeret[14] ad salutem. Vade[15] in
pace, vive cum[16] Christo, dege in Domino. Dominus sit tecum."
Quid plura dicam? Postquam Aethelredus[17] rex propter auctoritatem beatissimorum pontificum, Agathonis scilicet et Benedicti

---

[1] Ecfridi C   [2] prius C   [3] reconciliari F   [4] Aelfledam C   [5] Ethilredum C
[6] Merciorum C   [7] Ethilredo C   [8] Merciorum C   [9] *insert* mi C
[10] devotione F   [11] beatitudinis F   [12] Levison. sanctis C *and* F
[13] *insert* et C   [14] proficerit C   [15] vale C   [16] in C   [17] Ethilredus C

* cf. Luke 21. 19.   † Gen. 47. 29.   ‡ ib. 27. 4.

fear of the Lord, in accordance with the precepts of the rulers of the Apostolic See, and for the sake of the redemption of the soul of King Ecgfrith, who was the first to rob our bishop of everything and drive him, though innocent, from his fatherland, to deign to come to a reconciliation with him in a treaty of peace for the sake of the salvation of many. Moreover this king was not the only one whom the archbishop stirred up to make a settlement, but on every hand he diligently sought to make friends for him where once he had made enemies. He sent his letters to Aelffled, the holy virgin and abbess, urging her, in accordance with the authority of the Apostolic See, to make peace unhesitatingly with St Wilfrid the bishop; and Aethilred, King of the Mercians, he charged as follows, adjuring him by his love for himself and for Christ to receive him according to his former intention:

"To the most glorious and excellent Aethilred, King of the Mercians, Theodore, by the grace of God, Archbishop:—Everlasting salvation be yours in the Lord. Most beloved son, may your wondrous holiness know that I have made peace in Christ with the venerable Bishop Wilfrid, and therefore, beloved, I urge you with paternal love, and I charge you by the love of Christ, to grant your protection to his holy devotion to the utmost of your ability, with the help of God, all your life long, as you have always done; because for a long time, while deprived of his own possessions, he has laboured much in the Lord among the heathen. And so I, Theodore, a humble bishop, in my declining years, suggest this to your blessedness, for the Apostolic authority commends this as you know; and the most holy man I have named possesses his soul in patience even as the Scripture says, following in humility and gentleness his Head the Lord and Saviour, and awaiting a relief of the wrongs unjustly inflicted upon him. And if I have found grace in your sight, though it may seem difficult for you on account of the length of the journey, I would that my eyes could see your pleasant face and that my soul might bless you before I die. And now, my son, do as I have prayed you concerning this same most holy man, because, if you obey your father who, before long, will be departing from this world, it would greatly avail towards your salvation. Go in peace, live in Christ, and continue in the Lord. The Lord be with you."

What more shall I say? Afterwards King Aethilred, on account of the authority of the most blessed popes, to wit, Agatho, Benedict,

Sergiique, percipientium dignitatem apostolicae sedis, canonice et[1] libenter pontificem nostrum suscipiens, multa monasteria et regiones propriae iuris reddens habensque illum in summo honore dignitatis, usque ad finem vitae fidelis amicus indesinenter perseveravit.

CHAPTER XLIV

Quomodo Alhfrithus[2] rex suscepit pontificem nostrum

Factum est itaque, postquam vergentibus annorum multorum circulis, sancto rectore nostro aliquando honorifice in exilio degente, et tunc[3] monachis suis per diversa loca totius Brittanniae exterminatis et sub alienis dominis moerentes expectantesque a Domino redemptionem[4], ut postremo audierunt miserrimae cladis ruinam, Ecgfritho[5] Ultrahumbrensium[6] rege occiso[7] et cum omni optimo exercitus sui agmine a gente Pictorum oppresso. Et[8] post eum Aldfrithus[9] rex sapientissimus regnavit, qui sanctum Wilfrithum episcopum nostrum de exilio secundo anno regni sui venerabiliter secundum praeceptum archiepiscopi ad se invitavit; et primum coenobium cum possessionibus adhaerentibus in Hagustaldesiae[10] indulgens, et post intervallum temporis secundum Agathonis beatissimi[11] apostolicae sedis praesulis[12] et sanctae[13] synodus iudicio propriam sedem episcopalem in Eboraca[14] civitate et monasterium Inhripis[15] cum reditibus suis reddidit, expulsis de ea alienis episcopis. Quod tantum v annis in gaudio subiectorum suorum, de exilio sicut Iohannes apostolus et evangelista Ephesum[16] rediens, secure possedit.

CHAPTER XLV

De suscitata inimicitia inter eos

Nam antiquae inimicitiae suasores, quasi de sopore somni excitati, mare huius saeculi in gaudio serenum, procella flante[17] turbinis[18] invidiae folliculo, ad triste naufragium moventes, et facem dissensionis[19] extinctam resuscitavere. Quippe inter regem sapientissimum et sanctum virum praedictum aliquando pax et securitas et paene

---

[1] *omit* C   [2] Alfridus C   [3] tamen C   [4] redemptorem F   [5] Ecfrido C
[6] Ultraumbrensium C   [7] occisio F   [8] *omit* C   [9] Aldfridus C
[10] Hagustaldesae C   [11] b.A. C   [12] Mabillon. praesule C *and* F
[13] sancta F sancti C   [14] Euroica C   [15] Inhrypis C   [16] Effesum C
[17] flavente F   [18] *insert* de F   [19] dissensiones F

and Sergius, who assumed successively the dignity of the Apostolic See, received our bishop gladly and in a canonical manner, returned him many monasteries and lands in his own right, treated him with the utmost respect, and continued his faithful friend without ceasing until the end of his life.

CHAPTER XLIV

How King Aldfrith received our bishop. [686–687]

And so it happened that many years had passed away and our holy prelate was now living honourably in exile; his monks had been banished and scattered into various places throughout the whole of Britain where they were mourning under the power of alien lords and awaiting redemption from the Lord. At last the news came to them of a most woeful disaster in which Ecgfrith, King of the Northumbrians, had been slain and overthrown by the Picts, together with all the flower of his army. After him the most prudent King Aldfrith came to the throne; and, in the second year of his reign, he reverently summoned St Wilfrid our bishop from exile to his presence, in accordance with the archbishop's command. First of all he bestowed upon him the monastery at Hexham with all the possessions belonging to it; after an interval of time, in accordance with the judgment of the most blessed Agatho, the ruler of the Apostolic See, and of the Holy Synod, he restored to him his own episcopal see at York and the monastery at Ripon, together with their revenues, and drove the strange bishops out. Like John the Apostle and Evangelist returning to Ephesus, he possessed them in security and amid the rejoicings of his followers, for five years only after his exile.

CHAPTER XLV

Of the enmity which was stirred up between them.
[691–692]

But those who had instigated the old quarrel were aroused as though from sleep and began to disturb the sea of this world, now joyful and calm. Blowing with the bellows of envy they stirred up the storm blasts till dreadful shipwreck threatened; thus they lit again the torch of dissension once extinguished. At one time peace and quietness abounded between the prudent king and the holy man,

omnis boni gaudium abundavit[1]; aliquando vero aliquod spatium, olla fervente nequitiae, plures deterioravit, et sic iterum in concordia atque iterum in discordia alternatim[2] per multos annos in tali vicissitudine viventes manebant, usque dum postremo, maxima flamma inimicitiae exardescente, de regione Ultrahumbrensium[3] sanctus homo Dei a rege Aldfritho expulsus recessit. Nam prima causa est dissensionis eorum de antiqua origine descendens, quia ecclesia[4], quae sancto Petro apostolo dedicata est, territoriis et possessionibus suis iniuste privatur. Secunda causa[5] est, ut monasterium supradictum, quod in privilegium nobis donabatur, in episcopalem sedem transmutatur et libertatem relinquere, quam[6] sanctus Agatho et v[7] reges censuerunt fixe ac firmiter possidere. Tertia deinde causa[8] est, ut iussionibus et decretis Theodori archiepiscopi ab apostolica sede misso oportere cogebat oboedire[9], non illa significans canonica statuta, quae in principio episcopatus sui apud[10] nos[11] degens aut in novissimis[12] temporibus vitae suae constituit, quando omnes ecclesias nostras ad canonicam pacem unanimiter convocavit, sed magis ea decreta, quae mediis temporibus suis, quando discordia inter nos in Bryttania[13] exorta fuerat, statuit. Ideo sanctus pontifex noster haec renuens, ad amicum fidelem Aethelraedum[14] regem Merciorum accessit, eumque cum magno honore propter reverentiam apostolicae sedis suscepit, et in multa reverentia episcopatus eius, quam reverentissimus Sexwlfus episcopus vita obeunte ante regebat, sub protectione Dei[15] et illius degens mansit.

CHAPTER XLVI

De concilio Aetswinapathe[16]

Igitur Aldfritho[17] rege cum sancto archiepiscopo Berhtwaldo et totius paene Brittanniae episcopis congregata synodo in campo, qui dicitur Ouestraefelda[18], deinde legatis ad praesentiam sancti Wilfrithi episcopi missis, rogantes humiliter, ut eorum obtutibus dignaretur praesentari, promittentes per nuntios suos statuta canonica de antiqua fraude rationem[19] se reddituros, si ad illorum conventum venire non negaret. Quid plura dicam? Postquam vero in locum[20], ubi synodalis

[1] habundavit F *and* C   [2] aliter natim C   [3] ultraumbrensium C
[4] ecclesiam F   [5] *omit* C   [6] quod F   [7] quique C   [8] *omit* C
[9] ob. *before* oport. C   [10] caput F   [11] *omit* F   [12] novissimo F
[13] Brittannia C   [14] Ethelredum C   [15] *omit* F   [16] Aetsuinapaethae C
[17] Aldfrido C   [18] Onestraefelda C   [19] ratione F   [20] loco F

with the enjoyment of nearly every form of good; at another time the cauldron of evil boiled up and made many worse for a time, and so they continued living now in agreement and now in disagreement alternately, for many years, in such changing relations, until at last, when the flame of enmity was at its height, the holy man of God was banished by King Aldfrith and withdrew from Northumbria.

The first cause of their disagreement is of ancient origin, because the church dedicated to St Peter was unjustly deprived of its territories and possessions. The second cause is that the aforesaid monastery which was granted to us as our own property was changed into an episcopal see, thus losing the liberty which St Agatho and five kings had definitely established and firmly fixed. Then the third cause is that he kept compelling us to obey the commands and decrees of Theodore the archbishop who had been sent from the Apostolic See, not pointing to those canonical statutes which he made at the beginning of his rule among us, or in the last period of his life, when he called all our churches to harmony and ecclesiastical peace, but rather enforcing those decrees which he made in the middle of his rule, when discord had sprung up amongst us in Britain.

So our holy bishop, refusing these commands, went to his faithful friend Aethilred, King of the Mercians, who received him with great honour on account of his reverence for the Apostolic See, and he continued to live under the protection of God and the king, amid the profound respect of that bishopric which the most reverend Bishop Sexwulf had formerly ruled before his death.

CHAPTER XLVI

Of the Atswinapathe Council. [703?]

So, during the reign of Aldfrith, a synod was held in a place called *Ouestraefelda*, which was attended by the holy Archbishop Berhtwald and the bishops of nearly all Britain. They sent a deputation into the presence of St Wilfrid the bishop, humbly praying him to deign to be present with them, and promised by their messengers that they would take account of the canonical decrees concerning his former wrongs if he did not refuse to come to their gathering.

What more shall I say? After he had come to the place where the

disputatio debuerat esse, convenit[1], deinde non ita contigit, sicut[2] promissum fuerat; sed multae et magnae altercationum quaestiones ab eis exortae emerserunt, maxime ab illis pontificibus ecclesiarum,— cum voluntate tamen Aldfrithi regis et consensu quorundam abbatum id fecisse non dubium habetur,—qui pacem ecclesiarum Dei[3], avaritia instigante, nullatenus habere concupierunt, et multa falsa obicientes, quae nulla ratione veritatis comprobare potuerunt, insuper secundum statuta et iussiones Theodori archiepiscopi esse censendum sanctum pontificem nostrum confirmaverunt. Ille vero intellegens, quid essent argumentati, humiliter respondit, dicens, [4]praeceptis illorum consentire[5] eiusque[6] decretis secundum canonum normam censuit in omnibus libenter se velle oboedire. Deinde multis et duris sermonibus eorum pertinaciam obstinationis, quam per xx et duos annos contra apostolicam auctoritatem non timuerunt contentiose resistendo exercere, increpabat[7] et interrogavit eos, qua fronte auderent statutis apostolicis, ab Agathone sancto et Benedicto electo et beato Sergio sanctissimis papis ad Brittaniam pro salute animarum directis, praeponere aut eligere decreta Theodori archiepiscopi[8] quae in discordia, ut diximus, constituit.

CHAPTER XLVII

Quomodo ei insidiae patefactae sint[9]

Interea dum nullus modus locutionis decenter ab illis ordinatus inventus est[10], unus ex ministris regis[11] pontifici nostro valde devotus, quem ille a primaevo vagientis aetatuli incunabulo[12] enutrivit, ex tentorio regis latenter erupit[13], simulans alterius effigiem[14], cohortibus[15] se circumadstantium immiscens quasi ignotus, usquedum[16] ad pontificem nostrum perveniebat, pandensque ei causam iudicii illorum, revelabat indicando, dicens: "Hac omnino fraude te moliuntur decipere, ut primitus per scriptionem[17] propriae manus confirmes eorum tantummodo iudicium, quodcunque constituentes diffinient succumbere, ut, postquam isto alligatus fueris districtionis vinculo, de caetero in posterum permutare nullatenus queas. Ista

---

[1] conveniret C   [2] *insert* ei C   [3] *omit* C   [4–5] *omit* F   [6] eorumque C
[7] increpavit C   [8] episcopi F   [9] *There is no fresh chapter here in* C   [10] *At this point there is a note in* C *which looks as though it were intended for a chapter heading. It reads* De verna hoc dicitur. Unus...regis *are in capitals*
[11] *omit* F   [12] incunabulis F   [13] eripuit F   [14] effigie F   [15] chohortibus F *and* C   [16] usque F   [17] scriptioni C

discussion of the synod was to be, what had been promised did not take place. But many questions and great altercations arose among them, especially among those bishops of the churches who, being impelled by avarice, by no means desired to keep the peace among the churches of God; nor is there any doubt that they did it at the desire of King Aldfrith and with the consent of some of the abbots. They raised many false objections which they could not prove by any semblance of truth; in addition they affirmed that our holy bishop was to be judged according to the decrees and commands of Archbishop Theodore.

When St Wilfrid heard what they had asserted, he replied with all humility, declaring that he consented to their decisions, and he assured them that he was willing to obey his decrees gladly in all things which were in accordance with canon law. Then, with many sharp words, he rebuked their enduring obstinacy, with which for twenty-two years they had not feared to resist contentiously the Apostolic authority; and he asked them how with such effrontery they dared to choose in preference to the Apostolic decrees, delivered to Britain for the good of men's souls by the most holy popes, the holy Agatho, the elect Benedict and the blessed Sergius, the judgments of Archbishop Theodore, which he made, as we have said, in a time of discord.

CHAPTER XLVII

How their snares were revealed to him

Meanwhile, before they had found any proper or formal method of reply, one of the thegns of the king who was greatly devoted to our bishop, one whom he had brought up from babyhood's tender years, from the cradle indeed, stole out of the king's tent; he disguised his appearance and mingled with the crowds standing around, as though he were a stranger, until at last he reached our bishop. Then he clearly explained to him the reason of their decision, saying, "They are attempting by this treachery to deceive you utterly, in order that at the outset you may confirm by your own signature their sole judgment, so as to support whatever they may settle and decide: so that after you have been bound by this chain of constraint, for the rest you will never be able to make a change afterwards in any way. This will be the upshot of their judgment, that you shall surrender

siquidem erit illorum iudicii apertio, ut, quicquid in Ultrahumbrensium[1] aliquando terra[2] possidere visus fuisti vel in episcopatu vel in monasteriis vel in qualibet re, cuncta dimittas; et si quid in Myrciorum[3] regno subsecutus eras sub Aethelredo[4] rege, omnia reddendo archiepiscopo coacte relinquas, ipso donando[5] cui vult; et ad postremum temetipsum dampnando[6], de tuo[7] te sanctitatis[8] honore cum subscriptione degraderis." Haec dicens[9], subterfugiens discessit. Tunc sanctus vir summae virtutis et constantiae, ista audiens, cognito deceptionis argumento, cautior de subscriptione saepius replicata effectus est. Reddere vero responsa instanter quaerebant et aliquando minitantes arguebant eum, qui nollet mature confiteri subire arbitrium, cito se sententiam dampnationis subiacere sciret. Quibus respondens, ait: "Primum[10] archiepiscopi iudicium audiens, illum consonantem statutis sanctorum patrum regulis, toto mentis annisu subiacere amplector." Ad ultimum vero[11], diutius multis agnoscentibus, causam celare non poterant. Primo dixerunt sanctum pontificem nostrum[12] omnibus facultatibus spoliare taliter velle, ut nec in Ultrahumbrensium[13] regno nec in Mirciorum[14] minimam quidem unius domunculi portiunculam haberet. Huius autem iudicii inclementia, ab archiepiscopo et rege diffinita, et ipsos iam inimicos horruit, dicentibus, impium esse, tam famosum virum in circuitu nationibus absque ullo capitali crimine omnibus bonis[15] suis privare. Novissimum vero aliquid humanius pertractantes, censuerunt, ut monasterium tantummodo, quod construxit Inhripis[16] et dudum cum omnibus ad eum pertinentibus sancto Petro donans commendaverit,—perceptumque privilegium a sancto Agathone papa abbati familiaeque ibidem conversante[17] detulit,—redderent in possessionem, ea tamen interposita dictione[18] ut propria manus conscriptione firmiter contestaret, quod illic quietus consederet, saepta monasterii absque licentia regis non transmearet nec aliquid sacerdotalis officii attingeret, sed ut[19] suum de semetipso, quod dictu horribile est, gradum honoris abiecerit, sub testimonio confirmationis plurimum cogentes compulerunt. Quo audito, sanctus Wilfrithus episcopus noster constanter et intrepida[20] voce elevata locutus est, dicens: "Qua ex causa me com-

---

[1] Ultraumbrensium C   [2] terram F   [3] Merciorum C   [4] Ethelredo C
[5] donandum C   [6] donando C   [7] tua F   [8] sanctitate F   [9] *insert* subito C
[10] Primus F   [11] *insert* dum C   [12] famulum Dei C   [13] Ultraumbrensium C
[14] Merciorum C   [15] *omit* bonis F   [16] Inhrypis C   [17] conversatae C
[18] dicione C   [19] *omit* ut F   [20] intrepide C

all which you were seen to possess in the land of Northumbria, whether bishopric or monasteries or aught else; and whatever you have gained in Mercia under King Aethilred, you will surrender it all by force to the archbishop that he may give it to whom he wishes; and finally, by condemning yourself you will degrade yourself, by your own signature, from your holy office." When he had said these words, he departed by stealth.

Then the holy man, being extremely brave and firm, when he heard these things, perceived the proof of their deception and became more cautious about signing anything further. They asked him to return an answer on the spot, threatening at length that if he would not quickly acknowledge his submission to their judgment he would forthwith find himself placed under sentence of condemnation. His answer was, "I will first hear the decision of the archbishop, and if he is acting in agreement with the definite rules of the holy fathers, I am determined to submit with my whole heart."

Finally, when they could no longer hide their plan, seeing that so many saw what it was, they declared at first that they were determined to despoil our holy bishop of all his possessions so completely that he should not possess one fragment of a single cottage in Northumbria or Mercia. But the ruthlessness of the decision laid down by the archbishop and the king horrified even his very enemies, who said that it was impious to deprive of all his possessions a man who was so famous throughout all the nations and was not convicted of any capital offence. Finally, acting with a little more humanity, they decided that they would give into his possession the monastery only, which he had built at Ripon and had long ago consecrated to St Peter with all that belonged to it, and allow him the privilege granted by St Agatho the Pope to whatever abbot and brotherhood dwelt there; they added the proviso however that he should sign the strongest undertaking that he would remain quietly there; that he would not pass beyond the bounds of the monastery without permission from the king; that he would not in any way exercise the episcopal office. Thus they sought with the utmost urgency to compel him, under oath, to strip himself of his own accord (horrible to relate) of his honourable rank.

When St Wilfrid heard this he firmly replied in fearless tones: "Why do you force me to turn upon myself the sword of dire destruction to work mournful and miserable disaster, that is to say,

pellitis, ut tam lugubre calamitatis miseriae in memetipsum gladium dirae interfectionis, hoc est subscriptione[1] propriae dampnationis, convertam[2]? Nonne sine aliquo reatu suspicionis offendiculum faciam cunctis audientibus nominis mei divulgationem, quod[3] episcopi vocabulo, quamvis indignus, per XL prope annos nuncupabar? Necnon et ego primus post obitum primorum procerum, a sancto Gregorio directorum, Scotticae virulenta plantationis germina eradicarem[4]; ad verumque pascha et ad tonsuram in modum coronae, quae ante ea posteriore[5] capitis parte e summo abrasa vertice, secundum apostolicae sedis rationem totam Ultrahumbrensium[6] gentem permutando converterem? Aut quomodo iuxta ritum primitivae ecclesiae assono vocis modulamine, binis adstantibus choris, persultare responsoriis antiphonisque[7] reciprocis instruerem? Vel quomodo vitam monachorum secundum regulam sancti[8] Benedicti patris, quam nullus prior ibi invexit, constitueram? Et nunc contra me quomodo subitam dampnationis ipse[9] protulero extra conscientiam alicuius facinoris sententiam? Sed cum[10] de hac noviter orta quaestione, qua meum sanctitatis habitum violare estis conati, fiducialiter sedem appello apostolicam: vestrum autem quisquis deponere meum dignitatis gradum praesumit, a me hodie invitatus mecum pergat illuc ad iudicium. Debent etenim diligenter scire viri Romani sapientes, pro qua culpa vos me degradare[11] vultis[12], priusquam vobis solis ad ista consentiam." Haec audientes archiepiscopus et rex dixerunt: "Modo utique culpabilis factus, a nobis notatus dampnetur, quia magis illorum quam nostrum elegit iudicium." Et hoc promittendo rex addebat archiepiscopo: "Faciam enim, si iubes, absque haesitationis mora, ut, vi opprimentis[13] exercitus mei coactus, hac vice nostrum subire iudicium paratum se fateatur." Conciliales autem caeteri dicebant episcopi: "Recordari oportet, quod in nostram promissionis fidem huc usque perrexit, aliter non praesumens: pariter prospero itinere in pace revertamur ad domos nostras[14]."

---

[1] subscriptionem C   [2] conversatam C   [3] qua C   [4] eradicare F   [5] Mabillon. posteriora C *and* F   [6] ultraumbrensium C   [7] antifonisque C   [8] *omit* sancti F   [9] ipsi F   [10] *omit* cum C   [11] degradere C *and* F   [12] cupientes C   [13] opprimetis F   [14] dominum nostrum F

to subscribe to my own condemnation? Shall I not, without any guilt of mine, make suspicion to be a stumblingblock to all who hear the report of my name, seeing that for nearly forty years I have been called by the name of bishop, however unworthy I may have been? Was I not the first, after the death of the first elders who were sent by St Gregory, to root out the poisonous weeds planted by the Scots? Did I not change and convert the whole Northumbrian race to the true Easter and to the tonsure in the form of a crown, in accordance with the practice of the Apostolic See, though their tonsure had been previously at the back of the head, from the top of the head downwards? And did I not instruct them in accordance with the rite of the primitive Church to make use of a double choir singing in harmony, with reciprocal responsions and antiphons? And did I not arrange the life of the monks in accordance with the rule of the holy father Benedict which none had previously introduced there? And now how shall I pass a hurried sentence against myself, being unconscious of any crime? But now concerning this freshly-mooted scruple by which you are attempting to violate my sacred office, I appeal in all confidence to the Apostolic See, and let any one of you who presumes to lower my sacred episcopal dignity go to judgment with me there; I challenge him this day. For the wise Romans ought to investigate carefully for what fault you wish to degrade me, before I consent to that course at your bidding alone."

When the king and the archbishop heard this they said, "Now at any rate he is guilty; therefore let him be branded by us and condemned because he chooses their judgment rather than ours." To this proposal of the archbishop, the king added, "I will compel him, if you bid me, by force through the pressure of my army, and that without any delay or hesitation, to confess this time that he is prepared to accept our judgment." But the other bishops in council said, "We must remember that he came here under our safe conduct, without which he would not have ventured; let us all return home in peace and prosperity."

CHAPTER XLVIII

Qualiter ad Aethelredum[1] *regem reversus est*[2]

Post has igitur sermocinationes solvitur inutile concilium ex utraque parte, et[3] unusquisque domi revertens secessit; et ita, Deo protegente, servus suus, liberatus de manibus inimicorum, ad fidelissimum regem Aethelredum redibat indemnis. Noster autem sanctus pontifex pergens devenit ad Etheredum[4] regem, denuntians ei cunctam durae locutionis infestationem, quae a praesulibus contra illius praeceptum illata est. Tunc interrogans quoque regem, quomodo vel qualiter decrevisset de possessione terrarum propriarumque[5] facultatum, quae ab ipso donata sunt ei; rex vero respondit: "Maiorem non addo perturbationem destruendo monachorum vitam, quae ad ecclesiam beati Petri apostoli dedicata est; sed in eodem permanente statu, vita comite reservabo, quo[6] a me, Domino favente, conservata est, usque quo prius tecum nuntios proprios vel scripta proprietatis ad Romam permisero interrogare de his imminentibus causis, quomodo recta desiderans salvus inveniar." Hac responsione percepta, congaudentes divisi, unusquisque ad propria remeabat.

[CHAPTER XLIX]

De excommunicatione nostra

Inimici vero, qui haereditatem sancti pontificis nostri sibi usurpabant, annuntiantes, nos esse a sorte fidelium segregatos et eos, qui nobiscum participarent, et[7] in tantum communionem nostram execraverunt, ut, si quispiam abbatum vel presbiterorum[8] nostrorum, a fideli de plebe rogatus refectionem suam ante se positam signo crucis Dei benediceret, foras proiciendam et effundendam quasi idolothitum iudicabant et vasa, de quibus nostri[9] vescebantur, lavari prius quasi sorde polluta[10] iubebant, antequam ab aliis contingerentur.

---

[1] Aethel F   [2] *The chapter heading in* C *is* De redditu eius ad Aethelredum regem   [3] *omit* F   [4] Edilredum C   [5] *omit* que F   [6] quae C   [7] *omit* C   [8] presbiterum F   [9] *omit* F   [10] pulluta F

CHAPTER XLVIII

How he returned to King Aethilred. [702?]

After these discussions the fruitless council was dissolved by both parties, each one returning to his own home. And so, under the protection of God, His servant was freed from the hands of his enemies and returned uninjured to the faithful King Aethilred. Our holy bishop made his way into the presence of King Aethilred and declared to him the whole story of the attack upon him and the harsh charges made by the bishops contrary to the king's injunction. Then he asked the king also what sort of decrees he had made concerning the possession of the lands and the privileges which he had granted him. The king answered, "I will not raise up further trouble by destroying the livelihood of the monks which has been dedicated to the church of the Blessed Apostle Peter; but, so long as I have life, I will preserve it under the same conditions under which I have hitherto preserved it by the favour of God, until I have first sent my own messengers, or else letters of my own, with you to Rome to enquire about these pressing matters, so that I may find salvation in seeking to do the right." When he had made this answer, they rejoiced together and then parted, each one returning to his own place.

CHAPTER XLIX

Of our excommunication

But his enemies who usurped possession of our holy bishop's substance declared that we and those who participated with us were excommunicated from the heritage of the faithful; and they so utterly abjured communion with us that they decreed that if one of our abbots or priests was invited to eat with one of the faithful laity, and blessed the meal set before him with the sign of the cross of God, it must be thrown out of doors and cast away as if offered to idols; and the vessels from which our men fed, they ordered to be first washed, as though polluted with filth, before anyone else touched them.

CHAPTER L

De navigio eius pergenti[1] Romam

Haec miserabilis et lamentabilis ingruens calamitas a nobis comperta, ad Dominum incessabiliter die noctuque clamantes, in ieiunio et fletu cum omnibus subiectis nostris congregationibus fundentes precem[2] orationis offerebamus, quousque parati cum sancto pontifice nostro navem ascenderunt et, vehiculo navis transportati, ad litora australia, Domino praeviante, pervenerunt. Tunc vero pedestri gressu super terram simul gradientes, sanctis auxiliantibus apostolis, salvo spatioso itinere ad apostolicam venientes sedem, praesentati adstiterunt. Progeniculantes flexis poplitibus, obnixe obsecrantes postulabant ut hoc illorum legationis indiculum, quamvis rusticitate magis conscriptum quam urbanitatis facundia caraxatum appareat, pro sua consuetudinaria pietatis clementia non dedignanter susciperent. "Scire enim," dicebant, "vestram dignitatem hoc volumus, ut neminem per invidiam accusandum advenimus; sed tamen[3] ut, si quis in vestro beatissimo concilio contra nos[4] aliunde veniens aliquam[5] proferre ausus sit accusationis obiectionem, in quantum, vestra adiuvante clementia, valuerimus, aut excusare, si falsa, aut confiteri, si vera, parati sumus. Clementia ergo conditoris nostri et beatorum apostolorum principis protecti, ad hanc gloriosissimam sedem quasi ad matris gremium confugimus sufferendo, quicquid vestra beatissima imperaverit[6] auctoritas." Deinde itaque a beatissimo apostolico papa Iohanne sanctus pontifex noster Wilfrithus episcopus cum reverentissimis presbiteris et omni clero venerabili benigna pietate susceptus, glorificae sedis responsa expectantes, per aliquot[7] dies requiescentes, mansione voluntaria praeparata manserunt. Interim quoque legati a sancto archiepiscopo Berhwaldo[8] cum suis scriptis accusationis[9] ad apostolicam sedem directi, supplices petentes sibi praebendi a gloriosissima sede auditum legationis suae, qua fungebantur, simul pervenerunt. Tunc vero beatissimus apostolicus Iohannes papa cum coepiscopis[10] suis undique congregatis et omni venerabili clero ad synodalem locum veniens, praesentato Deo amabili Wilfritho episcopo cum fratribus

---

[1] persentique C   [2] prece F   [3] tantum C   [4] omit C   [5] aliquando C
[6] imperabit C   [7] aliquod C   [8] Berchtualdo C   [9] accusationes F
[10] episcopis C

CHAPTER L

Concerning his voyage on the way to Rome. [703?]

When we learned of the wretched and lamentable calamity that had befallen us, we cried to the Lord without ceasing day and night; with fasting and tears, we poured out our prayers and supplications, together with all the congregations attached to us, until the time when the preparations were made and the party embarked with our holy bishop, and, borne oversea by their ship, reached the southern shores, God going before them. Then, making their way together on foot overland, by the help of the holy Apostles, after a long journey, they arrived safely at the Apostolic See; on being presented, they urgently implored on bended knee that they would receive without disdain, as befitted their customary clemency and piety, this account of their errand, though it should appear to be written in rustic style instead of being inscribed with urbane eloquence. "For," said they, "we wish your Excellence to know that we have come to accuse no one through envy; but nevertheless, if any comes from elsewhere into your holy council and ventures to bring forward any hostile accusation against us, we wish you to know that we are prepared so far as we are able, with the help of your clemency, to offer our defence, if the charges are false, or to confess them, if they are true. So, protected by the clemency of our Creator and the chief of the blessed Apostles, we have fled for refuge to this most glorious see, as though to our mother's bosom, accepting whatever commands your most blessed authority shall lay upon us."

And so our holy prelate, Bishop Wilfrid, and the most reverend priests and all the venerable clergy were received by the most blessed and Apostolic Pope John with kindly piety; they rested several days in a dwelling which had been prepared for them freely, awaiting the answer of the glorious see. Meanwhile messengers from the holy Archbishop Berhtwald as well, also sent to the Apostolic See with his written accusation, arrived at the same time, humbly begging the most glorious See to grant an audience for the mission with which they were charged. Then when the most blessed Apostolic Pope John with his fellow-bishops, gathered together from every hand, and all the venerable clergy, had come to the place of meeting, Bishop Wilfrid the beloved of God and all his venerable

suis venerabilibus, primum petitionis suae cartula coram omni
conventu relegebatur, hoc modo continens[1]:

CHAPTER LI

De cartula petitionis suae

"Domino apostolico terque beatissimo universali papae Iohanni
Wilfrithus simplex et humilis servus servorum Dei episcopus.
Cognoscat sanctitas vestra, istas esse causas, pro quibus hanc sedem
apostolicam vestramque beatissimam praesentiam de ultima terrarum
parte iam vice tertia[2] adiuvandus adveni. Primo, quia unitas apostoli-
corum virorum individua semper esse solet, ut, quaeque a praedecessore vestro beatissimo Agathone papa iustissimis atque clementissimis
iudiciis decreta sunt, vestra pia auctoritas, quia multis non dubium
est ad salutem proficere, confirmet et corroboret: et ut pietas vestra
intelligere dignetur, quia in omnibus vestrae beatitudinis iussionibus
humiles et supplices subire parati sumus. Perturbationibus enim
nuper in Brittannia ortis ex parte eorum, qui contra decreta supradicti beatissimi Agathonis papae illiusque successorum venerabilium
patrum sibimet episcopatum et monasteria terrasque cum omnibus
meis facultatibus usurpabant, compulsus, hanc sacrosanctam apostolicam sedem appellavi, contestans eos per omnipotentem Deum
et beatum Petrum principem apostolorum, ut si quis aliquam contra
me accusationem haberet, ad vestram mecum praesentiam iudicandus
conveniret, sicut beati praedecessoris vestri Sergii papae scripta
cernebant[3]. Et ideo petitionum parvitatis meae paginam vestrae
gloriosissimae praesentiae pro instanti vobis notissima necessitate
offerendam curavi, et cum quibus vestrae solitae clementiae et
benignitatis[4] aures pulsare haec continens praesumo, ut omnia
rectitudinis pietatisque, quae a beatissimis antecessoribus vestris
dominis apostolicis sancto Agathone et electo Benedicto et beato
Sergio unanimiter erga meam parvitatem decreta sunt, vos largiflua
pietatis benevolentia confirmare dignemini. Et vestram inflexibilem
auctoritatem ex intima cordis intentione non solum ego, sed et omnes
qui mecum advenerunt fratres obsecrantes, humiliter postulamus,
ut, si quilibet accusatores contra nos aliunde venerint, per vestram

---

[1] continentem C *and* F   [2] terciam F tercia C   [3] decernebant C
[4] benignas C

brethren were presented to him and the document containing his petition was first read in the presence of the whole assembly, and this is how it ran:

CHAPTER LI

Of the document containing his petition

"To the Apostolic Lord and thrice-blessed universal Pope John, Wilfrid the simple and humble servant of the servants of God and bishop. Let your Holiness know that these are the causes why, for the third time, I have come to this Apostolic See and into your most blessed presence from the uttermost parts of the earth to seek your aid. First, because the unity of the apostolic men is ever indivisible, it is in order that your pious authority, since it undoubtedly avails for the salvation of many, may confirm and corroborate those matters which have been decreed by your predecessor the most blessed Pope Agatho in his most just and clement judgments, and that your piety may deign to understand that in all humility and subjection we are prepared to accept all the commands of your Blessedness. For I am compelled by the troubles which have been originated of late in Britain by those who, contrary to the decrees of the same most blessed Pope Agatho and of the venerable fathers his successors, have usurped for themselves my bishopric and monasteries and lands, with all my privileges, to appeal to this most holy and Apostolic See, adjuring those men by Almighty God and the Blessed Peter, chief of the Apostles, that, if anyone has any accusation to make against me, he should come to your presence with me to be judged, as the writings of your blessed predecessor Pope Sergius decreed. So I have caused to be delivered in your most glorious presence, on account of my urgent and manifest necessity, a document containing my unworthy petitions, and with these petitions, in the following terms, I venture to assail your ears trusting to your accustomed clemency and kindness, to the end that all the righteous and pious decrees made unanimously on my unworthy behalf by your most blessed predecessors, the Apostolic Lords, St Agatho, the elect Benedict, and the blessed Sergius, you may deign to confirm in your abounding benevolence and piety. And we humbly beg and beseech your inflexible authority, not only I myself but also all the brethren who have come with me, from the very bottom of our hearts, if any accusers

iussionem in medium producti, exponant accusationis causas; et si
vel minimam quidem confirmare potuerint, libenter vestri arbitrii
aequitatem sustinere parati sumus. Si autem mendacia tantummodo
vestrae beatissimae auctoritati, falsis commendata cartulis, afferre
ausi sint, detur nobis licentia, prout vestrae sanctitati placuerit, ipsas
accusationes expurgare. Necnon supplex et humilis vestram sanctitatem deprecor ut eandem auctoritatis instantiam[1] Aethelredo[2] regi
Merciorum de vitae nostrae solatio imperare dignemini, qua praedecessores vestri beatissimi apostolici sanctus Agatho, Benedictus et
Sergius demandabant, hoc est, ut ipsa monasteria cum terris[3] ad ea
pertinentibus, quae mihi ab ipso rege Aethelredo[4] eiusque fratre
Wilfario[5] vel aliis quibuslibet pro redemptione animarum suarum
perdonata sunt, nemo per invidiam vel nefandam cupiditatem auferre
et invadere contra vestra statuta atque illius supradicti regis voluntatem praesumat. Et adhuc summopere vestram almitatem obnixis
precibus humiliter deposco, ut omnia, quae antedecessor vester
saepe memoratus beatissimus Agatho in hac apostolica sede cum
universa synodo decreverat, ipsum regem Alfrithum[6] Aquilonensium
adimplere tranquillissimis[7] monitis obsecretis[8]. Quod si forte hoc
illi durum videatur pro mea causa esse, Eboracae[9] civitatis episcopatus
cum caeteris quam plurimis monasteriis in vestro pendeat arbitrio, cui
rectissimum gubernare censeatis. Tantum ipsa duo monasteria, quod
primum dicitur Hripis[10], et alterum, quod Agustaldaesei[11] vocatur,
quae a sancto Agathone papa huius[12] apostolicae sedis sub uno
privilegio adscripta sunt, per vestrae petitionis auxilium cum omnibus
terris atque possessionibus, ad ea pertinentibus, nobis restituantur.
Et post has petitiones hoc addam, quod iuxta statuta canonum de-
bitam venerationem cum fraterna caritate archiepiscopo Berhtwaldo[13]
dignanter semper exhibeo[14], et sic me libenter facturum promitto,
tantummodo si ipse praedecessorum vestrorum, beatissimi Agathonis
eiusque successorum, fundatissima erga meam parvitatem adimpleat
decreta."

[1] eadem auct. instantia C   [2] Ethelredo C   [3] ceteris C   [4] Ethelredo C
[5] Wlfario C   [6] Aldfridum C   [7] tranquillissimus F   [8] obsecrantis F
[9] Eboraicae C   [10] Hrypis   [11] Hagustaldesae C   [12] huic C *and* F
[13] Berhtvaldo C   [14] exhibebo C

have come against us from elsewhere, that they may be brought into your midst at your command and may put forward the reasons for their accusation; and if they can prove even the smallest point we are prepared to accept gladly your just judgment. But if they have dared to bring mere lies, backed up by false documents, to your most Blessed Authority, let us be granted liberty, according as it pleases your Holiness, to clear ourselves of these charges. However, in all humility, I pray your Holiness that you will deign to give your commands to Aethilred, King of Mercia, for the comfort of my life with the same force of authority with which your predecessors the most holy and Apostolic St Agatho, Benedict, and Sergius made their demands. That is to say that no one shall presume, either through envy or wicked cupidity, to take away or invade, contrary to your commands and to the will of the above-mentioned king, those monasteries and the lands belonging to them, which were given to me by King Aethilred himself or his brother Wulfhere or by any others for the redemption of their souls. And in addition I most humbly pray you with urgent prayers that of your kindness you will urge Aldfrith, King of the North, with peaceful counsels to fulfil all the decrees which were made by the most blessed Agatho your ever-remembered predecessor in this Apostolic See with the consent of the whole synod. If however this seem to him to be hard because I am concerned, let it rest with your judgment to decide who can best govern the bishopric of the city of York and the other numerous monasteries excepting only these two monasteries called Ripon and Hexham respectively, which were included by St Agatho the Pope of this Apostolic See within the terms of one and the same privilege. Let them be restored to us at your request with all the lands and possessions belonging to them. And to these petitions I add this, that, in accordance with the canons I always show due respect and brotherly love to Archbishop Berhtwald as is meet: and this I gladly promise to do still; only let him fulfil towards my unworthy self the well-founded decrees of your predecessors, the most blessed Agatho and his successors."

CHAPTER LII

De eo, quod Iohannes[1] papa praedecessorum scripta recensenda dixit

Postquam nostrae petitionis series recitata est et diligenter a gloriosissimis auscultata, ad habitaculaque nostra redire licentiam dederunt, introductis quoque ad praesentiam eorum honorabilem a sancto Berthwaldo[2] archiepiscopo cum scriptis suis viris directis ad[3] apostolicam sedem. Quorum multiplices et magnas accusationes contra hominem Dei Wilfrithum episcopum audientes, uniuscuiusque capituli examinationem ambobus praesentibus, hoc est accusatoribus[4] et[5] excusantibus[6], stabiliter audire in futuro tempore per ordinem promiserunt et[7] ipsos domum redire iusserunt. Tunc beatissimus Iohannes apostolicae sedis papa coepiscopis suis in synodali loco sedentibus dixit: "O sancta synodus, nostrum est primum sanctissimorum antedecessorum nostrorum percurrere canones et examinare scripta, de hac eadem inimicitia fraudis ex utraque parte olim ad hanc apostolicam sedem directa, et diligenter considerare, quid ter beatissimus Agatho in his causis censuerit, et post eum electus Benedictus necnon et praedecessor meus sanctissimus Sergius memoraliter retinere, quid de hac eadem re regibus et sancto archiepiscopo faciendum sit ab apostolica sede decreverunt. Deinde facilius, ex utraque parte in praesentia fraternitatis nostrae in invicem certantibus[8], Deo adiuvante et sancto Petro principe apostolorum, veritatis lumen, extincto mendacio et caecato[9], agnoscere valeamus et secundum normam sanctissimorum primorum praedecessorum canonice censeamus." Et hoc tale consilium beatissimi Iohannis universo synodo complacuit, et sic fecerunt.

CHAPTER LIII[10]

Itaque quadam die beatissimus Iohannes apostolicae sedis praesul et reverentissimi coepiscopi[11] eius, in sanctum concilium congregati, iusserunt utriusque[12], accusatorum et defensorum[13], electos viros sancto

---

[1] Iohannis C   [2] Berhtvaldo C   [3] *omit* C   [4] accusationibus F   [5] *omit* F
[6] excusationibus F   [7] *insert* iam C   [8] cernantibus C   [9] excaecato C
[10] *There is no chapter heading in either* MS *though it is obvious a new chapter begins here*   [11] episcopi F   [12] *insert* partis C   [13] defensatorum F

CHAPTER LII

*How Pope John said that the writings of his
predecessors were to be re-examined*

After the matter of our petition had been read and carefully listened
to by this most glorious company, we were given leave to return to
our dwellings; and the men who had been sent to the Apostolic See by
the Archbishop St Berhtwald were also brought into their honourable
presence with their writings; they listened to their manifold and
great accusations against Bishop Wilfrid the man of God, and promised
at some future time to conduct a thorough examination of each count
in order in the presence of both, that is both accusers and defendants;
thereupon they bade them go home.

Then the most blessed John, Pope of the Apostolic See, said to his
fellow-bishops who were sitting in the place of synod: "O Holy
Synod, first of all it is our duty to go through the canons of our most
holy predecessors and to examine the writings which were on former
occasions sent to this Apostolic See by both parties concerning this
same hostility and wrong, and to consider diligently and bear in mind
what the thrice-blessed Agatho decided in these matters, and after
him the elect Benedict, and my most holy predecessor Sergius; they
decided from the Apostolic See what should be done in this same
matter by the kings and the holy archbishop. Then, with the help of
God and of St Peter the chief of the Apostles, we shall the more
easily be able, after we have quenched and put out the fires of false-
hood, to perceive the light of truth, when representatives of both
sides are contending one against the other in the presence of our
brethren, and we shall decide in accordance with the canons and
the rule of our most holy predecessors." This plan pleased all the
synod of the most blessed John; and they acted accordingly.

CHAPTER LIII

[704]

And so, on a certain day the most blessed John the prelate of the
Apostolic See and his most reverend fellow-bishops gathered in holy
congregation ordered that chosen men of both parties, accusers and
defendants, should be present at the holy gathering; and this was

conventui praesentari, et mox ita factum est. Nam sanctus Wilfrithus
episcopus et venerabiles presbiteri et diacones eius praesentati sunt,
humiles et supplices honorabiles facies salutantes, promittentes se
cum intimo cordis affectu illius apostolicae sedis decreta suscipere
et adimplere; necnon et sancti archiepiscopi nuntii, secundum
praeceptum[1] sanctissimorum venientes, adstiterunt. Quibus datum
est tempus loquendi, ut unumquodcumque capitulum accusationis
eligerent, primum adversum nos dicerent, postea ad alia ordinantes
in conflictu accederent. Qui responderunt, dicentes: "Hoc est
primum capitulum nostrae accusationis, quod iste praesens Wilfrithus episcopus iudicia sancti archiepiscopi Berhtwaldi Cantuariorum ecclesiae et totius Brittanniae, ab hac apostolica sede emissi[2],
statuta coram synodo contumaciter renuens contempsit. Nos nostrae
partis sententiam detulimus; vos vestram defensionem dicite."
Stans itaque sanctus Wilfrithus episcopus noster, honorabili[3] senio
convectus[4], cum fratribus suis venerabilibus in conspectu totius
congregationis, dixit: "Humilis et supplex excellentissimam sanctitatem vestram deprecor, ut meae parvitatis dignemini veritatem huius
rei gestae a me audire. Eram enim in concilio sedens cum abbatibus
meis ac presbiteris[5] necnon et diaconibus; unum ex numero episcoporum illic congregatorum miserunt ad me, interrogantem[6] sermonibus regis nec minus et archiepiscopi, si ipsius solummodo archiepiscopi
iudicium consentire voluissem: et quicquid ille iudicando decrevisset,
an paratus fuissem adimplere omnibus votis annon. Ad istum ita
sciscitanti respondebam: 'Quae est illius iudicii sententia scire prius
oportet, quam confiteamur, utrum pati ea valeamus[7] exsequendo an
aliter.' Ille autem se nescire affirmabat nec alio modo archiepiscopum[8] velle revelando cuiquam nostrum[9] patefacere iudicii ex-
solutionem dicebat, antequam propriae[10] manus subscriptione coram
praesenti concilio fatentes confirmaremus, ut eius unicum per omnia
iudicium elegentes tenere nec ab eo ad dexteram neque ad sinistram
declinantes deviaremus. 'Istius tam angustam[11] districtionis coarta-
tionem,' dicebam, 'numquam antea a quoquam hominum coactam
audivi, ut omnino iuramentis nodo adstrictus fateretur decreta com-
posita, quamvis impossibilia, persolvere, priusquam sciret vim
decreti.' Attamen ibi coram senatu spopondi, quatenus in cunctis

---

[1] praeceptorum F   [2] emisso C *and* F   [3] honorabilis F   [4] confectus
Jones   [5] presbiteribus C   [6] interrogante F   [7] valemus C   [8] archiepiscopi C   [9] nostrorum C *insert* est F   [10] propria F   [11] augustam F

immediately done. For the holy Bishop Wilfrid and his venerable priests and deacons were introduced as humble suppliants; they saluted the honourable company and promised that they would accept and fulfil the decrees of that Apostolic See with the utmost goodwill. The messengers of the holy archbishop also came, in accordance with the command of the most holy men, and stood there. They were granted an opportunity of speaking, being allowed to choose any one section of their accusation and to speak first against us upon it. Afterwards they were to proceed in succession to the other counts under discussion.

They answered, "This is the first section of our accusation, that this Bishop Wilfrid here present contumaciously refused and despised, in the presence of the synod, the judgments of the holy Berhtwald, Archbishop of the Church of the Kentishmen and of all Britain, who had been sent forth from this Apostolic See. We have brought forward the opinion of our party, now do you declare your defence."

And St Wilfrid our bishop, bowed down by honourable age, arose amid his venerable brethren, and said in the presence of all the congregation, "As a humble suppliant I pray your most excellent Holiness that you will deign to hear from me the truth of this action of my unworthy self. I was present at the council with my abbots and priests and deacons too; they sent one of the bishops there assembled to ask me on behalf of the king and the archbishop if I would consent to the judgment of the archbishop himself alone, and whether or not I was prepared to fulfil with all my heart whatever he decreed. I answered the bishop's question in these words, 'We ought to know what is the substance of his decision before we declare whether we are able to accept and carry it out or not.' He asserted however that he did not know, and said that the archbishop would not declare the content of his decision by revealing it to any of our party until we had subscribed with our own hand in the presence of the council to a promise that we would choose his single judgment in all things for our observance and that we would not turn away from it to the right hand or the left. 'Never before,' said I, 'have I heard of a constraint as narrow and stringent as yours, enforced upon any man, so that he should actually promise after being bound by an oath to fulfil decrees made, however impossible they might be, and that before knowing the terms of the decree.' Nevertheless I promised there in the

archiepiscopi iudicium, in quibus consonans invenitur statutis
sanctorum patrum regulis et canonicis diffinitionibus et non dis-
crepans prorsus in ulla re a sancto Agathonis synodo caeterorumque
orthodoxorum ei[1] successorum repperiatur, toto mentis conatu
subiacere parati inveniemur[2]." Hanc excusationem sanctus pontifex
noster reddidit et silendo quievit. Tunc sancta synodus respondit:
"Wilfrithus Deo amabilis episcopus canonice[3] defensionis suae protectionem exposuit." Tunc[4] inter se graecizantes et subridentes, nos
autem[5] celantes, multa[6] loqui coeperunt et postremo dicentes accusatoribus: "Non ignoratis, carissimi fratres, habemus ex praecepto canonum nostrorum: *Quotienscumque clericis ab accusatoribus
multa crimina obiciuntur: et unum ex ipsis, de quo prius egerit, probare
non potuerit, ad caetera iam non[7] admittantur.* Sed tamen propter
honorem sancti archiepiscopi, ab huius apostolicae sedis monarchia
directo, et pro huius beatissimi Wilfrithi episcopi reverentia, diu
fraude spoliato, ut asserunt[8], Deo et sancto Petro principe apostolorum
revelante et aperiente, per multos dies vel menses omnia capitula
plene eventilantes, finem rei imponere desiderantes non fastidiose
curabimus." Post haec verba, pontifici nostro cum fratribus suis[9]
triumphali gaudio incoepto, a sancto synodo licentia[10] data, ad aliarum
dierum [11]conflictum praeparantes, ad mansiones suas redierunt. Alii
vero e contrario, primo ingressu conflictionis confusi, domum suam
adierunt, et nebulae mendaciorum, flante vento sapientiae, dispersae,
soleque veritatis per Dei adiutorium et sanctum Petrum illucescente,
per plura spatia dierum et mensium ab omni piaculo scelere degra-
dandi pure perfecteque excusatus, probabilis sanctus pontifex noster
apparuit. Nam per IIII menses et LXX conciliabula sanctissimae sedis
de fornace ignis examinandi, apostolica potestate hoc modo auxiliante,
purificatus, ut breviter[12] dicam, evasit: quia in sancto pascha[13], tertia
die, ter beatissimi Agathonis synodus adversum pravitates[14] haereti-
corum cum centum XXV orthodoxis episcopis constituta, ex quibus
unusquisque pro sua provincia et civitate veram fidem confessus et
subscriptione sua confirmavit. Haec coram omni populo more
Romanorum clara voce legebatur, in qua scriptura inventum est
inter caetera: *Wilfrithus Deo amabilis episcopus Eroboracae[15] civitatis,
apostolicam sedem de sua causa appellantem et ab hac potestate de certis*

---

[1] eius F   [2] inveniamur F   [3] canonicae C   [4] Tum C   [5] ac F   [6] multe C
[7] *omit* F   [8] assertur C   [9] *omit* F   [10]–[11] data...con- *omit* F   [12] *insert
after* evasit C   [13] pasca F   [14] pravitantes F   [15] Euroicae C

presence of the council that we should be found wholeheartedly to submit to the judgment of the archbishop in all things in which it was found to tally with the statutes, rules, and canonical definitions of the holy fathers and was not found in any way to be in conflict with the holy synod of Agatho and all his orthodox successors."

Our holy bishop offered this defence and was silent. Then the holy synod answered, "Bishop Wilfrid, beloved of God, has set forth, in accordance with the canons, the defence under which he seeks shelter."

Then they began to talk Greek among themselves and to smile covertly, saying many things which they concealed from us. Finally they said to the accusers, "You are not ignorant, dear brethren, of our practice in accordance with our canons: 'When many charges are brought against clerics, if the first one dealt with has not been proved, let not the accusers be allowed to proceed to the others.' But nevertheless, out of respect to the holy archbishop sent by the monarchy of this Apostolic See and out of reverence for this most blessed Bishop Wilfrid so long fraudulently despoiled, as it is asserted, we, with the help of God and St Peter the chief of the Apostles, in revealing and opening the matter, will take scrupulous care to sift all the charges thoroughly in the course of many days and months; for we desire to settle the matter finally."

After these words the joy of victory came upon our bishop and upon his brethren, and when permission had been granted them by the holy synod, they returned to their dwellings to prepare for the conflict which was to come. Their opponents, however, on the contrary, went to their homes in confusion at the beginning of the conflict and, the clouds of their lies being dispersed by the blast of the wind of wisdom, the sun of truth began to shine by the help of God and St Peter, and the holy bishop was seen after the lapse of many days and months to be proved absolutely and entirely free of all the crime which merited the punishment of degradation. For, to be brief, after being tested throughout the space of four months in seventy sittings of the council of the most holy See, he escaped from the fiery furnace of cross-examination, the apostolic power helping him in the following way: At holy Eastertide, on the third day of the feast, when the thrice-blessed Agatho was Pope, a synod consisting of 125 orthodox bishops was held to combat the corruptions of heretics and each one of these bishops

incertisque rebus absolutum et cum aliis CXXV *coepiscopis in synodo in iudicii sede constitutum et pro omni aquilonali parte Brittanniae et Hiberniae insulisque quae ab Anglorum et Brittonum necnon Scottorum et*[1] *Pictorum gentibus colebantur, veram et catholicam confessus fidem*[2] *et cum subscriptione sua corroboravit.* Itaque, quo audito, omnes cives Romani sapientes stupefacti sunt. Tunc Bonifacius[3] et Sizentius[4] et alii nonnulli, qui eum in diebus beatae memoriae Agathonis agnoscentes viderunt, dicebant, "istum esse praesentem Deo amabilem Wilfrithum episcopum, quem beatissimus Agatho purificatum de accusationibus[5], apostolica auctoritate absolutum, olim ad propria remisit, et iterum nunc—vae pro dolor!—infestatorum insidiae exorbitare de propria sede fecerunt. Qui per XL et eo amplius annos episcopatus officia fungebatur, et tam honorabilem senem cum fratribus venerabilibus accusatores falsidici et cum pseudographis[6] audaci temeritate et, ut ita dicam, unus diaconus et alii omnes sine aliquo ecclesiasticae dignitatis gradu in conventu apostolicae sedis excellentissimam personam ausi sunt accusare. Et ideo digni sunt poenas luere, in ima carceris angustia usque ad finem mortis macerati." Et tunc viri Romani verum eos dixisse affirmabant. Dixit autem beatissimus Iohannes apostolicae sedis papa: "Beatus Wilfrithus, Deo amabilis episcopus, in quo nullam criminis per tot conciliabula nostra examinando tam diligenter obiectionem invenimus, beati Petri apostoli et apostolorum principis auctoritate, qui habet potestatem solvendi ligandique ab occultis delictis, exsolutum sciat, et quod beatus Agatho et electus Benedictus sanctusque Sergius apostolicae sedis[7] praesules de eo censuerunt, nostrae quoque parvitatis humilitas cum totius[8] synodi consensu regibus et archiepiscopis[9] scripta iudicia, per manum beati Wilfrithi episcopi ad eos emissa, affirmare decrevit, hoc modo dicens:

---

[1] *omit* F   [2] f.c. C   [3] Bonifatius C   [4] Siszentius C   [5] accusatoribus F
[6] pseudogravis C   [7] *omit* sedis C   [8] cuncto eius F   [9] archiepiscopi F

confessed the true faith on behalf of his province and city, and confirmed his confession with his signature. Now this document was being read out in a loud voice before all the people after the Roman custom, and in it there occurred among other things these words: "Wilfrid, Bishop of York, beloved of God, appealing to the Apostolic See about his cause, and absolved by its power from definite and indefinite charges, and with 125 other bishops called together in synod set in the seat of judgment, confessed the true and catholic faith for all the northern part of Britain and Ireland and the islands, which are inhabited by the races of Angles and Britons as well as Scots and Picts, and corroborated it with his signature."

When they had heard these things all the wise citizens of Rome were amazed. Then Boniface and Sizentius and some others, who had known and seen him in the days of Agatho of blessed memory, said that "this same Bishop Wilfrid beloved of God was now present with them, whom the most blessed Agatho had formerly sent to his own home, purified and absolved from all the charges of his adversaries by Apostolic authority; and now once again, alas! the plots of his enemies had made him wander from his own see. For forty years and more he had held the office of bishop. False accusers, provided with forged documents, dared to accuse so honourable an old man together with his venerable brethren; and one mere deacon, so to speak, and others, all without any rank of ecclesiastical dignity, in their rash temerity, ventured to make charges against a person of the highest rank at a gathering of the Apostolic See. They are only fit to undergo punishment and to waste away in the deepest of dungeons until they die." Then the Romans declared that they had spoken the truth.

But the most blessed John, Pope of the Apostolic See, said: "The blessed Wilfrid, a bishop beloved of God, in whom we have found no reproach of guilt, though we have examined the matter so diligently in so many councils, let him be declared acquitted by the authority of the blessed Apostle Peter, chief of the Apostles, who has the power of binding and loosing from secret sins. And what the blessed Agatho, the elect Benedict, and the holy Sergius, the chiefs of the Apostolic See, have decided concerning him, we in our unworthiness, with the consent of the whole synod, have decided to confirm—even the judgments which were written and sent to the kings and archbishops by the hands of the blessed Bishop Wilfrid. The writing is as follows:

CHAPTER LIV

"'Dominis excellentissimis[1] Aethelredo[2] regi Merciorum et Alfrido regi Derorum et Berniciorum[3] Iohannes papa. De vestrae quidem eximiae religionis accessibus, gratia Dei cooperante[4], gaudemus, fervorem fidei cernentes in vobis, quam ex praedicatione principis apostolorum, Deo vestras animas illuminante, percepistis et efficaciter retinetis; ut[5] gaudium nostrum melior accessus amplificet! Illud vero animos nostros afficit et consacerdotum ac totius ecclesiae contristavit auditum[6] inextricabilis quorumdam dissensio, quod et ad correctionem oportet, Deo annuente, perducere, ut non contemptores pontificalium decretorum, sed ut oboedientiae filii ante Deum omnium iudicem comprobemur esse custodes. Dudum[7] enim sub apostolicae memoriae praedecessore nostro Agathone pontifice, dum Wilfrithus episcopus ad hanc sedem apostolicam veniens appellasset, et praesentibus eius contrariis, qui a Theodoro venerandae memoriae archiepiscopo sanctae Cantuariorum ecclesiae ex hac apostolica sede mandato et Hyldae[8] religiosae memoriae abbatissae ad eum accusandum huc prius advenerant, etiam hic episcopi de diversis provinciis cum suprafato sancto pontifice congregati, quae a partibus dicebantur, regulariter quaesierunt et sententialiter decreverunt, eandemque sententiam successores eius sancti pontifices praedecessores nostri secuti sunt. Nec hoc venerandae memoriae Theodorus praesul, qui ab hac apostolica sede directus est, contravenisse recognoscitur neque accusationem aliquam postmodum ad hanc sedem apostolicam demandavit, magis autem, ut ex eius dictis apparuit, et decretis pontificalibus obsecutus est. Succurrendum est itaque cum Dei praesidio, ne[9] perseveret in uno loco dissensio, dum in[10] caeteris consacerdotum ac plebium unanimitas maneat. Et haec de praeteritis memoravimus. De praesentibus quoque innotescere inclitae vestrae christianitati praevidimus, quod hii, qui de eadem insula Brittannia huc advenerunt[11], accusationes contra Wilfrithum episcopum detulerunt[12], ille superveniens cum fratribus suis, in accusatores eius quod excusaverunt retorserunt. Quorum conflictus apud conventum reverentissimorum episcoporum et sacerdotum, qui hic ad praesens

---

[1] eminentissimis C   [2] Aethilredo C   [3] Bernicorum C   [4] operante C
[5] et F   [6] auditis F   [7] Dum F   [8] Hildae C   [9] nec F   [10] *omit* C   [11] *insert* et C   [12] *insert* et F

CHAPTER LIV

"'To the most excellent lords, Aethilred, King of the Mercians, and Aldfrith, King of Deira and Bernicia, from Pope John. We rejoice in the increase of true religion among you by the help of the grace of God. We recognize the zeal of your faith, which you received through the preaching of the chief of the Apostles, when God illumined your hearts, and which you efficaciously hold; may your further growth make our joy the greater! But this matter which we have heard grieves our hearts and has saddened our fellow-clergy and all the Church, namely the inextricable dissension of certain men, which matter ought to be put right by the help of God, so that we may be proved in the presence of God, the Judge of all men, to be, not despisers of the pontifical decrees, but, as sons of obedience, their guardians. For some time ago, when Agatho our predecessor of Apostolic memory was Pope, Bishop Wilfrid came with an appeal to the Apostolic See. His adversaries were present, having come hither from Theodore of hallowed memory, Archbishop of the holy Church of the Kentish people, who was sent from this Apostolic See, and from the abbess Hild, of pious memory, in order to accuse him. Bishops also, from various provinces, were assembled here, with the above-mentioned holy prelate, and they duly enquired into what was said by the various parties and made their decree and sentence. And the holy bishops, his successors and our predecessors, have confirmed the same opinion. Nor is the Bishop Theodore of hallowed memory, who was sent forth from this Apostolic See, known to have contravened this, nor did he send any accusation afterwards to this Apostolic See; rather, as is clear from his words, he complied with the papal decrees. And so, with the help of God, we must see that dissension does not continue in one place while in others there is complete unanimity among priests and people. So much for the past. For the present also we have taken measures to make known to your renowned and Christian selves that those who came hither from the same island of Britain have brought accusations against Bishop Wilfrid; he followed with his brethren and turned upon his accusers the charges they made. We caused the debate between the parties to be conducted for some days before the assembly of reverend bishops and priests who were

inventi sunt, per dies aliquos fieri procuravimus; apud quos omnia,
quaequae in scriptis vel anterioribus vel modernis partes detulerunt
vel hic inveniri[1] potuerunt vel a partibus verbialiter dicta sunt,
subtiliter[2] inquisita ad cognitionem nostram perducta sunt, dum nec
ipsae principales personae, de quibus contentio omnis exorta est,
praesentes affuerint, quos necesse est, ut contentio omnis finem
accipiat, advenire et consedere[3]. Et idcirco commonemus Berht-
waldum[4] praesulem sanctae Cantuariorum ecclesiae, quem auctoritate principis apostolorum archiepiscopum ibidem confirmavimus,
reverentissimum fratrem nostrum, ut synodum convocet una cum
Wilfritho episcopo, et concilio regulariter celebrato, Bosam atque
Iohannem episcopos in synodum faciat advenire vocesque partium
audiat et consideret, quid sibi invicem partes valeant approbare. Et
siquidem, eo suffragante, apud synodum hoc regulariter determinare
valuerit, gratum nobis et partibus expedit; sin aliter acciderit[5], eos
synodaliter moneat et commonitionibus suis, et quaeque[6] consideret[7],
ad hanc sedem apostolicam simul occurrant, ut in ampliori concilio
flagitetur, ac[8] decidetur, quod hactenus non valuit terminari, atque
per gratiam sancti Spiritus, qui cum discordia venerant, revertantur
in pace. Scire autem debet, quicumque de eis advenire distulerit
vel, quod est execrandum, venire contempserit, seipsum deiectioni
submittat, et hinc abiciendus nec ibidem ab ullo praesulum sive
fidelium recipiendus. Qui enim suo inoboediens existit auctori, non
poterit inter ministros eius atque discipulos recenseri[9]. Vestra
proinde christiana et regalis sublimitas pro Dei timore et christianae
fidei reverentia et pace, quam Dominus Iesus Christus suis dedit
discipulis, subventum faciat atque concursum, ut haec, quae a Deo
aspirante perspeximus, ad effectum perveniant, ut pro huiusmodi
religioso annisu merces vobis ascribatur in coelis, quatinus et in hoc
seculo, Christo protegente, regnetis incolumes et aeterni regni eius
beatum consortium habeatis[10]. Ideo recordemini, o filii carissimi,
quid de hac eadem re beatissimus Agatho caeterique post eum con-
sona voce nobiscum praesules Romanae ecclesiae apostolica auctoritate sanxerunt. Quicumque enim cuiuslibet personae audaci temeritate[11] contempserit, non erit a Deo impunitus neque sine dampno

[1] invenire F   [2] suptiliter C   [3] consideret F   [4] Berchtwaldum C
[5] accederit F   [6] prodesse suis partibus unaquaeque *insert* C   [7] Mabillon.
considerat C *and* F   [8] ad C   [9] recesserit F   [10] habetis C   [11] temeri-
tati C

present here; before whom all the writings whether old or recent, which the parties brought forward, or which could be found here, and the verbal statements made by either party, were closely enquired into and brought to our knowledge. However the principal persons were not present from whom all the dissension arose; but it is necessary that these should come together and confer in order that all this contention may be brought to an end. And to this end we bid Berhtwald, the Bishop of the holy Church of the Kentish people, whom we have confirmed archbishop there by the authority of the chief of the Apostles, and who is our most reverend brother, to hold a synod with Bishop Wilfrid, and when the council has been regularly constituted, to cause Bishops Bosa and John to come into the synod, to hear what both sides have to say, and to consider what the parties in turn are able to prove to him. And if in his opinion it is possible to come to a regular conclusion before the synod, it will be satisfactory both for ourselves and for the parties at strife. But if it happens otherwise, let him give them a formal warning in the synod together with private admonitions and let him deal with each point; and let them present themselves together at this Apostolic See, that the matter may be thrashed out in a fuller council, and that a decision may be reached on a point which thus far it has not been possible to settle, and that by the grace of the Holy Spirit those who came in discord may return in peace. But if any one of these delays to come, or (what is to be execrated) does not deign to come, let him know that he will incur deprivation and that he will be repelled from this place, and, further, will not be received by any of the clergy or the faithful here. For he who is disobedient to his Head shall not be numbered amongst His servants and disciples. So may your most Christian and royal Highnesses, for fear of God and for reverence of the Christian faith and the peace which our Lord Jesus Christ gave to His disciples, lend your aid and assistance, so that these matters we have investigated by the help of God, may come to good effect; so that for such religious labours as these, you may be granted a reward in heaven, while in this world also you may reign unharmed under the protection of Christ and enjoy the blessed fellowship of His eternal kingdom. So remember, my dear sons, what the most blessed Agatho and the other dignitaries of the Roman church after him, in agreement with us, ordained by Apostolic authority about this matter. For whoever he may be, and of whatever rank, who despises us with

coelitus alligatus evadit. Incolumem eminentiam vestram gratia
superna custodiat.'"

CHAPTER LV

Qualiter iussus patriam redire sanctas reliquias
secum portavit[1]

Transactis[2] itaque ibi multis mensibus[3], paene cotidie in conflictu
diligenter examinatus, postremo tamen in victoria omnino excusabilis
apparuit. Iam[4] vero sancto pontifici nostro[5] volenti ad sedem
apostolicam manere et in[6] sua senectute sibi mundum crucifigere
vitamque ibi finire, apostolicus antistes et universa sancta[7] synodus
humiliter oboedientiam suam olim promittenti singulariter praecipientes, illum apostolica auctoritate de certis incertisque causis post
longam afflictionem pure absolutum patriam remeare iudiciaque con-
scripta regibus et archiepiscopo portare et maerorem[8] subditorum
sedare gaudiumque amicorum renovare in nomine Domini iusserunt.
Ille autem sanctus pontifex noster sciens oboedire[9], cum sociis loca
sanctorum circumiens moreque suo ab electis viris sanctas reliquias
nominatim congregans aliaque indumenta purpureaque[10] et serica ad
ornamenta ecclesiarum lucratus, cum benedictione sanctorum
patriam remeavit, pergens per plana et aspera camporum et montium
longo itinere, usquedum Galliarum regionem pervenit.

CHAPTER LVI

De patroni[11] nostri aegrotatione et Michaelis adventu[12]

Deinde igitur, iter agentibus, sanctus pontifex noster maximo
languore infirmitatis correptus, equo primitus vehitur; postremo
tamen inter manus maerentium et lacrimantium ad Deumque
clamantium in feretro portatus, ad Meldum civitatem vix vivus
deducitur, nihil de morte eius dubitantes. Quippe qui nihil alicuius
cibi aut liquoris quattuor diebus et quattuor noctibus degustavit,
sed in excessu iacens spiritus, tantum halitus et calida membra
vivum eum demonstrabant. Quinta demum die, mane illucescente,

---

[1] *No chapter heading in* C [2] Trans F [3] *insert* actis F [4] Ibi F [5] non C
[6] *omit* C [7] *omit* F [8] Mabillon. memorem C *and* F [9] obediens F
[10] *omit* que C [11] patronis F [12] *No chapter heading in* C

bold temerity, he shall not be unpunished by God, nor, being found guilty by Heaven, shall he escape without loss. May the heavenly grace keep your Eminences unharmed!'"

CHAPTER LV

How he was ordered to return home and took holy relics with him. [704]

So, after many months had passed away with almost daily examinations and debate, at last he appeared victorious and altogether free from guilt. But although our holy bishop wished to remain in the Apostolic See and crucify the world to himself in his old age and finish his life there, yet, inasmuch as he had previously promised his humble obedience, the Apostolic chief and the holy synod one and all charged him to depart to his country, completely absolved by the Apostolic authority from every charge, definite and indefinite, after a long period of affliction. They bade him, in the name of the Lord, to carry their written decisions to the kings and the archbishop, and to soothe the grief of his followers and renew the joy of his friends. But our holy bishop, in all obedience, visited with his friends the shrines of the saints, and according to his habit, collected from elect men holy relics authenticated by the names of saints, buying also vestments of purple and silk to ornament the churches. With the blessing of the saints he made his way homewards, over hill and dale, by smooth paths and rough, until, after a long journey, he reached the kingdom of Gaul.

CHAPTER LVI

How our patron was sick and how Michael appeared to him. [705]

Then, as they were journeying, our holy bishop was seized with a very great infirmity of body. At first he was borne on horseback, but at last he was carried on a litter by his friends who mourned and wept the while and called upon God, until he was brought, scarcely alive, to the town of Meaux, his comrades never doubting that he would die. In fact he had not tasted any food or drink for four days and four nights; but though he was unconscious, yet his breathing and the warmth of his limbs proved that he was alive.

ecce! angelus Domini in veste candida sancto pontifici nostro apparuit, dicens: "Ego sum Michael summi Dei nuntius, qui misit me ad te indicare, quod tibi adduntur anni vitae pro intercessione sanctae Mariae genetricis[1] Dei semperque virginis et pro subditorum tuorum lacrimis, ad aures Domini pervenientibus; et hoc tibi erit signum, quod ab hac die in dies melioratus sanaberis et ad patriam tuam pervenies[2], tibique substantiarum tuarum carissima quaeque[3] redduntur, et in pace vitam consummabis. Paratus quoque esto, quia post IIII annorum spatium iterum visitabo te. Iam enim memento quod in honore sancti Petri et Andreae apostolis domos aedificasti, sanctae vero Mariae semper virgini intercedenti pro te nullam fecisti. Habes hoc emendare et in honorem eius domum dedicare." Et post haec verba angelus Domini assumptus ab oculis eius discessit. Sanctus itaque pontifex noster, quasi de somno excitatus surgens, inter choros canentium et flentium resedit, dicens: "Ubi est Acca presbiter noster?" Qui statim cum gaudio[4] invocatus advenit, gratias agens Domino cum omnibus, quod eum sedentem et loquentem vidissent. Deinde vero[5], remotis fratribus de domo, solo fidelissimo presbitero suo Acca, qui nunc est beatae memoriae gratia Dei episcopus, per ordinem, sicut supra[6] diximus, visionem omnem revelavit, et statim sanctus presbiter praefatus acuti ingenii intellexit, gratias agens Domino, eo modo pontifici nostro pro intercessione sanctae Mariae[7] matris Domini et pro subditorum suorum precibus annos vitae additos, sicut Ezechiae regi Iudae xv annos adiectos, quorum v pro electione David patris sui, alii autem v pro intercessione Esaiae prophetae in templo Dei, alii v pro regis ipsius bonitate et ploratu ad parietem converso anni vitae adduntur.

CHAPTER LVII

Qualiter reversus mare transierit[8]

Tunc ergo sanctus pontifex noster, manibus et facie lavatis, omnibus nostris mira hilaritate gaudentibus, vitam ei[9] a Domino concessam gratulanter confitentibus, sumpto aliquantulum cibo, secundum

---

[1] genitricis F   [2] perveneris F   [3] *omit* C   [4] gladio F   [5] ergo C
[6] *omit* F   [7] virgini *inserted and afterwards erased in* C   [8] *No chapter heading in* C   [9] *omit* F

At last on the fifth day as the morning was breaking, lo! an angel of the Lord in shining raiment appeared to our holy bishop and said, "I am Michael the messenger of the most high God, who sent me to tell you that years of life have been added to you by the intercession of St Mary, Mother of God and ever Virgin, and by the lamentations of your followers, which have reached the ears of the Lord; and this shall be a sign to you: from this day you will begin to grow better day by day, and you will reach your native land; and all the most precious of your possessions will be returned to you, and you will end your life in peace. Also be prepared; for after the space of four years I will visit you again. Now remember that you have built churches in honour of the Apostles St Peter and St Andrew; but you have built nothing in honour of St Mary, ever Virgin, who is interceding for you. You have to put this right and to dedicate a church in honour of her." After these words the angel of the Lord was taken up from his sight and departed.

And so our holy bishop, as though aroused from sleep, rose up and sat amongst the company of those who were chanting and weeping. "Where is Acca our priest?" he said. He immediately came with great joy at his call, thanking God with all the others because they saw him sitting up and talking. Then when the brethren had been sent from the chamber, and his faithful priest Acca, he who is now bishop of blessed memory by the grace of God, was alone with him, Wilfrid revealed the whole vision at length as we have described it. Forthwith the said holy priest, who was a man of acute mind, gave thanks to God, understanding that in this way years of life had been added to our bishop through the intercession of St Mary the Mother of the Lord, and through the prayers of his followers, as fifteen years were added to Hezekiah, King of Judah: of these five were added because of the election of his father David, another five for the intercession of the prophet Isaiah in the temple of God, and the remaining five years of life for the goodness of the king himself and because he wept turning his face to the wall.

CHAPTER LVII
How he returned across the sea. [705]

Then our holy bishop, when he had washed his face and hands, and all were rejoicing with wondrous joy and were thankfully confessing that his life had been granted him by God, took a little food, and

Ionathan[1] illuminatis oculis refocilatus est, et post paucos dies, convalescente eadem infirmitate, coepto itinere usque ad mare pervenerunt, [2]cuius magnitudinem navigio superantes, in Cantuaria regione portum salutis Deo adiuvante invenerunt[3]. Illic autem archiepiscopo Bergtwaldo[4] invento, sancti pontificis nostri nuntii cum eo loquebantur. Qui eis spopondit mitigare iudicia dura, olim in synodo statuta, quia apostolica auctoritate coactus et per nuntios[5] scriptis directis territus est et tremebundus pacifice sine simulatione, sicut rei eventus probavit, sancto pontifici nostro reconciliatus est. Deinde itaque cum multitudine[6] abbatum suorum cum muneribus iuxta Lundoniam civitatem ab oriente laeti obeuntes inventi sunt. Postremo tunc[7] ad Aethelredum[8] regem, qui ante regnum[9] regebat Myrciorum[10] populorum[11], semper fidelissimum amicum, nimirum pro nimio gaudio lacrimantem, sanctus pontifex noster veniens[12], osculantes et amplexantes se invicem, honorifice ab amico more suo susceptus est. Qui ei[13] salutationis verba ab[14] apostolica sede emissa et statuta de se iudicia, signata cum bullis et sigillis, humiliter ostendit. Ille vero, statim apertis et recitatis apostolicae[15] sedis litteris, prosternens se in terram, oboedienter spopondit, dicens: "Hujus apostolicae[16] auctoritatis scriptis ne unius quidem litterae apicem umquam in vita mea condempnabo neque non[17] facientibus consentio, sed ut impleantur secundum vires meas adiuvabo." Sicut enim promiserat, ita sine dubio effecit. Iam enim merces, Deo donante, aeterna retribuetur ei in bono. Nam statim Coenred, quem regem post se constituit[18], invitavit et adiuravit eum in nomine Domini et in sua caritate oboedire praeceptis apostolicae sedis. Ille autem voluntarie sic facere promisit.

CHAPTER LVIII

*Quomodo propter contemptum eius Aldfrithus
rex periit*[19]

Denique post non multi temporis spatium, Aethelredo amico suo dicente[20], sanctus pontifex noster electos nuntios Badwinum presbiterum et abbatem magistrumque Alfrithum ad Aldfrithum[21] Ultrahumbrensium regem sibique notos emisit, dicens[22] ad eum: "Sanctus

---

[1] Ionatham F   [2-3] *omit* F   [4] Berchtwaldo C   [5] *insert* suos C   [6] multitudines C *and* F   [7] tamen C   [8] Ethelredum C   [9] *omit* C   [10] Merciorum C   [11] *omit* F   [12] *insert* mitissime eum salutavit C   [13] eis F   [14] *omit* F   [15-16] *omit* C   [17] *omit* C   [18] *insert* ad se C   [19] *No chapter heading in* C   [20] docente C   [21] Alfrithum C   [22] dicentes C

like Jonathan he was revived and his eyes were enlightened; and a few days afterwards, when he was healed of this same infirmity, they set out and came to the sea: they crossed its full extent by ship and, by the help of God, they found a safe harbour in the land of Kent. There the messengers of our holy bishop, when they had found Archbishop Berhtwald, had converse with him. He promised to mitigate the severity of the former decrees of the synod, for he was compelled by the Apostolic authority and terrified by the writings which the messengers had brought; and thus with trembling he was reconciled to our holy bishop, and, as events proved, this was no simulation of peace. And so they were found joyfully making their way towards the city of London from the east, attended by a great crowd of their abbots and laden with gifts.

Then finally our holy bishop came to King Aethilred who had once reigned over the kingdom of Mercia and was always a most faithful friend of his. The king actually wept through excess of joy; they kissed and embraced each other, and Wilfrid was as usual most honourably received by his friend. Then he gave the words of salutation that had been sent from the Apostolic See and humbly showed the king the decrees which had been made concerning him, signed with bulls and seals. As soon as the writings from the Apostolic See were opened and read, the king bowed himself to the ground and obediently made a promise in these words: "As for the writings of this Apostolic authority I will never in my life disobey one single jot or tittle in them nor will I consent to those who disobey them; but I will do my best to get them fulfilled." And what he had promised he carried out. And for this, eternal reward will be bestowed upon him for his good, by the gift of God. For he at once summoned Coenred whom he had appointed king in his place, and begged him, in the name of the Lord, and out of love for him, to obey the precepts of the Apostolic See. This he willingly promised to do.

CHAPTER LVIII
How King Aldfrith perished for despising him. [705]

Not long afterwards, on the advice of his friend Aethilred, our holy bishop sent chosen messengers well known to himself, Badwini, a priest and abbot, and Alfrith the teacher, to Aldfrith, King of Northumbria, and sent him messages to this effect:

pontifex noster salutat te pacificis verbis postulatque a te, ut licentiam sibi veniendi ad praesentiam tuam concedas cum litteris salutationis apostolicae sedis et iudiciis de sua causa apostolica auctoritate[1] constitutis." Quibus rex in prima vice nihil dure et austere respondit; sed, conductione facta et statuta die iterum revertendi ad se, tunc respondere promisit. Fratres vero secundum praeceptum regis altera vice in die conductionis revertentes ad eum sciscitantesque ab eo, quid ad responsionem esset dicturus. Quibus rex, sicut consiliarii eius persuaserunt, respondit: "O fratres mihi ambo venerabiles, petite a me vobismet ipsis necessaria, et ego propter reverentiam vestram donabo vobis. De causa vero Wilfrithi domini vestri nolite me ab hoc die diutius flagitare, quia, quod ante praedecessores mei reges et archiepiscopus cum consiliariis suis censuerunt, et quod postea nos cum archiepiscopo, ab apostolica sede emisso, cum omnibus paene Brittaniae[2] nostrae[3] gentis praesulibus iudicavimus, hoc, inquam, quamdiu vixero, propter apostolicae sedis, ut dicitis[4], scripta numquam volo mutare." Et hanc sententiam plene postmodum mutavit, et vere poenituit eum[5].

CHAPTER LIX

Deinde namque nuntii tristem nuntium portantes recesserunt ab eo, vultum eius ultra non videntes, veneruntque ad dominum[6] suum. Nam ultio divina nihil morata, sed secundum prophetiam praesulis apostolicae sedis vinculis alligatum infirmitatis districte regem compressit. Qui statim, ut erat sapientissimus, agnoscens, ab apostolica potestate perculsum se esse, poenitentia ductus, confessus est peccatum suum, in Wilfrithum episcopum contra apostolicae sedis iudicia commissum, dicens significando: "Si aliquo modo ad me viventem[7] venire per invitationem potuisset, statim piaculum meum emendarem[8]." Et tamen votum vovit Deo et sancto Petro, si de illa infirmitate sanatus surrexisset, secundum sancti Wilfrithi episcopi desiderium et apostolicae sedis iudicium omnia sanare. "Sin vero, Deo volente, defunctus fuero, praecipio in nomine Domini haeredi, quicumque mihi in regnum successerit, ut cum Wilfritho episcopo pro remedio animae meae et suae pacem et concordiam ineat." Haec

---

[1] potestate C   [2] Brittanniae C   [3] vestrae C   [4] dicatis F   [5] *omit* F   [6] deum F
[7] venientem F   [8] emendare F

"Our holy bishop salutes you with words of peace and asks you to grant him permission to come into your presence with letters of greeting from the Apostolic See and the judgments decreed in his case by the Apostolic authority."

The first time, the king did not make them a harsh or stern answer, but arranged a meeting and a day for them to come back to him and promised to give his answer then. So the brethren came back a second time on the day of the meeting, in accordance with his command, and asked him what his answer would be. The king replied as his counsellors persuaded him. "Brethren, both of whom I respect, ask of me anything that you need for yourselves and I will give it out of regard for you. But in the matter of Wilfrid your lord, from this day importune me no more about it. My predecessors, the kings and the archbishop, with their counsellors, arrived at a certain decision which was agreed to by myself and the archbishop who was sent forth from the Apostolic See with almost all the prelates of our people of Britain. This, I say, as long as I live I will never change because of writings sent from the Apostolic See as you declare." This declaration he entirely changed later on and sincerely repented.

CHAPTER LIX

Thereupon the messengers left him, bearing this unhappy message, and saw his face no more, but returned to their lord.

Now the divine vengeance did not tarry but, as the prelate of the Apostolic See had prophesied, laid hold upon the king binding him fast by the chains of sickness. Being a prudent man he realized that he had been struck by the Apostolic power, and, moved by penitence, confessed the sin which he had committed against Bishop Wilfrid in defiance of the judgments of the Apostolic See. He said, in witness thereof: "If only he could have somehow come to me at my invitation while I am still alive, I would at once amend my crime." But nevertheless he made a vow to God and St Peter that if he rose healed from his bed of sickness he would remedy everything in accordance with the desire of St Wilfrid the bishop and the judgment of the Apostolic See. "But if by God's will I die, in the name of God I bid my heir, whoever it may be who shall succeed me in the kingdom, to make peace and a settlement with Bishop Wilfrid for the good of my soul and his own."

verba fidelissimi testes audierunt nobisque indicaverunt, ex quibus
est Aelfleda abbatissa et sapientissima virgo, quae est vere filia regis,
necnon et Aethelburga abbatissa, et multi alii testes haec firmaverunt[1].
Regem vero languor oppressit, loquela illum per multos dies deseruit,
postremo diem obiit, et post eum Eadwlf per parvum spatium
regnavit. Ad quem sanctus pontifex noster de exilio cum filio suo
proprio veniens, de Hrypis quasi ad amicum nuntios emisit, quibus
austere et dure, persuasus a consiliariis[2] suis, pro antiqua nequitia
respondebat, dicens: "Per salutem meam iuro, nisi de regno meo in
spatio sex dierum discesserit, de sodalibus eius quoscumque invenero,
morte peribunt." Et post haec aspera verba, coniuratione facta
adversum eum, de regno quod duos menses` habuit, expulsus est, et
regnavit pro eo puer regius, cui nomen erat Osred, filius Aldfrithi[3]
regis, et sancto pontifici nostro filius adoptivus factus est.

[CHAPTER LX]

In primo anno Osredi regis Berhtwaldus[4] Cantuariorum ecclesiae
et paene totius Brittanniae archiepiscopus de austro veniens[5], habens
ex praecepto apostolicae sedis Aquilonalium regem cum omnibus
episcopis suis et abbatibus et totius regni eius principibus ad synodalem locum de causa beati Wilfrithi episcopi diligenter invitare[6], et
ita factum est. Nam in unum locum iuxta fluvium Nid ab oriente
congregati rex cum principibus et tres episcopi eius cum abbatibus
necnon et beata Aelfleda abbatissa, semper totius provinciae con-
solatrix optimaque consiliatrix, Berhtwaldus[7] quoque archiepiscopus
et Wilfrithus episcopus simul in una die advenerunt. Deinde,
sedentibus rege et episcopis cum principibus eorum in synodali loco,
tali modo archiepiscopus loqui incipiebat: "Oremus Dominum
nostrum Iesum Christum[8], ut pacis concordiam in cordibus nostris
per Spiritum sanctum indulgeat. Habemus enim et ego et beatus
Wilfrithus episcopus scripta apostolicae sedis, parvitati[9] enim meae
per nuntios directa et per semetipsum similiter allata, et[10] ut ea in
praesentia reverentiae vestrae recitentur[11], humili prece deposcimus."
Quibus venerabiles domini licentiam dederunt, et[12] coram synodo,

---

[1] adfirmaverunt C   [2] conciliariis F   [3] Aldfridi C   [4] Berhtualdus C
[5] venientes F   [6] *insert* et vitare F   [7] Berchtualdus C   [8] *omit* I.C. C
[9] parvitatis C   [10] *omit* F   [11] recitantur F   [12] *omit* F

These words were heard by most faithful witnesses and told to us. Of these, one is the abbess and most prudent virgin Aelffled, who is indeed the daughter of a king, and another is the abbess Aethilberg; and it has been confirmed by many other witnesses. But the king was overcome by his weakness; his power of speech deserted him for many days, and at last he died. After him Eadwulf reigned for a short time. Our holy bishop coming to him from exile with Eadwulf's own son, sent messengers from Ripon as if to a friend. But the king, persuaded by his counsellors because of their deep-rooted malice, replied harshly and austerely: "By my salvation I swear that if he has not left my kingdom in six days, any of his companions whom I can find shall perish." After these rough words a conspiracy arose against the king, and he was driven from the kingdom over which he had reigned for two months.

In his place reigned a boy of royal birth whose name was Osred, the son of King Aldfrith, and he became the adopted son of our holy bishop.

CHAPTER LX

[706]

In the first year of King Osred, Berhtwald, Archbishop of the Church of the Kentish people and of nearly all Britain, came from the south, having, in accordance with the precept of the Apostolic See, earnestly to invite the king of the northern regions with all his bishops and abbots and the chief men of his whole kingdom to the place of synod to consider the case of the blessed Bishop Wilfrid; and he carried out the command. The king and his chief men, three of his bishops and their abbots, as well as the blessed abbess Aelffled, always the comforter and best counsellor of the whole province, all gathered together in one place near the river Nidd and on its eastern side. Archbishop Berhtwald also and Bishop Wilfrid arrived together on the same day. The king and the bishops and their chief men took their seats in the place of synod and the archbishop began to speak in these words: "Let us pray our Lord Jesus Christ to grant us concord and peace in our hearts by the Holy Spirit. Both I and the blessed Bishop Wilfrid have writings from the Apostolic See, for some have been sent by messengers to my unworthy self, and others likewise have been brought by him. We humbly ask that these may be read in your revered presence." The

omnibus audientibus, utriusque libri a principio usque ad finem legebantur. Post lectionem[1], cunctis tacentibus, Berthfrithus[2], secundus a rege princeps, ad archiepiscopum dixit: "Nos, qui interpretatione indigemus, quid apostolica auctoritas dicat, audire delectat." Et respondit ei[3] archiepiscopus, dicens: "Iudicia apostolicae sedis longo circuitu et ambagibus verborum, unum tamen intellectum de eadem re[4] utrique libri ostendentes, quorum in[5] brevi sermone sensum tantum explicabo. Apostolica namque potestas, quae primum Petro apostolo[6] ligandi solvendique donata est, sua auctoritate de beato Wilfritho episcopo censuit, ut in praesentia mea, licet indignus, et omnis conventus[7] praesules ecclesiarum huius provinciae, antiquam inimicitiam pro animarum salute relinquentes, beato Wilfritho episcopo in bono reconcilientur. Nam his coepiscopis meis e duobus ab apostolica sede iudiciis optio datur, utrum voluerint, eligant, ut aut cum Wilfritho episcopo pacem plene perfecteque ineant et partes ecclesiarum, quas olim ipse regebat, sicut sapientes mecum iudicaverint, restituant, aut si hoc optimum noluissent, omnes simul ad apostolicam sedem pergerent ibique maiori concilio diiudicarentur. Si quis vero contempnens,—quod absit,—neutrum ex his duobus implere voluisset[8], sciat se, si rex sit aut laicus, a corpore et a[9] sanguine Christi excommunicatum; si vero episcopus aut presbiter, quod est execrabilius et dictu horrendum, ab omni gradu[10] degradari. Haec sunt iudicia apostolicae sedis brevi sermone exposita." Episcopi vero resistentes dixerunt: "Quod praedecessores nostri olim, Theodorus archiepiscopus, ab apostolica sede emissus, et Ecfrithus[11] rex censuerunt et postea in campo, qui Eostrefeld[12] dicitur, una nobiscum paene totius Britanniae[13] episcopi tuaque, archiepiscope, praesentia excellentissima cum rege Aldfritho iudicavimus, quomodo immutare quis valeat?" Interea autem beatissima Aelfleda abbatissa benedicto ore suo dixit: "Vere in Christo dico testamentum Alfrithi[14] regis in ea infirmitate, qua vitam finivit qui votum vovit Deo et sancto Petro dicens: 'Si vixero, omnia iudicia apostolicae sedis quae[15] ante renui audire, de beato Wilfrido episcopo replebo. Si vero diem obiero, dicite tamen haeredi meo

---

[1] *insert* autem C   [2] Berectfrithus C   [3] *omit* F   [4] *omit* C   [5] *omit* C
[6] *insert* et principi apostolorum C   [7] Mabillon. conventui C *and* F
[8] noluisse C   [9] *omit* C   [10] *insert* ecclesiasticae dignitatis C
[11] Aecfrithus C   [12] Eostraefeld C   [13] Brittanniae C   [14] Aldfrithi C
[15] Raine. quas C *and* F

venerable lords gave them permission and the documents of both were read before the synod for all to hear from beginning to end.

After the reading all were silent and Berhtfrith, a chief man next in rank to the king, said to the archbishop, "We who need a translation should be glad to hear what the Apostolic authority says." The archbishop answered him, "The judgments of the Apostolic See are expressed in roundabout and enigmatic language, but nevertheless both documents show the same meaning in the matter. I will explain the bare sense in brief. The Apostolic power to bind and to loose, which was first given to Peter, has decided of its own authority in the matter of the blessed Bishop Wilfrid that, in the presence of myself, though unworthy, and of the whole assembly, the prelates of the churches in this province, leaving the old enmity, for the salvation of their souls, be reconciled for good with the blessed Bishop Wilfrid. For to these my fellow-bishops a choice is offered out of two decrees made by the Apostolic See: let them choose which of the two they will, either to make a complete and perfect peace with Bishop Wilfrid and to restore to him such parts of the churches he formerly ruled as wise counsellors and myself shall settle, or if they are unwilling to take this, the best course, to go all together to the Apostolic See, and there be judged in a greater council. If anyone show his contempt (which God forbid!) and will do neither of these, let him know that, whether he be king or layman, he is excommunicated from the body and blood of Christ: but if he be a bishop or priest who acts thus—which is more horrible still and dreadful to speak of—he is to be degraded from all holy orders. These in brief are the decrees of the Apostolic See."

The bishops however resisted and said, "Who can anywise alter that which was once decided by our predecessors, Archbishop Theodore who was sent forth from the Apostolic See, and King Ecgfrith; and what we and the bishops of almost the whole of Britain and in your most excellent presence, archbishop, afterwards decreed with King Aldfrith in the place called *Eostrefeld*?"

Meanwhile the most blessed Aelffled the abbess spoke with holy words: "I tell you truly in Christ the testament of King Aldfrith in the illness which brought his life to a close. He vowed a vow to God and to St Peter saying, 'If I live, I will fulfil all the decrees of the Apostolic See concerning the blessed Bishop Wilfrid which I once refused to obey. But, if I die, bid my heir, my son, in the name of the

filio in nomine Domini, ut pro remedio animae meae iudicium [1]de Wilfritho episcopo apostolicum[2] repleat." Haec ea[3] loquente, Berechfrithus[4], praefatus regis princeps, respondens dixit: "Haec est voluntas regis et principum eius, ut mandatis apostolicae sedis et praeceptis Alfrithi regis in omnibus obediamus[5]. Nam quando in urbe, quae Bebbanburge[6] dicitur, obsessi et undique hostili manu circumcincti in angustiaque rupis[7] lapideae mansimus, inito consilio inter nos, si Deus nostro regali puero regnum patris sui concedisset, quae mandavit apostolica auctoritas de[8] Wilfritho episcopo, adimplere Deo spopondimus, et statim post vota, mutatis animis inimicorum, concito cursu omnes cum iuramento in amicitiam nostram conversi sunt; apertis ianuis de angustia liberati, fugatis inimicis nostris, regnum accepimus." Postquam haec verba finita sunt, episcopi sibi mutuo separati ab aliis inire consilium[9] coeperunt, aliquando cum eis archiepiscopus, aliquando vero sapientissima virgo Aelfleda, et huius sancti concilii[10] talis finis extitit, ut omnes episcopi et rex cum optimatibus suis pure pacis concordiam cum Wilfritho episcopo inierint, quam inter se usque ad finem vitae conservaverunt, reddentes ei duo optima coenobia, quae sunt[11] Inhripis[12] et Inagustaldesiae[13], cum omnibus reditibus suis. Et illa die omnes episcopi se in invicem osculantes et amplexantes panemque frangentes communicaverunt; gratias agentes Deo omnis sancti huius beatitudinis, in pace Christi ad sua loca remearunt.

CHAPTER LXI

Mirabilis Deus in sanctis suis*, qui pro amore totius ecclesiae salutifera pace animas praesulum coronavit. Et haec est maxima beatitudo ex utraque parte, tam illorum, qui per longa spatia annorum possessionem suam possidebant et voluntarie ad emendationem in pace Christi ante suum obitum pontifici nostro reddiderunt, quam nostrorum, qui, per diversa exilia dispersi, tristes sub alienis dominis servi eramus et nunc in pace omnium ubique reconciliatorum cum domino nostro, capite carissimo, spem vitae[14] gerentes, gaudentes et exultantes in benedictione vivimus.

[1-2] *omit* C   [3] eo F   [4] Berhtfrithus C   [5] obediemus F   [6] Bebbanburg C
[7] *omit* F   [8] *insert* sancto C   [9] *omit* F   [10] consilii F   [11] erant C
[12] Irhypis C   [13] Inhagustaldaesae   [14] *insert* cum Domino C

* Psa. 67. 36 (Vulg.).

Lord, that he fulfil for the good of my soul the Apostolic judgment concerning Bishop Wilfrid.'"

When she had finished her speech, Berhtfrith the aforesaid chief man of the king made answer: "This is the will of the king and of his chief men, that we obey the mandates of the Apostolic See and the commands of King Aldfrith in all things. For when we were besieged in the city called Bamborough and surrounded on every hand by a hostile force and were sheltering in a narrow place in the stony rock, taking counsel amongst ourselves, we vowed that if God granted our royal boy his father's kingdom, we would fulfil the Apostolic commands concerning Bishop Wilfrid. As soon as our vow was made, the minds of our enemies were changed; with all haste they all plighted their friendship to us with an oath; the gates were opened, we were freed from our narrow quarters, our enemies were put to flight, and the kingdom became ours."

After these words were finished, the bishops separated from the rest and began to take counsel together; sometimes the archbishop consulted with them and sometimes the prudent virgin Aelffled. The end of this holy council was that all the bishops and the king with his counsellors made a complete peace with Bishop Wilfrid, which they kept until the end of their lives; they returned him the two best monasteries, Ripon and Hexham, with all the revenues belonging to them; and on that day all the bishops kissed and embraced one another and communicated in the breaking of bread. They gave thanks to God for all this holy blessedness, and went to their homes in the peace of Christ.

CHAPTER LXI

"God is wondrous in His holy places," who, out of love for the whole Church, crowned the souls of the prelates with healthful peace. And this has been the source of the greatest blessedness on both sides; on the part of those who, though they had held their possessions through a long period of years, nevertheless voluntarily, in order to make amends in the peace of Christ, gave them up to our bishop before his death; as well as on our part, who had been scattered into exile in many places and had served in sadness under foreign masters, and now in peace with all men who were everywhere reconciled to our master, had hope of life, and lived in blessedness with our beloved lord and master, rejoicing and exulting.

CHAPTER LXII

Laetitia huius saeculi luctu miscebitur, et omnis res ad finem respicit. Nam cum tempus, quod Michael archangelus praedixerat, appropinquaret, sanctus pontifex noster pergens ad Agustaldaesiae[1], extimplo tali languore correptus, quasi olim in Meldum civitate fatigatus est, ut inde validiorem sustineret languorem. Tunc omnis familia cum intimo cordis maerore[2] consueta arma orationum arripiens, die noctuque indesinenter canentes et deprecantes Dominum concedere ei inducias vitae, saltem ad loquendum et domos suas ad disponendas possessionesque dividendas, et ne nos quasi orbatos sine abbatibus relinqueret. Huius autem luctuosae calamitatis fama longe lateque pervolavit, et omnes abbates eius de suis locis et anachoritae concito cursu pergentes die et nocte festinanter, nihil secundum traditiones hominum de morte eius haesitantes, undique congregati, absque spe praesentium[3], tamen ad viventem pervenerunt, domumque ingressi, genuflectentes et unanimiter omnes in luctu rogantes Dominum, ut in se promissionem suam expleret dicentem: *Ubicumque fuerint duo vel tres [4]congregati in nomine meo, ibi sum in medio eorum**, dicit Dominus[5], et ut[6] pontifici nostro aliquod spatium vitae concederet. Et, Deo concedente, ita factum est, ut[7] et omnem vitam nostram in diversis locis secundum suum desiderium sub praepositis a se electis constitueret et substantiam suam intus et foris Deo et hominibus suo iudicio dispertiret, quod ante non perfecerat[8]. Nam ex illa die, quasi de somno excitatus, accipiens intellectum et memoriam loquendique facultatem, integrae sanitati redditus est, et nos Deo gratias agentes[9] miroque gaudio laetificati, unusquisque viam suam adiit.

[1] de Hagustaldesae C [2] memore F [3] *insert* et absentium C [4-5] *omit* F *insert* et reliqua F [6] *omit* F [7] *omit* F [8] Mabillon. praefecer. C praeficerat F [9] *omit* F

* Matth. 18. 20.

CHAPTER LXII

[708?]

But the joy of this world will be mixed with grief, and all things look toward their end. When the time drew near that the Archangel Michael had foretold, our holy bishop was on his way to Hexham; he was suddenly struck down with the same disease as had afflicted him in the town of Meaux, but his sickness was much greater than then. Then the whole household in the deepest grief of heart seized their accustomed weapons of prayer, and day and night they chanted without ceasing, praying to the Lord to grant him an extension of life, at any rate so that he could speak to them, and dispose of his monasteries and divide his possessions, and not leave us as it were orphans, without any abbots. The report of this mournful calamity spread far and wide and all his abbots and anchorites came hastening from their homes by day and by night; not hesitating on account of the rumours about his death, they gathered together from every side, and although those present with him had no hope, yet they reached him while he was still alive. They entered the house, and, kneeling down, with one accord they all prayed to the Lord in their grief that He would fulfil to them His promise that, "wherever two or three are gathered together in my name, there am I in the midst of them," saith the Lord, and that He would grant our bishop a longer space of life. And by God's permission it came to pass that he arranged the lives of all of us in various places according to his desire, under the superiors chosen by himself, and shared his substance both within and without between God and men according to his judgment; for he had not yet done these things.

From that day, as though roused from sleep, he received back his intellect and memory and his power of speech, and was restored to complete health. We gave thanks to God and rejoicing with great joy each one went his way.

CHAPTER LXIII

Sanctus itaque pontifex noster in gaudio suorum et pace perfecta vivens et omnia ea[1], quae prius hominibus defuisse[2] ei videbantur, per spatium anni et dimidii post infirmitatem plene perfecteque emendavit. Nam non multo tempore ante beatae memoriae obitum Inhripis[3] cum duobus abbatibus et fratribus valde fidelibus, omnes numero VIII, ad se invitatis, gazofilacium aperire claviculario praecepit et omne aurum et argentum cum lapidibus pretiosis in conspectu eorum deponere et in quattuor partes secundum suum iudicium dirimere iussit, qui nihil moratus, praecepto sancti patris oboediens, sic omnia complevit. Sanctus autem[4] pontifex noster ad fideles testes dixit: "Scitote, fratres mei[5] dilectissimi, cogitationem meam, quam ante olim cogitavi, ut sancti Petri apostoli sedem iterum appellarem et viderem, unde liberatus fui frequenter, Deoque volente, vitam meam illic finirem, et unam optimam ex his IIII partibus ad munera offerenda per ecclesias sanctorum mecum deducere donaque portare ad ecclesiam[6] sanctae Mariae matris Domini dedicatam, ad sanctum Paulum apostolum munera pro anima mea offerre. Si vero Deus aliquid aliud providerit, ut frequenter senibus evenire solet, et dies obitus mei me occupavit[7], vobis fidelibus praecipio in nomine Iesu Christi, ut per nuntios ad supradictas ecclesias munera mea mittatis. Ex tribus vero aliis partibus unam pauperibus populi mei pro redemptione animae meae dividite: alteram autem partem praepositi coenobiorum duorum saepe dictorum inter se dividant, ut cum muneribus regum[8] et episcoporum amicitiam perpetrare potuerint. Tertiam vero partem his, qui mecum longa exilia perpessi laboraverunt, et quibus terras praediorum non dedi, secundum uniuscuiusque mensuram dispertite illis, ut habeant, unde se post me sustentent[9]." Iterum alia vice post spatium temporis testibus fidelibus dixit: "Fratres, recolite, quod hunc Tatberhtum presbiterum, propinquum meum, [10]qui nunc usque meus comes fuit[11] individuus, huius[12] coenobii[13] constituo Inhripis[14] praepositum, ut regimen mecum[15], quamdiu

---

[1] e.o. C   [2] difuisse F   [3] Inhrypis C   [4] autem *after* fideles *in* F   [5] mi F   [6] *insert* sanctorum F   [7] occupaverit C   [8] regis C   [9] sustentant F   [10-11] nunc comes F   [12] huiuscemodi F   [13] *omit* F   [14] Inhrypis C   [15] meum C

CHAPTER LXIII

[708?]

And so our holy bishop lived to the joy of his friends and in perfect peace and all those matters, which previously he seemed to men to have left undone, he completely settled during the year and a half after his illness. A short time before his ever-memorable and blessed death, he ordered his treasurer to open his treasury at Ripon in the presence of two abbots and some very faithful brethren, eight in number altogether, whom he had invited, and to put out in their sight all the gold, silver and precious stones; and he bade the treasurer divide it into four parts, according to his direction. Without delay the treasurer obeyed the words of the holy father, and thus completed his task.

Our holy bishop then said to these faithful witnesses: "Dearest brethren, know this thought of mine which I have long since had in mind, that I should again visit the see of the holy Apostle Peter where I have so often been delivered from trouble and should there end my life, God willing. I intended to take with me the best of the four portions of this treasure to offer gifts in the churches of the Saints; to carry presents to the church dedicated to St Mary the Mother of the Lord; and to offer gifts to St Paul the Apostle for the welfare of my soul. But since God has provided for me otherwise, as often happens to old men, and the day of my death has overtaken me, I bid you, my faithful brethren, in the name of Jesus Christ, to send messengers to carry my gifts to the churches I have named. Of the other three parts, divide one among the poor of my people for the redemption of my soul: the second part let the heads of the two oft-mentioned abbeys divide among themselves so that they may be able to purchase the friendship of kings and bishops. The third part you are to share among those who have laboured and suffered long exile with me and to whom I have given no lands and estates; distribute it according to the needs of each man so that they may have the means to maintain themselves after I have departed."

After a space of time he spoke once again to the faithful witnesses: "Remember, brethren, that I appoint as head over this monastery at Ripon this Tatberht the priest. He is my kinsman and has been up till now my inseparable companion; while I live he is to rule with

vixero, habeat et post obitum meum sine scrupulo possideat. Ideo namque haec statuta dico, ut[1], me Michael archangelus visitans, paratum inveniat; signa enim obitus mei multa frequentant."

CHAPTER LXIV

Post has ergo sermocinationes, secundum iussionem sancti pontificis nostri pulsato signo, tota familia Hryporum simul in unum congregata est. Ad quam introgressus est sanctus pontifex noster, et[2] residens loqui incipiebat, hoc[3] dicens: "Frater noster reverentissimus Celinus[4], aliquamdiu praepositus debitae nostrae observantiae, multum in Domino laboravit et nunc ad pristinum statum conversationis atque ad deserta loca revertere et contemplativam vitam, sicut olim, exercere et soli Deo servire concupiscit, et hoc ei diutius nolo renuere. Admoneo tamen vos, ut regulariter vitae vestrae institutionem conservare dignemini, usquedum, Deo volente, iterum veniam ad vos. Nam hii duo abbates nostri Tibba et Ebba[5] praesentes, emissi a Ceolredo rege Merciorum, invitantes me ad colloquium eius, et hoc pro nostrorum coenobiorum statu[6], quae in regno eius sunt, me consentire suaserunt: qui enim omnem vitam suam meo iudicio disponere promittit. Et iterum cum revertero ad vos, Deo volente, vita comite adducam mecum, quem inveni dignum virum vestrae praepositionis principatui. Sin vero aliquid propter frequentes infirmitates meas, Deo providente, aliud contigerit, quemcumque hi testes, qui nunc iuxta me sedentes, Tibba et Ebba[7] abbates, Tatberhtus et Hathufrith[8] presbiteri magisterque Aluhfrithus, venientes vobis dixerint, illum suscipite et abbatem constituite et oboedientiam, quam Deo mihique promisistis et huc usque perfecistis, secundum praeceptum meum illi reddite." Geniculantes lacrimantesque, inclinato capite in terram, omnia praecepta eius adimplere promiserunt, pronique orantes, sanctus pontifex noster benedixit eos et Domino commendavit, et ab eo die ultra faciem eius simul non viderunt.

---

[1] *insert* si F   [2] *omit* F   [3] *insert* modo C   [4] Caelinus C   [5] Eabba C
[6] *omit* F   [7] Eabba C   [8] Hadufrith C

me and after my death he is to possess it without any question. I make these decrees in order that, when the Archangel Michael visits me, he may find me prepared; for many signs of death gather round me."

CHAPTER LXIV

[709]

After these conversations, a bell was rung at the command of our bishop and the whole community at Ripon gathered together. Our holy bishop entered, sat down, and began to speak: "Our most reverend brother Caelin has, for some time, taken the lead in our religious duties and has laboured much in the Lord. He now desires to return to his former manner of life, to go back to the desert places, and to live a life of contemplation, as he once did, serving God alone. And this I will no longer deny him. However I admonish you to keep your rule of life worthily until I return to you, if God wills. But our two abbots Tibba and Eabba are here, sent from Ceolred, King of Mercia, asking me to go to confer with him, and they have persuaded me to consent to this for the sake of the position of our monasteries in his kingdom; for he promises to order his whole life after my instruction. And when I return to you alive, if God so wills, I will bring with me the man whom I have found fit to preside over you. But if in the providence of God it happens otherwise on account of my many infirmities, I bid you receive and make abbot whomsoever these my witnesses who are now sitting near me, namely the abbots Tibba and Eabba, the priests Tatberht and Hathufrith, and the teacher Aluhfrith, shall come and announce to you. And the obedience which you have promised to God and to me and have hitherto performed, you must render to him in accordance with my commands."

Then they knelt weeping, and with heads bowed to the ground they promised to fulfil all his commands; and as they prayed, prostrating themselves, our holy bishop gave them his blessing, and commended them to God. From that day, as a community, they never saw his face again.

CHAPTER LXV

Pergens igitur sanctus pontifex noster cum pace et benedictione
omnium, tam principum quam subditorum Ultrahumbrensium, ad
australia regna tetendit, ibique abbates suos omnes in adventu eius
gaudentes invenit. Illic enim quibusdam supradicta testamenta ex
ordine narravit et unicuique eorum secundum suam mensuram aut
cum terris vitam[1] monachorum suorum augmentavit aut cum
pecunia corda eorum laetificavit, quasi prophetiae[2] spiritu ante
obitum suum haereditatem haeredibus dispertiens. Postremo ad
monasterium eius, quod in Undolum positum est, in quo olim
Andreae apostoli dedicavit ecclesiam, pervenerunt; ibique statim a
languore infirmitatis coangustatus, ita ut intellegeret vicinum sibi
esse finem huius vitae, et paucis verbis admonuit eos, ut memores
essent omnium bonorum, quae ante locutus est. Nam omnem vitae
suae conversationem memorialiter prius enarravit presbitero Tat-
berhto[3], videlicet propinquo suo, quadam die equitantibus illis[4] per
viam, quasi praesciens[5] obitum suum; necnon recordatus est omnes
terras in diversis locis, quas abbatibus ante dederat aut tunc dare
iussit, ut erat coenobium[6] Inhegustaldesiae[7], quod Accan presbitero,
qui post eum fuit beatae memoriae gratia Dei episcopus, in possessionem dare praecepit. Postquam pauca locutus est, benedixit eos,
sicut Iacob benedixit filios suos, et cum quiete, non cum gemitu et
murmure, caput ad cervical lectuli inclinavit et requievit; illi vero
in choro die noctuque indesinenter psalmos canentes et cum fletu
miscentes, usquedum in psalmo centesimo tertio ad versiculum
illum pervenerunt in quo dicitur[8]: "*Emitte spiritum tuum, et crea-
buntur, et renovabis faciem terrae*.*" Tunc[9] sanctus pontifex noster
emisit spiritum suum, et omnes stupefacti sunt, audientes ea hora
sonitum quasi avium advenientium, nube testium confirmante.
Abbatem ordinatum acceperunt, qui pro amore patris sui sancti
pontificis nostri multa bona facere consuevit. Nam omni die pro eo
missam singularem celebrare et omni hebdomada[10] quintam feriam,
in qua obiit, quasi dominicam in epulis venerari[11]: et anniversaria die
obitus sui universas decimarum partes de armentis et de gregibus

[1] *omit* F   [2] prophetice F   [3] T.p. C   [4] illi C   [5] praescientiae F
praesciente C   [6] c.e. F   [7] Inhagustaldaesae C   [8] dicit C   [9] tamen C
[10] ebdomada C *and* F   [11] venerare F

* Psa. 103. 30.

CHAPTER LXV
[709]

Then our holy bishop went forward with the peace and blessing of all, both the chief men and subjects of Northumbria, and came to the southern lands, where he found all his abbots rejoicing at his coming. There he repeated the above-mentioned will at length to certain of them and for each of them in due proportion he either increased the livelihood of their monks by gifts of land, or rejoiced their hearts with money, as though, endowed with the spirit of prophecy, he were sharing his inheritance among his heirs before his death. Finally they came to his monastery at Oundle where he once dedicated a church to the Apostle Andrew. Here he was immediately seized by sickness, and knew that the end of his life was at hand. In a few words he urged them to be mindful of all the good words which he had spoken to them before. For he had on a former occasion narrated from memory the whole story of his life to the priest Tatberht his kinsman, on a certain day as they were riding along together, as though he foresaw his death; besides this he recounted all the lands in various localities which he had previously given to abbots or now willed to give; thus he bade that the monastery at Hexham should be given to the priest Acca, who after him by the grace of God was bishop of blessed memory. After speaking a few words he blessed them, just as Jacob blessed his sons; then in peace, without sigh or murmur, he leaned his head upon the pillow and rested. The others sang psalms together day and night without ceasing, mingling their singing with their tears, until they reached the verse in the 103rd Psalm which runs "Send forth Thy Spirit, and they shall be created, and Thou shalt renew the face of the earth." Then our holy bishop breathed his last and they were all amazed, for they heard at that hour the sound as it were of birds approaching, as a cloud of witnesses confirm. They then received the abbot who had been appointed, who, for the love of his father our holy bishop, was wont to do many good works. He decided to celebrate a private Mass for him every day, and every week to celebrate Thursday, the day on which he died, as a feast as though it were Sunday. He determined on the anniversary of his death to divide his whole share of the tithes of the herds and flocks among the poor of his people, to the glory of God, all the days of his life, apart

[1]pauperibus populi sui dividere omnibus diebus[2] vitae suae ad gloriam Dei constituit, absque his elemosinis, quas omni die pro se et pro anima episcopi sui semper nominatim simul indigenis et Deo dabat.

CHAPTER LXVI[3]

Dominus itaque noster sanctum pontificem[4], magnum virum et fidelem servum, sicut credimus, apud se inter suos sanctos miraculorum virtutibus hominibus declaravit. Nam quadam die abbates undique advenientes, sanctum corpus pontificis in curru deducentibus, aliisque petentibus[5] sanctum corpus lavare et diligenter honorificeque indui, sicut dignum erat, licentiam perpetraverunt. Tunc enim quidam ex abbatibus nomine Bacula sindonem suam supra faciem terrae expandit, et super eam sanctum corpus deposuerunt fratres, suis manibus lavantes ecclesiasticeque induentes et ad praefinitum locum cum hymnis et canticis cum timore Dei portabant et supra domum quasi residentium avium cum sonitu iterum audierunt et statim iterum avolantium in coelum cum suavi modulamine pennarum. Sapientes autem qui illic aderant dixerunt, certe se scire, angelorum choros cum Michaele[6] venisse et animam sancti pontificis in paradisum deducere. Deinde, extento foris tentorio, sanctum corpus balneaverunt et balneum ibi in terram fuderunt, et habitatores cellae ligneam crucem ibidem postea erexerunt, ibique Dominus multa mirabilia facere consuevit. Nostri vero sanctum corpus lintheis induentes et in curru[7] ponentes psalmodiamque canentes, coepto itinere usque ad Hrypense monasterium pervenerunt; quibus mox familia tota cum sanctis reliquiis in obviam exivit. Paene nullus se a lacrimis et fletu abstinuit; elevata voce cum hymnis et canticis introduxerunt ad se et in basilicam, quam sanctus pontifex noster olim in honorem sancti Petri apostoli aedificavit et dedicavit, corpus sanctissimi viri honorifice deposuerunt anno aetatis suae septuagesimo sexto. Quantos vero per quadraginta sex annos episcopatus sui episcopos[8] et presbiteros et diacones[9] ordinaverat et quantas ecclesias dedicavit, quis[10] enumerare[11] potest? Cuius laus manet in aeternum. Et dignum haeredem Tatberhtum presbiterum secundum praeceptum sancti pontificis nostri circumdantes abbates deduxerunt. Iterum itaque praefatus abbas sinodem suam, paululum a pedibus

[1-2] omit C   [3] Chapter heading in F de signo circuli properly belongs to Chap. LXVIII   [4] insert nostrum F   [5] ab iisque petentibus tes C   [6] Michahel eo C   [7] cursum C   [8] omit sui episcopos C   [9] diaconos C   [10] quamvis F   [11] omit F

from those charities which he always gave every day to God and to the needy, for himself and for the soul of his bishop and always in his name.

CHAPTER LXVI

So our Lord proved to men by virtue of miracles that the holy bishop (a great man and a faithful servant as we believe) was with Himself and among His saints. For on a certain day the abbots came from every quarter, some to carry away the holy body of the bishop in a chariot and others intending to wash the holy body and to clothe it carefully and honourably as was fitting; and they obtained permission to do so. Then a certain abbot named Bacula spread out his robe upon the ground, and the brethren laid the holy body upon it, after washing it with their own hands, and clothing it in ecclesiastical robes, and so they carried him to the appointed place with hymns and canticles in the fear of God. Once again above the monastery they heard as it were the noise of birds settling down with a sound and flying away again into the sky, their wings making sweet melody. The wise men who were present said that they knew of a truth that bands of angels had come with Michael to take the soul of the holy bishop to Paradise. Then they put up a tent outside, bathed the holy body and emptied the bath on to the ground in the same place. The people who inhabited the monastery afterwards built a wooden cross on the spot, and the Lord used to perform many marvels there. Then our brethren clothed the holy body in linen, placed it in a carriage, and setting forth singing psalms, came to the monastery at Ripon. Forthwith all the community came to meet them bearing holy relics. Hardly any of them could keep from tears and weeping. Raising their voices in hymns and canticles, they brought in the body of the most holy man with honour and placed it in the church which our holy bishop had once built and dedicated to the honour of St Peter the Apostle. He was in his seventy-sixth year, and who can tell how many bishops, priests, and deacons he had ordained, and how many churches he had dedicated during the forty-six years of his episcopate? His praise remains for ever. The abbots surrounded and led in his worthy heir the priest Tatberht, according to our holy bishop's command.

And once again the abbot above mentioned gave his robe to his

ministrantium sordidatam, puero suo ministro involutam dedit,
praecipiens ei, ut ad abbatissam sancti pontificis nostri nomine
Cynethrith[1] eam deduxisset sibique talem servaret, usquedum
iterum, Deo volente, ad eam pervenisset. Quae praeceptis abbatis
primitus oboediens, postremo tamen mundare eam praecepit. Et hoc
audiens quaedam debilis paupercula sanctimonialis, per multos
annos, ut in euangelio cementarius, aridam manum et inutilem habens,
ad abbatissam accedit, cum lacrimis genuflectens[2], adiuravit eam,
dicens: "In nomine Domini Iesu Christi[3] et pro anima sancti
episcopi tui indulge mihi mea decrepita membra in hoc lavacro
lavare. Credo enim indubitata fide, hanc meam manum incurvatam
et brachium longo tempore emarcuatum in eo lavacro per sancti
sudoris[4] ammixtionem, Deo volente, posse sanari[5]." Abbatissa vero
religiosa, renuere timens, secundum fidem suam licentiam dedit.
Illa etenim statim cum una manu alteram insensatam calefactae
aquae lexivae immersit sindonemque tetigit et stipitem aridae manus
cum vestimento fricans lavavit. Deinde—quid magis moror in verbis?
—digiti erecti, manus vivificata, brachio roborato, a tactu sindonis
per fidem sanabatur, sicut mulier in evangelio Moerisa nomine a
profluvio sanguinis sanata est, quae tetigit fimbriam vestimenti Iesu:
uterque gratias agens Domino, in mirabilibus suis laudabant eum

CHAPTER LXVII

Alio quoque in tempore Dominus sanctum suum pontificem
nostrum miranter laudabilem more suo hominibus ostendit. Nam
supradictum coenobium in Undolum, ubi pontifex noster viam[6]
patrum iniit[7], nobiles quidam exules cum exercitu causa iniuriae
suae spoliantes, totum combusserunt, excepta una domu[8], in qua
sanctus pater noster obiit; quam diligenti cura[9] cum titionibus et
lampadibus sine causa accendere nitebantur. Nam contra naturam
[10]ignes eorum[11] de tecto[12] stipuloso quasi[13] madefactis facibus extin-
guebantur. Postremo tamen unus ex eis audaci animo introgressus,
foenum[14] aridum intus facilius accendere putans, vidit hominem
iuvenem stantem in albis et in manu sua crucem tenentem auream.

---

[1] Cynethryth C   [2] genuflectans C *and* F   [3] Christi Iesu F   [4] sideris F
[5] satiari F   [6] via C   [7] ruit C   [8] domo C   [9] curru F   [10-11] *omit* F
[12] tecti C   [13] quas F   [14] poenum F

boy servant, folded up and somewhat soiled by the feet of those who had been ministering; he bade him take it to the abbess of our holy bishop, Cynithrith by name, telling her to keep it as it was until he came again to her, if God so willed. At first she obeyed the abbot's commands, but afterwards she gave orders to wash it.

There was a certain nun both poor and weak who for many years had had a withered and useless hand like the mason in the Gospel. When she heard this, she came to the abbess and kneeling before her begged her with tears, saying, "In the name of the Lord Jesus Christ and by the soul of your holy bishop, grant that I may wash my decrepit limbs in this water. For I believe with unwavering faith that this crooked hand of mine and this arm which has long been withered can be healed, if God so wills it, in this water, through the mingling therewith of the holy sweat." The pious abbess, not daring to refuse her, gave her permission in accordance with her faith. Then at once with one hand she plunged the other lifeless limb into the warm soapy water and touched the robe; then she washed the stump of her withered hand, rubbing it with the garment. Thereupon (why should I make a longer story of it?) her fingers were straightened, her hand was revived, and her arm strengthened and she was healed through her faith by touching the garment, just as the woman in the Gospel, named Moerisa, was healed of the issue of blood when she touched the hem of Jesus' garment. And both of them giving thanks to God praised Him in His wonderful works.

CHAPTER LXVII

On another occasion also the Lord manifested to men His saint, our wondrous and praiseworthy bishop, in accordance with His wont. For certain exiles of noble birth who were ravaging with an army, because of some wrong done to them, burned the whole of the above-mentioned monastery at Oundle, where our bishop had been gathered to his fathers, with the exception of the one house where our holy father died: this they diligently attempted to set fire to, for no reason, by means of firebrands and torches. But their fires were extinguished contrary to nature as though the torches were damped down by the thatched roof. At last one of them boldly entered, thinking that he would more easily set fire to the dry hay within, and saw a young man in white who stood holding a golden cross in his

Ille autem, statim ut vidit, stupefactus est et[1] in excessu mentis foras rediens, dixit: "Recedamus dehinc[2]: ecce! angelus Domini hanc domum defendit." Et ab ea recesserunt. Deinde etiam, quod multorum testimonio comprobatur, erat sepes[3] magna spinea, quae totum[4] monasterium circumcingebat, et[5] eam statim flamma ex hac parte devorante, exardescebat usque ad locum, ubi crucem ligneam in loca[6] balnei erectam diximus. Ibi erectione crucis ignis illa vorax extimplo evanescit[7]. Ex altera vero parte monasterii ignis ardens, per arentem spineam sepem cito circumiens usque ad angulum[8] eminus supradicti domus, ibique minuato lumine extinguebatur, ibique ea sola parte sepis incontaminata manente. Homines quoque malivoli[9] supradicti, vindicante Deo, perierunt. Nam quidam nobilissimi ex his erant cum exercitibus suis post intervallum temporis in clara luce excaecati; nihil videntes, ab hostibus suis improvidi undique circumacti moxque prostrati et occisi sunt, paucique ex sociis eorum evaserunt, signo crucis[10] muniti. Tali igitur prodigio sanctus Dei Wilfrithus precibus iniurias suas vindicavit[11].

CHAPTER LXVIII[12]

De signo circuli

Igitur postquam sanctus pontifex noster migravit ad Dominum, ubique abbates eius cum subiectis suis, antiquorum hostium insidias timentes, dixerunt: "Quamdiu vixit optimum caput vitae nostrae, frequenter a regibus et principibus Brittanniae varias temptationes sustinuimus, quibus omnibus propter sanctitatem pontificis et sapientiam multorumque amicorum subsidium finem venerabilem semper imponere consuevit; nunc autem nostrum est plene perfecteque credere, intercessorem nostrum per signum sanctae crucis coaequari apostolis Dei Petro et Andreae, quos maxime diligebat et substantiam suam cum subditis dedicavit, in conspectu Dei sine cessatione nostrae defensionis tutorem existere." Et mox huius credulitatis signum in caelo apparuit. Nam anniversaria die sancti pontificis nostri, undique pontifices nostri, undique abbates sui[13] ab

---

[1] omit est et F   [2] hinc C   [3] sepis C and F   [4] omit C   [5] omit F   [6] loco F
[7] evanuit C   [8] angelum F   [9] manivoli F   [10] omit C   [11] After muniti in place of last sentence F reads frequentabat preces et iniurias suas vindicabat
[12] No fresh chapter in F. Chapter-heading in C   [13] suos F and C

hand. As soon as he saw him he was amazed and rushed out, beside himself, crying, "Let us depart from here, for lo! an angel of the Lord is defending this house." And they went away from it.

Again, as is proved by the witness of many, a great hedge of thorn, which surrounded the whole monastery, was at once devoured on one side by flames which burned it up to the place where, as we have said, the wooden cross was erected on the site of the bath. At the place where the cross was erected that devouring fire immediately died away. The fire burned on the other side of the monastery and quickly crept round the parched thorn-hedge to the projecting corner of the above-mentioned house, and there the flame sank and went out, so that this was the only part of the hedge remaining undestroyed.

These evil-minded men mentioned above perished by the punishment of God. For certain of the most noble of them, with their troops, a short time afterwards, became blinded in the full light of day, and seeing nothing, they were hemmed in by their enemies on every side without knowing it, and were soon overthrown and slain. A few of their companions escaped by defending themselves with the sign of the cross. And so with such a miracle Wilfrid, the saint of God, by his prayers avenged his wrongs.

CHAPTER LXVIII

Of the sign of the arc

So, after our holy bishop had departed to be with the Lord, his abbots and their followers everywhere, fearing the snares of their old enemies, said, "While the most worthy ruler of our life was alive, we frequently endured various trials from the kings and princes of Britain, all of which were wont to end honourably for us, owing to the holiness and wisdom of our bishop and the help of many friends. But now it is for us to believe fully and perfectly that our intercessor by the sign of the holy cross has been made equal to the Apostles of God, Peter and Andrew, whom he specially loved, and to whom in company with his followers he dedicated his substance, and that, in the sight of God, he guards and defends us without ceasing."

And soon a sign to warrant this belief appeared in the sky. For on the anniversary of our holy bishop, our bishops and their abbots

oriente et occidente, ab aquilone et austro ad sollempnem diem congregati, in unum convenerunt, vigiliasque vespere facientes in ecclesia, ubi membra sancti episcopi nostri requiescunt; fratribusque vero quibusdam ea hora foris stantibus hebetioris ingenii, signum in caelo apparuit, cuius visionem alternatim usque mane reticuerunt. Crastina die audientes nuntiatum grave tulerunt, musitantes[1] pro peccatis suis sibi non esse revelatum. Cuius honestatis levamen et solamen mox subvenit. Nam cum, sollempnitatis convivio et coena finita, in crepusculo vespertino[2] abbates cum omni familia ad completorium orationis exierunt, statim in caelo signum admirabile viderunt, quod est candidum circulum, totum coenobium circumdantem, quasi per diem arcus coeli absque variis coloribus. Namque huius candidi circuli principium, incipiens a cornibus basilicae nostrae sancto Petro dedicatae, e[3] regione, ubi membra nostri episcopi[4] requiescunt, in australem tendens dexteramque[5] partem coenobii ample circumiens, usque ad aquilonem pervenit; deinde continuato circulo in euro-notum[6] orientis coeli sursum adhaerens finem defixit. Nos vero[7] adorantes laudavimus Dominum mirabilem in sanctis suis, perspicue[8] intellegentes murum auxilii divini circa vineam familiae Domini electam, sicut evidenter de nobis timentibus rei eventus probavit. Nam quia in omnibus regnis Citra-Ultraque-Humbrensium vita nostra sub abbatibus electis utebatur, fratribus[9] videntibus, concurrerunt quasi quidam[10] arcus tendentium et sagittas mittentium ac[11] in semetipso retorquerunt[12]. Nos autem *in nomine Domini magnificabimur*[13]★.

---

[1] *Interlinear gloss in* C id est silenter loquentes   [2] vespertio F   [3] et F
[4] pontificis C   [5] dextramque F   [6] nothum C *and* F   [7] *omit* F   [8] *Interlinear gloss in* C id est manifeste   [9] *insert* fratres C   [10] *omit* F   [11] *omit* F
[12] in semetipsis rectorquentium C   [13] vocabimur F. *In* C *there is an insertion in a later hand* Explicit R : C : 24s

★ cf. Psa. 19. 6 (Vulg.)

gathered and came together from every side, from the north and south, from the east and west, to celebrate the solemn day; they kept vigils at even in the church where the limbs of our holy bishop rest. As certain brethren of a duller spirit were standing outside at that hour, a sign appeared in the sky. They kept silence among themselves about this vision until morning. On the following day, when the others heard of it, they were deeply grieved, murmuring to themselves that it had not been revealed to them on account of their sins. But comfort and solace soon came for their frankness. For when the feast which accompanied the solemnity was over, the abbots went out with the whole community to compline in the evening twilight. Suddenly they saw a wonderful sign in the sky, namely a white arc, surrounding the whole monastery, like a rainbow by day, but without its various colours. For this white arc starting from the gables of our church dedicated to St Peter, opposite where the limbs of our bishop rest, and stretching southwards, made a wide sweep round the right-hand side of the monastery until it reached the north. Then, continuing towards the south-east quarter of the morning sky and tending upwards, it ended there. We worshipped and praised the Lord who is wonderful in His holy places, and clearly understood that the wall of divine help was around the elect vineyard of the Lord's family, as events manifestly proved to those who were in fear for us. For while our life was spent in all the kingdoms on both sides of the Humber under elect abbots, in the sight of our brethren certain of those who assembled and as it were drew their bow and shot their arrows turned their shafts back upon themselves. But "we shall be magnified in the name of the Lord."

NOTES

PREFACE

PREFACE. The preface is copied almost word for word from the *Anonymous Life of St Cuthbert* (ed. Stevenson, *Bedae Opera historica minora*, 1841, p. 259). Internal evidence proves that this work was written before Eddius's Life and that therefore Eddius must have followed the *Life of St Cuthbert*. It has since been shewn by Dr Levison (*S.R.M.* VI. 193) that the Introduction to the *Life of St Cuthbert* is no more than a compilation from the *Epistula Victorii ad Hilarum*, a Latin translation of the *Life of St Antony* written by St Athanasius, and the *Life of St Martin of Tours* by Sulpicius Severus. Thus the result is that the work of no less than four authors finds its way into Eddius's introductory chapter!

ACCA. Fifth Bishop of Hexham; died 740. He seems to have acted as patron and adviser to men of letters. Most of Bede's theological works are dedicated to Acca. But there are special reasons why it should have been Acca who urged Eddius to write the Life, for the former had come into close contact with Wilfrid himself. He had voluntarily accompanied Wilfrid into exile; he was with the saint when he visited the South Saxons (*H.E.* IV. 14). He went to Friesland with him and visited St Willibrord (*H.E.* III. 13). He was with him at Rome, and when Wilfrid lay in a trance at Meaux his first words on his recovery were, "Where is Acca our priest?" It was to Acca too that he related his vision (see ch. LVI). Wilfrid made him Abbot of Hexham, and, after his death, Acca became bishop as well (see *D.N.B.* s.v. Acca). It is therefore natural that Acca should have urged Eddius to write a Life, both as patron of letters and as a follower fulfilling a pious duty to the memory of his beloved master.*

In the Chapter Library at Durham there stands a beautifully carved fragment of a cross called Acca's Cross. It is so called because it is supposed to be one of the two mentioned by Symeon of Durham as standing over the grave of Acca at Hexham. (See *A.E.E.* v. 170. Haverfield and Greenwell, *A Catalogue of the sculptured and inscribed stones in the Cathedral Library, Durham* (Durham, 1899), pp. 53 ff.).

TATBERHT. We know no more of him than we learn from Eddius. It was to him that Wilfrid related the story of his life probably as he

---

* For a fuller account of his life see A. S. Cook, *The Old English* Andreas *and Bishop Acca of Hexham.* (*Connecticut Academy of Arts and Sciences*, vol. 26, pp. 245–332). Cook attempts to shew that the Old English poem *Andreas* was the work of Acca, who was really glorifying St Wilfrid in the person of St Andrew.

rode on his last journey to Oundle. He was one of those to whom Wilfrid gave his last instructions and to whom he left the monastery at Ripon (see chs. LXIII–LXVI). The name Tatberht also occurs in the *Liber Vitae* (Surt. Soc. XIII. 6) under the heading of "Nomina Abbatum gradus presbyteratus." Presumably it is the same man.

FERIUNTQUE, ETC. This is a quotation from Horace (*Odes*, II. 10). But Eddius is quoting from St Jerome, for the quotation, together with the sentence that introduces it, is copied from St Jerome's *Liber Hebraicarum Quaestionum in Genesim* (Migne, XXIII. 983).

CHAPTER I

WILFRID'S BIRTH. The miracle associated with the birth of Wilfrid may be compared with others to be found in the lives of the saints, especially the Celtic saints. A ball of fire was seen over the place where St Declan was born. Similar portents were connected with the infancy of St Brigid, St Comgall, St Mochaomhoc, St Columba (cf. Reeves, *Adamnan's Life of St Columba* (1857), p. 192 *n.*), with St Cuthbert, St Brendan of Clonfert, and St Maedoc of Ferns. (*Lives of Irish Saints*, C. Plummer, II. 45, 177.)

There are also classical examples to be found in Virgil, *Aen.* II. 682, Livy, I. 39, and in Pausanias, II. 26. 4 (the case of Aesculapius).

This particular miracle seems to owe its form to the Biblical miracle of the burning bush. For a full discussion on the subject of ecclesiastical and mediaeval miracles see Hast. *E.R.E.* s.v. Miracles.

CHAPTER II

EANFLED. Daughter of Edwin of York, was born in 626 on the night after Edwin so nearly lost his life through the treachery of the West Saxon prince Cwichelm. As a thankoffering the child was dedicated to Christ and was the first Northumbrian to receive baptism (*H.E.* II. 9). After Edwin was slain at *Haethfelth* in 633, Paulinus fled to Kent taking with him Aethilburg the widowed queen and the little Eanfled (*H.E.* II. 20). About 643 she was married to Oswiu, King of Northumbria, and at her request he gave a site at a place called Ingetlingum (Gilling?) to found a monastery in memory of that Oswini who was murdered by her husband's orders (*H.E.* III. 14). She was a deeply religious woman, kept her own chaplain, and observed the Roman method of keeping Easter as opposed to the Celtic.

CUDDA. "Ex sodalibus," i.e. probably one of the king's thegns. The name stands second on the list of abbots in the *Liber Vitae* after "Biscopus," i.e. Benedict Biscop (Surt. Soc. XIII. 8). If this is the

same man, it was probably he who gave St Cuthbert the sarcophagus in which he was afterwards buried and would be the venerable Abbot Cudda of whom we read in *Vit. Cuth.* c. 37.

THE PSALTER. We learn from ch. III that this was the Psalter according to Jerome's version. (See note, ch. III.)

CHAPTER III

ERCONBERHT. King of Kent, 640–664. Eanfled's mother, Aethilburg, was sister of Eadbald, Erconberht's father. Hence Eanfled and Erconberht were cousins (*H.E.* v. 19).

THE PSALTER. The Psalter here referred to is called the Gallican Psalter and was made by Jerome from the LXX about 389. The Roman Psalter which he made in 383 was no more than a revision of the old Italic version.

FIFTH EDITION. "Quintam editionem." This phrase, which is also used by William of Malmesbury, has never been explained. There was no fifth edition of the Psalms in the seventh century. Raine suggests that it is the Greek word κοινή referring to the common version or Vulgate (Raine, *H.Y.* I. 5). My colleague Dr Pace suggests that "quintam" is a scribal error for "antiquam," which on the whole seems a better explanation.

BISCOP BADUCING. Baducing is the patronymic of the man more usually known as Benedict Biscop. We read much about him in Bede. He was a man of noble birth (*H.E.* v. 19) and founded monasteries at Wearmouth and Jarrow. He had previously been a thegn of Oswiu of Northumbria. But at the age of twenty-five he decided to renounce the world and to make his way to Rome (*H.A.* 2). This was the occasion of his journey with Wilfrid. As a result of this visit he attempted to introduce the Roman system of Church organization in Northumbria. This was the first of five visits to Rome in the course of which he assimilated much Roman culture. His great hobby seems to have been the collection of Roman manuscripts, vessels, vestments and pictures. He evidently fired Wilfrid with similar enthusiasms. He brought over skilled masons and glass-workers from Gaul to help him in building the monastery of St Peter at Wearmouth. It is not easy to gauge Benedict's influence both in art and learning, for in the second half of the seventh century traces of Italian influence are to be found in the churches of Northumbria, and, according to some authorities, in the crosses and slabs as well. (See *A.E.E.* I. 175.) He was also the instructor of Bede. Biscop died in 690.

WILFRID'S JOURNEY. By 720 the journey to Rome had become quite common even for women, as we learn from Boniface's correspondence. And by 747 Boniface is urging that these pilgrimages

should be forbidden to English women because of the large number who succumbed to moral temptations on the way and never reached Rome. (See Kylie, *English Correspondence of St Boniface*, King's Classics, pp. 64 ff. and 188 ff.)

CHAPTER IV

DALFINUS. Who was Dalfinus? From the Fasti of the Church of Lyons it is clear that the archbishop at this time was Aunemundus. An account of both Aunemundus and Dalfinus is given in *Gallia Christiana* (ed. Piolin, IV. 43), derived from an old Lyons breviary. From this it appears that Dalfinus was Count of the city of Lyons and brother of the archbishop. It is this count who offers his daughter to Wilfrid and the match would have been an excellent one from a worldly point of view. As Wilfrid was still in the lower orders of the Church, celibacy was not binding upon him. Generally speaking, celibacy was not enforced on any except the regular clergy until well into the eleventh century. (See Hast. *E.R.E.* s.v. Celibacy.)

Compare also the story of the priest Alchmund and his descendants in Symeon of Durham (*Hist. Dunelm. Eccl.* bk III. 1, Rolls Series, LXXV. 80).

CHAPTER V

ST ANDREW'S ORATORY. This may have been the oratory under St Peter's or another in the Via Labicana. However, it is much more likely to have been the monastery of St Andrew on the Coelian Hill, the home of Gregory and Augustine and consequently, as Raine truly says, "a most sacred place to any pilgrim from England" (Raine, *H.Y.* I. 8). Possibly it was the sight of the gospels in this monastery which led him to make his gift later on to the church at Ripon. See ch. XVII.

BONIFACE. An interesting find was made at Whitby in 1879, when a leaden bulla was discovered in an ancient shell-heap. The bulla which is about the size of a shilling bears the inscription BONIFATII ARCEIDIAC. This shell-heap has produced several finds connected with Wilfrid, but there is apparently no other reason for connecting the Boniface of the bulla with Wilfrid's spiritual instructor. We know nothing of him except what Eddius tells us here and in ch. LIII.

THE POPE. It is not certain whether this was Eugenius or St Martin I. Eugenius was elected in September 654 while St Martin was still alive but in exile. It is therefore probable that it was Eugenius, who is described as a "weak but kindly prelate" (Bright, *E.E.C.H.* p. 219 *n.*).

CHAPTER VI

TONSURE. It is important in view of the later controversies to differentiate between the three forms of tonsure.

1. The Oriental type, which consisted in shaving the whole head (cf. *H.E.* IV. 1). The authority of St Paul was claimed for this because we read of his having shorn his head in Cenchrea (Acts 18. 18).

2. The Western or Petrine form. This consisted in leaving a circlet of hair and shaving the crown. As Eddius explains, it symbolized the crown of thorns. It was also declared to symbolize the crown of Christ's royal priesthood.

3. The Celtic form. There is some doubt as to the form of this tonsure. Some hold that it left the hair long at the back while the upper part of the front was left bare, nothing more than a band of hair being left round the forehead from ear to ear (J. Dowden, "An examination of original documents on the question of the form of the Celtic Tonsure," *Proceedings of the Society of Antiquaries of Scotland*, XXX. 325 ff.). Others consider that the hair was shaved to a line from ear to ear behind which the hair was grown. The Celtic form was common to all Celts both insular and continental. (See ch. XLVII.) Cf. Plummer's *Bede*, II. 353 ff.

The tonsure was originally part of the ceremony of ordination, but towards the end of the seventh century was separated from it. As Wilfrid was not ordained priest until later (see ch. IX), and as we read he introduced the Benedictine rule to the north on his return to England, this was probably the occasion of his undertaking monastic vows.

BALDHILD. C reads "Brunechild." It is suggested by Raine that the author or scribe had been reading the life of Columbanus who had been persecuted by Brunechild; she is compared with Jezebel as here. Brunechild however died in 613. The insertion of this name may of course be an interesting reminiscence of Brynhild, the heroine of the Volsunga Saga. Some of the MSS of both Fridegoda's *Vita Wilfridi* and of Bede's *Ecclesiastical History* read "Brunechild" probably following the Eddius MS.

Baldhild however is said to have been an Anglo-Saxon slave. She married Clovis II (who died in 656) and was at this time acting as regent for her son Clothaire III. She was said to have been beautiful and pious. She gave great gifts to the Church, and died in the monastery of Chelles in 680. After her death she was canonized. It is therefore very unlikely that she was responsible for the persecution of the Church and the death of Aunemundus. It seems much more reasonable to believe the tradition of the times, namely that the death of Aunemundus was brought about by Ebroin, the mayor of

the palace (see Mab. *AA.SS.O.S.B.* saec. IV. pt I. 639. See also note, ch. xxv). Eddius by his reference to the part played by the dukes seems to imply that it was by no means entirely the work of the queen. It may well be that the reason why Wilfrid's life was spared was because he was of the same nationality as the queen. Eadmer (*Vita Wilf.* ch. VII) of course declares that it was due to the terror of the English name. The other solution however seems more probable. In any case it is difficult to reconcile Eddius's narrative with what is known from other sources of contemporary Gaulish history.

JOHN THE APOSTLE. The story of the boiling oil is related by Tertullian (*De Praescriptionibus adversus Haereticos*, ch. 36) and that of the poison by Isidore of Seville (*De ortu et obitu Sanctorum*, ch. 72).

CHAPTER VII

CONFESSOR. After his adventures at Lyons, Wilfrid has now earned the title of "Confessor," that is one who has confessed his religion in the face of great danger but has not actually suffered death.

OSWIU. Oswiu ruled in Bernicia from 643, and over the whole of Northumbria probably from 655. He died in 671. He made his son Alhfrith under-king in Deira (Florence of Worcester, I.25), who according to Bede (*H.E.* III. 14) seems to have rebelled against his father. Alhfrith must have had a strong bias in favour of the Roman form of worship—otherwise it is difficult to account for his disposition to aid Wilfrid even before he saw him (cf. *H.E.* V. 19). The decision to settle the growing controversy between the Celtic and the Roman Churches and the synod of Whitby were probably largely due to Alhfrith's influence.

COENWALH ruled over Wessex from 643, but was driven out by Penda King of the Mercians in 645. He took refuge with Anna King of the East Anglians and father of Aethilthryth. Here he accepted Christianity. His treatment of Agilberht (see ch. IX, note) so closely resembles Oswiu's treatment of Wilfrid that it seems as though the two kings must have followed a common policy. One of his last acts was to receive Benedict Biscop on his return from Rome. He died in 672 (*H.E.* III. 7, IV. 12). See *D.C.B.* I. 593.

CHAPTER VIII

AET STANFORDA. This has usually been said to be Stamford in Lincolnshire owing to a statement of John Wessington, a fifteenth-century prior of Durham who declared that it was this Stamford. This, he says, was afterwards given to the monastery of Durham by

William the Conqueror. But the difficulty is that one can hardly expect a Northumbrian king to be giving away land in Mercia. Smith in his edition of Bede's works suggests Stamford Bridge near York. It is not known that this was ever Church property, but considering how little is known of the history of Northumbria from the eighth to the eleventh century, this is hardly an insuperable objection. Other suggestions are Stainforth near Doncaster and Stainforth near Giggleswick.

HIDES. Lat. "tributariorum." We have no means of deciding the exact size of the hide at this time. It was the amount of land belonging to a household. In the eleventh century, and probably for two or three centuries before that, in the south of England, it was generally identified with the ploughland and reckoned as 120 acres.

RIPON. Lat. "Inhrypis." Alhfrith had founded the monastery here. It appears from Bede (*H.E.* III. 25) that this had originally been given to Eata, Abbot of Melrose. Cuthbert and other brethren were sent to form a new settlement here, but rather than accept Alhfrith's continental Easter they had returned to Melrose, leaving the monastery vacant.

CHAPTER IX

AGILBERHT. Bede declares him to have been of Gaulish nationality, and implies that he was consecrated in Gaul (*H.E.* III. 7). Apparently, though a consecrated bishop, he had no see when he came to Wessex in 648 and was appointed successor to Birinus as Bishop of the West Saxons. Coenwalh (see ch. VII and note) could not understand his speech, and so he appointed another bishop named Wini to Winchester, and the diocese was divided. Agilberht was highly offended and went north, where we find him taking part in the synod of Whitby. He was afterwards appointed to the see of Paris, where he died an old man (*H.E.* III. 7, 25, 26, 28).

It is noticeable that Wilfrid was ordained by the stranger bishop rather than by his own bishop, Colman, who was of the Celtic school.

FOREIGN. Lat. "transmarinus." Probably Eddius means a bishop of foreign birth and consecration.

CHAPTER X

COLMAN. Here called Bishop of York and Metropolitan. This is not an accurate description, as the headquarters of the bishops from Iona were at Lindisfarne. There had been no bishop in York after Paulinus's flight in 633. Nor should Colman be described as Metropolitan, for even Paulinus was not really archbishop, seeing he

did not receive the pallium from the Pope until 634 (*H.E.* II. 20). The first Archbishop of York was therefore Egbert who received the pallium in 735.

Saint Colman, the date of whose birth is unknown, came from Ireland, probably from Mayo, and became a monk at the monastery of Hii or Iona. He was consecrated Bishop of the Kingdom of Northumbria in 661. After leaving Lindisfarne as described in the chapter, he returned to Hii, taking with him some of the bones of St Aidan, the founder of the house, and such of his followers as refused to accept the Roman usages. In 668 he left Hii with his company and settled in Inishbofin off the coast of Mayo, where he died in 676. (See *D.N.B.* s.v. and *H.E.* III. 25, 26, IV. 4.)

STREUNESHALH. This is usually identified with Whitby though the name itself corresponds with the modern form Strensall, the name of a place near York. But recent early Anglo-Saxon finds at Whitby have made the traditional identification practically certain.

HILD or HILDA (614–680), abbess of Whitby, was of royal lineage. Her father was Hereric, nephew of Edwin. After living at the court of Edwin she was baptized by Paulinus at the age of thirteen. She was going to her sister as a nun at the convent of Chelles near Paris, but was recalled by St Aidan, and after being for eight years abbess of a religious house at Hartlepool she got possession of an estate at Whitby, and founded a mixed monastery which soon became the most famous religious house in north-east England. She opposed Wilfrid when he appealed to Rome in 679 (see ch. LIV). During the last six years of her life she suffered from ill-health, but, busy to the last, she died in 680 at the age of sixty-six (*H.E.* IV. 21).

THE EASTER QUESTION. This difficult question, which caused so much division in the early Church, really turned on two main issues: first what is the first day on which Easter Sunday may be celebrated, and secondly, what is the day on which the Paschal full moon falls. The first question was answered differently by the Celtic and the Roman Church, the former declaring that it might be celebrated on the Sunday between the fourteenth and the twentieth day of the moon (not twenty-second as the C-text reads), while the latter maintained that it could only be celebrated between the fifteenth and the twenty-first. Although Eddius does not make it very clear, both schools of thought were agreed that Easter must take place on Sunday (*H.E.* III. 25). According to tradition St John had declared that Easter should be celebrated on the fourteenth day of the moon, no matter what day of the week it fell upon. Those who held this view were called Quartodecimans and were condemned as heretics by the Council of Nicaea. Apparently Eddius makes Wilfrid charge his adversaries with being Quartodecimans, though it is plain from

Bede (*l.c.*) that he knew they were not.* (See ch. XIV and note.)

The other point of contention was the question as to the date of the Paschal full moon. This question was answered by the adoption of cycles. The Roman Church used a nineteen-year cycle. The first person to draw up such a cycle was Victorius of Aquitaine. This was adopted in Rome about 457. It comprised 532 years starting with the supposed date of the crucifixion and ran from A.D. 28 to 559. This cycle was improved upon by Dionysius Exiguus who drew up a cycle which ran from 1 B.C. to A.D. 532 and from A.D. 532 to 1063. This was finally adopted by the Roman Church. It is usually held that the Celtic Church used an older eighty-four-year cycle (see *H.E.* II. 2 and V. 21), but there is evidence that the Celtic peoples had some knowledge of the Victorian but not the Dionysian nineteen-year cycle (see Chad. *O.E.N.* pp. 24 *n.* and 48 *n.*). For a fuller account of the whole subject see *En. Britt.* s.v. Easter, and Plummer's *Bede*, II. 348 ff.

TONSURE. See ch. VI and note.

COLMAN'S RETIREMENT. The bitter spirit which Eddius shews towards all Wilfrid's opponents is illustrated here by his unkind reference to Colman.

CHAPTER XI

COLMAN'S SUCCESSOR. We learn from Bede (*H.E.* III. 26) that Tuda was elected to take Colman's place. He had only been bishop for a few months when he was carried off by the plague which swept across England in 664. Eddius ignores Tuda altogether and makes it seem as though Wilfrid succeeded Colman. From Bede (*H.E.* III. 28 and V. 19) it is clear that Alhfrith was the moving spirit in the election, and from his account it looks as though Wilfrid was intended to be bishop only over Deira in the first instance and Tuda bishop over Bernicia, but that on Tuda's death, Wilfrid was made bishop over the whole of Northumbria. If this is the case it would partly but not entirely explain Theodore's high-handed action later on (ch. XXIV), and also explain how Chad came to be bishop—not as bishop over the whole of Northumbria but merely as successor to Tuda in Bernicia. Theodore's objection according to Bede was solely on the ground of his orders (*H.E.* IV. 2). When Chad ceased to be Bishop of York, Wilfrid took his place. But the weakness of Bede's story is that it gives no reason for Chad's removal from the diocese. Eddius's story at least explains this point clearly enough. See ch. XIV, note.

* As Colman actually points out in this chapter, they celebrated Easter on the 14th day of the moon only when it fell on a Sunday.

HIS DISCOURSE WAS PURE. It is a remarkable fact that the whole of this passage from this point to the end of the chapter with the exception of about three words is taken from the *Vit. Anon. Cuthb.* and is of course a description of that saint (see Preface and note). The words of St Paul quoted here are also quoted in the other Life in the same place.

CHAPTER XII

QUARTODECIMANS. This of course was an unfair accusation. The Celts were not Quartodecimans, as Wilfrid must have known (cf. chs. XIV and XV). It seems, however, as though Eddius were definitely putting these words into Wilfrid's mouth. If not it follows that Wilfrid is deliberately stating what he knows to be untrue. In view of Bede's account of Wilfrid's speech at the synod of Whitby (*H.E.* III. 25), it looks as though it is Eddius who is to blame rather than Wilfrid.

WILFRID'S CONSECRATION. Of the bishops who were alive at that time, there were Cedd of Essex and Jaruman of Mercia, both of whom were open to objection because they had been consecrated by the Celtic party. Then there was Agilberht's successor or rather supplanter, Wini, who was open to objection on moral grounds. Deusdedit, Archbishop of Canterbury, and Damian of Rochester were probably dead, so that only Boniface of East Anglia remained. He could hardly have been objected to on either moral or orthodox grounds for he had been consecrated by Archbishop Honorius. But probably Wilfrid wished to be ordained by at least three bishops in accordance with Roman usage. The Celtic usage permitted consecration by a single bishop. (See Hast. *E.R.E.* s.v. Ministry.)

This passage is the main source of information concerning the Gallic method of consecrating a bishop. The carrying of the newly-consecrated bishop by his brethren is mentioned by Gregory of Tours (*History of the Franks*, III. 2) in his account of the consecration of St Quintanus at Auvergne. For other references to this Gallic custom see E. Martène, *De Antiquis Ecclesiae Ritibus*, II. 28, ed. 1788, where he adds that it was still (1700) in use at Orleans.

Of the golden chair, all we know is that Gregory the Great presented a golden chair to Gregory of Tours, so he was evidently familiar with this custom (Bened. *Vit. Greg.* Migne, III. 3. 8). Bright compares the "sella gestatoria" of the Pope (Bright, *E.E.C.H.* p. 242).

YORK. It seems likely that Wilfrid desired the change of position from Lindisfarne, which was so closely connected with the Celtic form of worship, to York with its memories of Paulinus.

CHAPTER XIII

THE HEATHEN RITE. The magical rite practised by the
heathen high priest is interesting. A somewhat similar instance is to
be found in the *Gesta Herewardi* (Gaimar's *Lestorie des Engles*, Rolls
Series, CXI. I. 384–390). When William the Conqueror had attempted
in vain to drive Hereward and his followers from the Isle of Ely, an
old woman dressed as a witch is set on a lofty station. Mounted
upon it she delivers a long harangue against the isle and its inhabitants.
Apparently the lofty station added to the effectiveness of the
incantation. Compare also the Norse witchcraft as described in the
sagas, where a platform was erected on which the performer could
work spells (cf. *Laxdale Saga*, ch. XXXV; *Thorfinn Saga Karlsefnis*,
ch. III; Du Chaillu, *The Viking Age*, I. 397). Spells for binding and
loosing were very familiar. Cf. Bede's "litterae solutoriae" (*H.E.* IV.
20). For another example of binding cf. the story of the incident at
St Edmund's shrine (Aelfric's *Lives of the Saints*, II. 329, E.E.T.S.).

CHAPTER XIV

CHAD. St Ceadda, better known as St Chad, a Northumbrian
and disciple of St Aidan. The date of his birth is unknown. In 664
on the death of his brother Cedd, who was Bishop of the East Saxons
and Abbot of Lastingham, Chad succeeded him in the latter office
(*H.E.* III. 23). After the events related in this and the following
chapter he ruled over Lichfield for two and a half years, and then,
in 672, fell a victim to the pestilence, which carried off so many of
the clergy. Bede gives a picturesque account of his death (*H.E.* IV. 3).
It is to be noted that although Eddius is violently prejudiced against
him, he speaks highly of his humility and sanctity. This fact, even
more than Bede's account, helps us to realize how deep was the
respect in which he was held by his contemporaries, for Eddius is
always a violent partisan and, generally speaking, gauges the characters of all Wilfrid's contemporaries by their attitude towards his hero.
Bede, it may be noted, says nothing about Wilfrid's intercession with
Wulfhere on Chad's behalf.
  It is not easy to explain why Oswiu changed his mind about
Wilfrid and appointed Chad. Dr Levison (*S.R.M.* VI. 167 ff.)
attempts to shew from Bede (*H.E.* III. 28) that Chad was consecrated to the see, not to replace but to assist Wilfrid. But Bede's
words will hardly bear such an interpretation. No facts are forth-
coming to explain Oswiu's action and we can only surmise that it
was in some way connected with his quarrel with Alhfrith, an attempt perhaps to avenge himself on his son by turning out his
protégé. But see notes, chs. VII. and XI.

WULFHERE. Son of Penda, reigned over Mercia from 659 to 675. He is always highly praised by the chroniclers for his generosity to the Church. He was certainly strongly in favour of Christianity. How far this was political and how far the result of conviction, it is not easy to decide. The chief blot on his fame is his transaction with Wini, who according to Bede bought from him the bishopric of London "for a price" (*H.E.* III. 7).

EGBERT. King of Kent, 664–673. We know little of his life or history, save that he seems to have been friendly with Oswiu and to have consulted him over the consecration of Wighard.

PUTTA. Afterwards Bishop of Rochester, from the arrival of Archbishop Theodore in 669 until the sack of Rochester by Aethilred, King of Mercia, in 676. He was extraordinarily skilled in Church music, which he had learned from the disciples of Pope Gregory; after he lost his see, he made no effort to regain it but used to go about teaching church music wherever he was required (*H.E.* IV. 2, 12).

DEUSDEDIT. Succeeded Honorius as Archbishop of Canterbury after an interval of a year and a half from the death of the latter in 653. He was a West Saxon by birth. Little is known of his episcopate. (See Bright, *E.E.C.H.* pp. 199 ff.)

AEDDE. This is possibly the author of the work. See Introduction.

AEONA. Nothing more is known of him beyond this single mention by Eddius. His name is an unusual one.

MASONS. Benedict Biscop also brought with him masons and glass-makers from Gaul (Bede, *H.A.* 5).

RULE OF ST BENEDICT. The rule of St Benedict was of course introduced to England by St Augustine and his fellow-monks in 597. The monastery he established, was probably the first Benedictine house outside Italy. The Scottish monastic rules were observed at Lindisfarne and in Northumbria generally, until St Wilfrid in accordance with his general Romanizing policy introduced the rule of St Benedict. Eddius seems here to suggest that he had recently learned the rule during his stay in Kent. This does not seem possible, for he must have learned about it during his visits to Italy and Gaul. See also the note on the tonsure he received at Lyons, ch. VI.

CHAPTER XV

THEODORE. After the death of Deusdedit, Wighard was chosen primate "with the consent of the Church of the English nation" (*H.E.* III. 29). He was sent to Rome to receive consecration and the pallium from Pope Vitalian, but died of plague in Rome. The Pope appointed Theodore of Tarsus to succeed him but owing to various

hindrances it was more than three years before the new archbishop arrived in 669. He was a man of learning with a knowledge of Greek and Latin. Although apparently he was sixty-seven years of age when he reached these shores, he was extremely active both mentally and physically. It was during his first general survey of his province that he restored Wilfrid to his see. Theodore's great work was to organize the English Church on a permanent basis. At this time some of the sees were vacant and some were filled irregularly. At the synod of Hertford in 673 (*H.E.* IV. 5) the united English Church met together for the first time to confirm such arrangements as had already been made, and to consider others. Amongst other things Theodore suggested that "more bishops be made as the multitude of believers increases." For the present this was passed over, but Theodore kept this aim steadily before him and it was for this reason that he came into collision with Wilfrid.

LICHFIELD. Bede says that it was Theodore and not Wilfrid who arranged for Chad to go to Lichfield (*H.E.* IV. 3). When it is a choice between Eddius and Bede, Bede is usually to be preferred. (See Introduction.)

CHAD'S RECONSECRATION. It seemed rather unnecessary that Theodore, as Eddius declares, should have consecrated Chad "through all the ecclesiastical degrees." His reconsecration as bishop was to be expected; he had been consecrated by Wini and two bishops of the Celtic school (*H.E.* III. 28). Bede merely states that he "completed his consecration afresh in the Catholic manner" (*H.E.* IV. 3). See *D.C.B.* s.v. Chad.

CHAPTER XVI

METROPOLITAN. See note, ch. X.

THE CHURCH AT YORK. Paulinus built first a wooden church and then put a stone building over it. Bede tells us that he left the work unfinished when he fled from the north at the death of Edwin (*H.E.* II. 14). Bede explains that the walls were not raised to their proper height when Paulinus left, but Eddius speaks of an apparently completed, or almost completed church, so it seems likely that Oswald did something, though, in the course of the thirty-six years during which the headquarters of the Northumbrian bishops were at Lindisfarne, it is clear that little regard was paid to the church. Wilfrid's church was not destined to last long for we learn from the *A.S.C.* that it was burnt down in 741.

MOST CHRISTIAN KING. This phrase afterwards became a formal and hereditary title of the French kings. See Ducange, s.v. Christianitas, and Plummer's *Bede*, II. 86. The same title is given to Ecgfrith and Aelfwini in ch. XVII.

GLASS. There is a discrepancy here between Eddius and Bede. The latter says that in 675 Benedict Biscop brought glassmakers with him from Gaul, "a kind of workmen hitherto unknown in England" (Bede, *H.A.* 5), but Eddius dates the renovation of the church at York between 669 (restoration of Wilfrid to the see) and 671 (death of Oswiu). As we have seen that Wilfrid brought over masons and artisans of almost every kind (ch. XIV) it is quite probable that Eddius is correct.

CHAPTER XVII

RIPON. All that remains of Wilfrid's work is a certain crypt which is now reached by a mediaeval staircase on the south side of the nave. The crypt, like that at Hexham, is partly covered with plaster, but underneath has been found blue and gold paint which is said to be contemporary with the crypt.* There is a great similarity between the crypt here and that at Hexham; the latter can be definitely assigned to Wilfrid. The similarity is in fact so great that there is little doubt that the Ripon crypt as it now stands is Wilfrid's work too. Wilfrid probably brought the idea of an underground sepulchral chamber, approached by stairs, from Rome or Gaul. The crypts were intended to hold a sarcophagus and reliquaries and were so arranged as to permit worshippers to see the holy objects without any confusion or overcrowding (*A.E.E.* II. 1925, 163). An opening in one of the walls in the Ripon crypt is still called "St Wilfrid's needle."

The monastery buildings were probably about 200 yards away from the church itself. Leland in his Itinerary (cf. Surt. Soc. LXXIV. pp. 83 ff.) declares that the old abbey stood "where now is a chapel of our Lady in a bottom." There are still a few remains of this chapel near the site of the present Deanery. It is also recorded in ch. LXVIII that the brethren at Ripon "went out...in the evening twilight" from their feasting hall to compline.

DRESSED STONE. It is easy to recognize the mediaeval additions in the crypt because they are of much rougher work than that of Wilfrid.

VARIOUS COLUMNS. Possibly from Roman remains in the district, just as happened at Hexham. Aldborough (Isurium) was only seven miles away.

AISLES. L. "porticibus." On the meaning of this word cf. *A.E.E.* II. (1925), pp. 88 ff., 330, 369. Baldwin Brown translates it "side-chapels."

ECGFRITH. Second son of Oswiu, whom he succeeded as king of Northumbria in 671. He was slain by the Picts in 685 in the

* Compare the reference to 'gold and silver and varied purples' in the text.

disastrous battle at Nechtansmere. For the picturesque account of Cuthbert's vision of his death, see *Vit. Cuth.* ch. XXVII. See also ch. XIX and note.

AELFWINI. As Eddius calls him king here and in ch. XXIV, it is probable that he was under-king of Deira in succession to Oswiu. See ch. XXIV and note.

ALTAR WITH BASES. Perhaps a reminiscence of Ezra 3. 3 (Vulg.), "Altare Dei super bases suas."

CONSECRATED PLACES. This is a very interesting reference to what happened to the earlier British churches, which had been deserted probably at the time of the Saxon conquest of Elmet in the days of Edwin (cf. *Historia Brittonum*, Appendix, in T. Gale, *xv scriptores*, Oxford, 1691, p. 117).

RIBBLE, YEADON, ETC. These conjectural identifications of the place-names are based on suggestions made by Prof. Chadwick. Raine's suggestions (*H.Y.* I. 26) are all philologically impossible.

PURPLE MANUSCRIPTS. Manuscripts were occasionally treated with purple and written with gold and silver letters. The famous Codex Argenteus which contained the Gothic gospels of Ulfilas, and the Gallican Psalter in the Abbey of St Germain-des-Prés, are both of this kind. Each belongs to the fifth or sixth century. For other examples see Ducange, s.v. membranum. For a discussion of the whole subject see Sir E. Maunde Thompson's *Handbook of Greek and Latin Palaeography*, pp. 40 ff.

CASE. Lat. "bibliotheca" may mean either the binding of the book or the case in which the book was kept. It was a fairly common thing to decorate the covers, especially of Gospels, with very elaborate work, gold, silver, jewels and enamel. One of the earliest examples of this elaborate decorative work still preserved, is a sixth-century Gospel presented by Theodolinda, Queen of the Lombards, to the church of Monza, north Italy, in 616, where it is still to be seen. Separate cases were well known too, and Gregory of Tours in his *History of the Franks* (III. 9) tells how Childebert I in 530 robbed a church, probably at Narbonne, of "20 Gospel cases (*capsae*) all of pure gold and adorned with precious stones." Later on similar cases called cumdachs were quite common in Ireland (see Margaret Stokes, *Early Christian Art in Ireland*, pp. 88 ff.) and were used not only for Gospels but for other sacred writings. Rupert, a twelfth-century monk of Deaux, says: "The books of the Gospels are also very rightly decorated with gold and silver and precious stones, for in them the gold of heavenly wisdom shines, the silver of faithful eloquence glitters, and the precious stones of miracles sparkle" (*De divinis Officiis*, II. 23, Migne, CLXX. 53).* The Anglo-Saxon Riddle No. 27 refers to a Bible Codex, and may be compared.

Among the gospels recorded as belonging to the cathedral at York at the beginning of the sixteenth century are two of St Wilfrid's texts adorned with silver and gold (Raine, *H.Y.* III. 387).

OUR CHURCH. This shews that the author of the Life belonged to the Ripon monastery. (See Introduction.)

CHAPTER XVIII

IN HIS SAINTS. Lat. "sanctis suis" of course means "holy places," but here Eddius seems to have wilfully misread the meaning. Cf. ch. LXI.

ONTIDDANUFRI. Has not been satisfactorily identified.

CONFIRM. The rites of confirmation and baptism were not definitely separated in the Western Church for many centuries after this, though the custom of administering them at the same time was not universal. (See *E.R.E.* s.v. Confirmation).

GREAT PLAGUE. There were many visitations of the plague during the seventh century. Bede speaks of it in 664 (*H.E.* III. 27) and there were renewed outbreaks of it to the end of the century. Thus at Jarrow in 685 only the Abbot Ceolfrith and a little boy (probably Bede himself) were left to carry on the services (*H.A.* 14). According to Canon Fowler it was a virulent bilious fever (*Adamnan's Life of Columba*, J. T. Fowler, Oxford, 1920, p. 224).

CHAPTER XIX

AETHILTHRYTH. Commonly known as St Audrey, daughter of Anna, King of the East Angles. Ecgfrith was her second husband, and was very much younger than his saintly wife. According to Bede, it was Wilfrid who encouraged her in her desire to remain a virgin, and when, much against her husband's will, she retired to Coldingham monastery, 672, it was from Wilfrid that she received the veil. This fact helps to account for Ecgfrith's later hostility. She was not at Coldingham long, for she became Abbess of Ely about 673 and died of the plague in 679 or 680 (*H.E.* IV. 17). On the derivation of the word "tawdry" and its connection with the saint see *N.E.D.* s.v.

BATTLE WITH THE PICTS. It is clear from this passage and from Bede that Ecgfrith was supreme over some part of Pictland. But it was evidently an uneasy rule, even though on this occasion Ecgfrith won a telling victory.

A TROOP OF HORSEMEN. This is the first mention of cavalry in English history (cf. Chad. *O.E.N.* p. 159, n. 1).

★ The Lindisfarne Gospels also had an elaborate cover or case made by a cunning metal-worker, an anchorite called Billfrith. (*A.E.E.* v. 334.)

BEORNHAETH. This seems to be the father of the Berht who ravaged Ireland in 648, and was killed by the Picts in 699. Compare Plummer's note in *A.S.C.* s.a. 699 and 710. The name occurs in the *Liber Vitae* among the "nomina regum vel ducum" (Surt. Soc. XIII. 1). Probably it is the same man.

CHAPTER XX

WULFHERE. Eddius's partisanship is well seen by comparing his description of Wulfhere in this chapter with that in ch. XIV. See Introduction. The battle described here must have taken place after the Council of Hertford in 673, at which Ecgfrith can hardly have been present if he had been at war with Mercia, and before 675, when Wulfhere died. Soon after this, presumably as the result of the battle, Lindsey was restored to Northumbria (*H.E.* IV. 12). Symeon of Durham (*Hist. de Sanct. Cuth.* ch. VII, Rolls Series, LXXV. 200) says that Wilfrid was present at the battle with Ecgfrith.

CHAPTER XXI

SAXONS. The name Saxon is here applied to the Mercians. Apparently Eddius knows nothing of the distinction drawn by Bede (*H.E.* I. 15), where he puts the Mercians down as Angles in contra-distinction to the Saxons of Essex, Wessex and Sussex (see Chad. *O.E.N.* ch. IV).

BATHS. It is clear from this and other passages that bathing had a religious significance and was probably a memorial of baptism. Bathing in cold water was a form of penance, as we see in the story of St Cuthbert bathing by night in the sea (Bede, *Vit. Cuth.* 10). It was on the other hand considered a mark of piety to abstain from hot baths; while in other cases it was apparently a form of asceticism to abstain from baths of any sort. Thomas of Ely, for instance, says of Sexburg, sister and successor of Aethilthryth of Ely, that she fled "from the use of baths as though from a poisoned seedbed" (Thomas of Ely, *Anglia Sacra*, ed. Wharton, 1691, I. 596), while St Audrey herself was "so pure of heart that she had no need to wash her body" (*Liber Eliensis*, ed. Stewart, p. 50).

CHAPTER XXII

THE CHURCH AT HEXHAM. This account of Wilfrid's church at Hexham and the much fuller account given by Richard of Hexham in the twelfth century (Twisden, *Decem scriptores*, Lon. 1652, col. 290) throw more light than any other documents on the architecture of the seventh century, shewing, as they do, the transition which was at this time taking place from the early Christian to the Romanesque

forms. The church was, according to Eddius, a great advance on anything which had so far been built in England. In 1908, during some explorations beneath the floor of the choir, the foundations of the apse of St Wilfrid's church were discovered and its plan was revealed. From this, according to C. C. Hodges, who helped to carry out the explorations, it was found that the greatest length was 165 ft., the extreme width across the transepts was 126 ft., and the outside width of the nave 70 ft. (See C. C. Hodges and J. Gibson, *Hexham and its Abbey*. Hexham, 1919, pp. 38 ff.) Its design seems to have been inspired by the larger churches of the basilica type which Wilfrid had seen in Gaul and Italy. William of Malmesbury declares that "those who have visited Italy allege that at Hexham they see the glories of Rome once again!" (Will. Malms. *Gest. Pont. Ang.*, Rolls Series, LII. 255). This appearance would of course be enhanced by the fact that Roman worked stones from Corstopitum, the abandoned Roman city near Corbridge, were largely used in its construction. The crypt stands nowadays very much as it has always stood. For further details and the comparison with the crypt at Ripon see ch. XVII, note. One of its most interesting features is the stone with the inscription from which the name of Geta was erased after he was murdered by his brother Caracalla at the beginning of the third century. This stone is built into the wall of the crypt. (For a fuller account of Hexham Church see *A.E.E.* II. 1925, 149 ff.)

OF BLESSED MEMORY. A curious phrase to use of a living man. It occurs again in chs. LVI and LXIV. Other examples of this usage are to be found in contemporary writings. For collected examples see G. D. Hoffmann, *Beobachtungen aus denen deutschen Staatsgeschichten und Rechten*, 1762, III. 67 ff.

CHAPTER XXIV

IURMINBURG. Ecgfrith certainly married again before Aethil-thryth's death, which did not take place until 679 or 680. It was a lawful marriage according to the church law which permitted a second marriage when husband or wife left the other by solemn profession in a religious order before the consummation of marriage. The marriage was then declared to be dissolved (see *Cath. Enc.* s.v. Divorce). This would cover the case of Ecgfrith, and make his second marriage ecclesiastically legal. Iurminburg objected to Wilfrid's secular pomp, evidently jealous for her husband's sake. Wilfrid's attitude to the king's first marriage would naturally stir up the hostility of the latter against him. After her husband's death she took the veil. Her name appears in the *Liber Vitae* in the list of queens and abbesses between Eanfled and Aelffled (Surt. Soc. XIII. 3).

DIVISION OF THE DIOCESE. Theodore had already made up his mind that the tribal dioceses were becoming unwieldy, for at the synod of Hertford (673) he had proposed "that more bishops should be made," but the proposal was not ratified. Ecgfrith possibly made use of Theodore for his own ends and convinced him that it was useless to expect Wilfrid's consent (see also note on ch. XI). This may account for the fact that Theodore did not appeal to Wilfrid first. Eddius's story that Theodore was bribed is quite incredible considering what we know of the archbishop's character.

THE CONSECRATION. It was laid down by the councils of the Church that a bishop must be consecrated by at least three fellow bishops (see note, ch. XII). The Pope, however, from the sixth century onwards, ordained bishops by his own authority. Possibly Theodore considered that his position as archbishop gave him the same privilege. Otherwise the consecration was not canonical.

NOT SUBJECTS OF THE DIOCESE. The three bishops were Bosa, Eata and Eadhaeth. The original intention was to make two new bishoprics in Wilfrid's diocese for Bernicia and Deira; the other diocese was to be the newly acquired province of Lindsey, and so was not, in spite of Eddius, part of Wilfrid's old diocese at all. Eddius is again amazingly inaccurate in his description of these three men as being " picked up elsewhere," etc. Bosa had been educated under Hild at Whitby (*H.E.* IV. 21). Eata was one of Aidan's twelve English pupils, and was Abbot of Lindisfarne (*H.E.* III. 26), while Eadhaeth accompanied Chad from Northumbria, when he went to Kent to be consecrated Bishop of York (*H.E.* III. 28). They were therefore all three closely connected with the Celtic church.

ON THE ADVICE OF HIS BROTHER-BISHOPS. But Wilfrid states explicitly in his appeal to the Pope (ch. XXX) that some bishops had supported Theodore. They certainly refused to take part with Theodore in the consecration of the three bishops. Nevertheless even if they supported Wilfrid on this occasion in his appeal to Rome, they apparently changed their minds later. For we do not hear that any of them supported him between the time when he was driven from his see and his restoration.

ON THIS DAY TWELVEMONTH. This refers to Aelfwini's death, 679, which took place at the battle of the Trent. Aethilred, King of the Mercians, fought with and apparently defeated the Northumbrians (*H.E.* IV. 19, 20). Peace was brought about by the mediation of Theodore. Aelfwini was only eighteen years old.

THE NEW BISHOPRICS. On Wilfrid's expulsion, Bosa became Bishop of all Deira with his seat at York. Eata superintended Bernicia either from Lindisfarne or Hexham, and Eadhaeth became first Bishop of Lindsey.

CHAPTER XXV

EBROIN. Mayor of the Palace in Neustria under Theodoric or Thierry III, King of Neustria and Burgundy, was, like the other mayors of the Palace from 639–751, virtually ruler of the realm. The kings were mere shadows, and have justly come down to posterity with the title of "les rois fainéants." Ebroin had a great influence in Austrasia and Burgundy too. He defeated and slew Leodogar (St Leger), Bishop of Autun, who attempted to defend the rights of Burgundy, and remained master of Burgundy and Neustria until he was assassinated in 681. He seems to have been a sinister influence over a large part of Western Europe during the third quarter of the seventh century. It was he who kept Theodore imprisoned for some months when he was on his way to England in 668.

GREATER EXILE. If this has any technical meaning, it probably refers to a decree of exile pronounced by the king which condemned not to death but to the loss of all rights and privileges. (See J. Hoops, *Reallexikon der germanischen Altertumskunde*, s.v. Friedlosigkeit.)

WINFRID. St Winfrid was Bishop of the Mercian Church in succession to St Chad. He had long been a deacon of the church and is described by Bede (*H.E.* IV. 3) as a "good and modest man." Soon after the Council of Hertford he was deposed by Theodore for disobedience (*H.E.* IV. 6); Bede does not state the reason, but we are tempted to assign the same reason for it as for the deposition of Wilfrid. Bede does not mention this journey to the continent but says that he retired to a monastery "Ad Baruae," Barrow-on-Humber in Lincolnshire. Eddius's story certainly looks somewhat doubtful in the face of Bede's silence.

CHAPTER XXVI

FRIESLAND. Wilfrid was obviously aware of the hostility of Ebroin or it is unlikely that he would have taken the unusual course of landing in Frisia. Thus he avoided Neustria altogether and travelled through Austrasia. So it is quite possible that Eddius's story that Ebroin's hostility was due to his Northumbrian enemies, is simply a baseless charge.

ALDGISL. Not otherwise known, though mentioned also in the parallel passage in Bede (*H.E.* V. 19).

THE FRISIAN LANGUAGE. Apparently Wilfrid found the difference in language no bar to his preaching. Frisian was so closely connected with his own tongue that the difference would be little more than one of dialect.

WILLIBRORD. Unfortunately the results of Wilfrid's preaching were not lasting. Ten years after, Wihtberht, a hermit from Ireland,

preached for two years to these same people but laboured in vain (*H.E.* v. 9). Willibrord, who was brought up by Wilfrid in the monastery at Ripon, set out for Frisia in 690 with twelve companions. With the help of Pippin, Duke of the Franks, he was most successful, and won many converts. He was consecrated Archbishop of the Frisians by Pope Sergius in 695. Wilfrid visited his old pupil again in Frisia on his last journey to Rome. Eddius does not mention this incident, but only Bede (*H.E.* III. 13) on the authority of Acca, from whom he probably heard it. Willibrord died about 739 in the monastery of Epternach (*H.E.* v. 10, 11).

CHAPTER XXVII

BUSHEL. A liquid and dry measure which varied in different places and at different times. In Roman times it was equal to two gallons (see Ducange, s.v. modium).

SOLIDI. A golden solidus was at this time equal in value to forty silver denarii (see Ducange, s.v.).

CHAPTER XXVIII

DAGOBERT. This was Dagobert II, King of Austrasia, 676–679 (?). After the death of his father he was dethroned by Grimoald, Mayor of the Palace, and sent to an Irish monastery. The nobles however refused to obey Grimoald's son whom he put in Dagobert's place, because he was not of noble birth. Dagobert was recalled by the Austrasians during their struggles with Ebroin after the death of Childeric. It was on this occasion that Wilfrid invited him over from Ireland and sent him back to Austrasia in royal state. This was obviously one cause of Ebroin's hostility to Wilfrid. Dagobert was assassinated very soon after Wilfrid's visit, probably in 679.

STRASSBURG. Arbogastus Bishop of Strassburg died in 679. He was succeeded on Wilfrid's refusal by Florentinus (*Gallia Christiana*, v. 782).

DEODATUS. Bishop of Toul, 679–680. His name appears in an official account of the Council held in 679 (see ch. XXIX and note).

PERCTARIT, KING OF CAMPANIA. Berhthere or Perctarit was not King of Campania but of Lombardy, and ruled at Milan (661–688). He had a troubled reign and was for nine years in exile (662–671). He was fleeing from the usurper Grimoald when this incident occurred, and found shelter in Pannonia with the Khan of the Avars. (See T. Hodgkin, *Italy and her Invaders*, VI. 242 ff.) The story Perctarit tells, occurs nowhere else except in Eddius.

CHAPTER XXIX

A G A T H O. Pope from 678–681. He was a Sicilian, who seems to have been greatly loved for his kindness and geniality. His chief act during his Pontificate was the settling of the Monothelite controversy. (See ch. XXXIII, note.)

C O E N W A L D. Nothing further is known about him except that William of Malmesbury declares that he supported the charges "in harsh and bitter terms" (William of Malmesbury, *Gesta Pontificum*, bk III, Rolls Series, LII. 222).

T H E C O N S T A N T I N I A N. This church was built by Constantine the Great during the latter part of his reign; hence its name. It was dedicated to our Saviour until some time in the seventh century, when its dedication was changed to that of St John the Evangelist. Hodgkin (*Italy and her Invaders*, VI. 260) suggests the year 653 for the change, but from this reference it would seem as if the rededication must have taken place at least some 30 years later.

A G A T H O ' S S P E E C H. Agatho's speech as given here is for the first part identical with the speech delivered at a Council of which an official account has been preserved among the Concilia. This Council had apparently no special reference to Wilfrid, but dealt generally with the trouble in the English Church. (See Haddan and Stubbs, *Councils and Ecclesiastical Documents*, III. 131–141.) It may well have been a Council held in 679 and slightly before the one described here, to discuss Coenwald's embassy. Deodatus of Toul, who accompanied Wilfrid, is recorded as being present; so Wilfrid must have been in Rome though not admitted to the Council. Plummer (*Bede*, II. 325) is inclined to think that the official account of the Council is only another version of Eddius, and that it does not represent a distinct Council.

A N D R E W. Bishop of Ostia, 680–685. The incumbent of this diocese was perpetual deacon of the Sacred College of Cardinals.

J O H N. Bishop of Porto, 680–692. The bishop who held this see was perpetual sub-deacon of the same College. It was in their official capacity that both these bishops took the important part in the proceedings which is assigned to them. (See P. B. Gams, *Series Episcoporum Ecclesiae Catholicae*, IV. VIII.)

S E C R E T A R I U M. This word has two meanings: (1) as here, a room where bishops received the greetings of their people, transacted business, held meetings of the clergy, or sat in synod; (2) a vestry or sacristy. (See Ducange, s.v.)

S E C R E T A R Y. Lat. "notarius." One of the official scribes always attached to the Holy See and to the bishops' courts. (See Ducange, s.v.)

CHAPTER XXX

ENGLAND. Lat. "Saxoniae." A word often used by Latin writers
for England as a whole. For other collected examples see Plummer,
Bede, II. 368 and Chad. *O.E.N.* p. 56. See also ch. XIX, note.

HANDED DOWN. "Traditas" must refer here to "kanonum"
with a confusion of case and gender. Eddius evidently had "normam" in mind.

WITHOUT THE CONSENT OF ANY BISHOP. See note,
ch. XXIV.

MY OLD SEES. Lat. "parrochiis." The word "parochia" is here
used in the sense of a bishop's see, as ordinarily, but loosely, to
describe the newly constructed sees made from his old see.

CHAPTER XXXII

THE ANSWER OF THE SYNOD. It is important to notice that
the synod did no more than fulfil Theodore's original intention
while at the same time rectifying the mistake which he had made in
dividing up Wilfrid's see without his consent. The comprehensive
curse with which the answer ends is of a type not uncommon in the
Papal decrees and charters of the time.

CHAPTER XXXIII

MANY DAYS. It was during this time, in March 680, that Wilfrid
attended a synod of the Western Church on Monothelitism, and, in
the absence of Theodore, answered for the orthodoxy of the North
of Britain, Ireland and the islands. (See ch. LIII and note.)

RELICS. For an account of the extraordinary lengths to which the
traffic in relics was carried, see the article on Relics, *E.R.E.* s.v. No
church was considered complete which did not contain relics of the
saints. The crypts at Hexham and Ripon were probably both built
for the preservation and exhibition of relics.

DAGOBERT. See ch. XXVIII and note. No more is known of the
death of Dagobert than is told us by Eddius. Mabillon suggests
that the bishop who is referred to here may be either Faramandus,
or Waimerus a former Duke of Campania, both of whom had been
put into bishoprics by Ebroin, but were of course not recognized by
the Church. (Mab. *AA.SS.O.S.B.* 1677, Saec. IV. pt I, 695 n.)

EBROIN. Wilfrid was present at the conference in Rome in
March 680. Ebroin was murdered apparently before May of the
same year. Now a charter quoted in the *Vita Condedi anachoretae
Belcinnacensis* bears the date of the seventh year of Theodoric III,
i.e. 680, and is subscribed by Waratto who was Ebroin's successor

as mayor. Therefore Ebroin must almost certainly have been dead by this time, for we know that Wilfrid did not hasten back from Rome to Gaul. It looks then as though we must regard this part of the story at any rate, and perhaps the whole of it, with considerable suspicion.

CHAPTER XXXIV

WILFRID'S RETURN. The assurance with which Wilfrid shews the decrees of the synod to Ecgfrith and the way in which they are received by the king and the assembled counsellors, throw an interesting light on the attitude of the northern rulers towards the papal claims to supremacy. They did not categorically deny the right of the Apostolic See to settle the internal disputes of the Church, but they declared that the writings had been bought—a decision which was as insulting to the Papal See as it was to Wilfrid. "The allegation," says Bright, "shews that Rome had already a bad reputation for venality, which afterwards grew worse." (Bright, *E.E.C.H.* p. 337.)

QUEEN. Iurminburg. See ch. XXIV and note.

RELIQUARY. Lat. "chrismarium." A vessel containing the chrism or consecrated oil for baptism, confirmation and the anointing of the sick. It was often used as a case for keeping relics. For many examples of this see Ducange, s.v. chrismarium.

CHAPTER XXXVI

REEVE. Lat. "praefectum." This official was apparently a king's reeve charged with the administration of a royal estate or borough. This would in all probability carry with it the administration of the surrounding districts. (Cf. H. M. Chadwick, *Anglo-Saxon Institutions*, p. 344.)

OSFRITH. Not otherwise known.

ROYAL BOROUGH. A royal estate probably used as an administrative centre for the surrounding districts. This would account for the presence of the prison here. (See H. M. Chadwick, *op. cit.* pp. 254 ff., etc.)

BRONINIS. Not identified. None of the suggestions (Burnswark, Brunanburh, etc.) are entirely satisfactory.

THEGN. Lat. "comes," equivalent to O.E. "gesith." (Cf. H. M. Chadwick, *op. cit.* pp. 333 ff.)

PRISON ILLUMINATED. Possibly a reminiscence of Peter in prison, Acts 12. 7.

WILFRID'S ANSWER. This incident like many others in his life (e.g. the shipwreck on the Sussex coast, ch. XIII, his attitude to the hostile bishop, ch. XXXIII) reveal Wilfrid very clearly as a man of great courage, physical as well as moral.

CHAPTER XXXVII

AEBBE. If this is the Aebbe who was abbess of Coldingham, then
it is quite obvious that she must have been alive long after 683,
which is the supposed date of her death. See ch. XXXIX, note. There
were however two other abbesses named Aebbe at the end of the
seventh century. One is found in the third cartoon of the remarkable
roll in the Harley collection of MSS in the British Museum, containing
pictures of the life of St Guthlac. The picture illustrates St Guthlac
receiving the tonsure at Repton, and the abbess in the picture is
called Ebba, but in the text Aelfthryth (see W. De Gray Birch,
Memorials of St Guthlac, p. xxxix). The other Aebbe was abbess in
the isle of Thanet (see Kemble, *Codex Diplomaticus*, Nos. 8, 10, 14,
15, 989).

CHAPTER XXXVIII

TYDLIN. Not known elsewhere.

FETTERS LOOSED. This again seems to be a reminiscence of
the prison experience of Paul and Silas, Acts 16. 26. Compare Bede's
story of the Northumbrian prisoner who could not be bound (*H.E.*
IV. 20).

CHAPTER XXXIX

COLDINGHAM. In County Berwick, Scotland. There are still
to be seen at Kirkhill on the coast two miles east of the modern
Coldingham some remains of a chapel of later date. On St Abb's
Head itself, three miles north-east of Coldingham, there are also to
be seen remains of a chapel and other monastic buildings which are
also later.* It was a double monastery of monks and nuns. The date
of the foundation by Aebbe is not certain. It was here that Ecgfrith's
wife Aethilthryth entered, when she left her husband. It was destroyed by fire, in 679, according to the *A.S.C.*, but this can hardly
be the case, for the date of Wilfrid's imprisonment was 680. More
than that Bede (*H.E.* IV. 23) declares that the fire took place after
Aebbe's death, and she was alive in 681.

AEBBE. Daughter of Aethilfrith, King of Northumbria, sister of
St Oswald and Oswiu, and aunt of Ecgfrith. She does not seem to
have been a very successful abbess for there were many troubles at
Coldingham during her days (*H.E.* IV. 23). St Abb's Head takes
its name from her, and also Ebchester, Co. Durham, which was
originally a Roman town presented to her by her brother. Here

---

* It is probable however that earlier work might be found if the site were
carefully examined. See MacGibbon and Ross, *Ecclesiastical Architecture
of Scotland*, I. 437, and *Historical Monuments (Scotland) Commissions,
County of Berwick*, p. 43 (Edinburgh, 1915).

she founded another monastery. She was a great friend of St Cuthbert, but it was while staying with her and seeing the scandalous lives of some of the inmates that the saint is supposed to have made up his mind to exclude women from his monastic church at Lindisfarne. The date of Aebbe's death is unknown, but it is supposed to have taken place about 683 (but see note, ch. xxxvii). Her relics were transferred from Coldingham to Durham in the eleventh century by Aelfred, sacrist of Durham. (Symeon of Durham, *History of Church of Durham*, Rolls Series, lxxv. 88.)

CHAPTER XL

BERHTWALD. The only other place where this sub-king is mentioned is in William of Malmesbury (*G.P.*, Rolls Series, lii. 351, 352), where we are further told that he was the son of Wulfhere, and, in addition, we are given a charter in which Berhtwald grants land to the monastery at Malmesbury.

AETHILRED. He succeeded to the throne of Mercia in 675 on the death of his brother Wulfhere. He carried on the war with Northumbria which his brother had been waging. It was brought to a conclusion about 679 through the mediation of Archbishop Theodore. During the latter part of his life he was a pious and peaceful prince, though he seems to have been troubled by civil strife (see *A.S.C.* 697). He abdicated his throne in 704 (see ch. lvii), and retired to the monastery of Bardney of which he became the abbot. The date of his death is unknown.

AETHILRED'S QUEEN. This was Osthryth, daughter of Oswiu and sister of Ecgfrith. She was murdered in 697 by "the Southumbrians" (*A.S.C.* 697). In the epitome appended to Bede it is explained that the murder was performed by the chief men of the Mercians (*H.E.* v. 24).

ECGFRITH. See ch. xvii and note.

CENTWINI. According to Bede (*H.E.* iv. 12) Centwini divided the kingdom of Wessex on the death of his brother Coenwalh in 672 and ruled with others. The *A.S.C.* says that Aescwini, a distant cousin, succeeded to the throne on the death of Coenwalh's queen Sexburg. Possibly Centwini was the strongest among these "subreguli." We know next to nothing of his life except that he fought with the British and drove them to the sea (*A.S.C.* 682). Aldhelm says that he entered a monastery before his death (*Aldhelmi Opera*, ed. Giles, p. 115). He is supposed to have died in 685.

CHAPTER XLI

AETHILWALH. King of the South Saxons, had according to Bede been baptized in Mercia, owing to the influence of King Wulfhere, some twenty years before this time. His wife Eabe, daughter of Eanfrith, King of the Hwicce, was also a baptized Christian. Wulfhere had ravaged the Isle of Wight and the province of the Meonwaras in 661, and had bestowed them on Aethilwalh. He was killed in 686 by Ceadwalla who had aspired to the West Saxon throne and had been driven into exile among the South Saxons. (*H.E.* IV. 13.) Apparently from Eddius's account, the king had either reverted to heathenism or at any rate forgotten the Christian teaching of his earlier days. Under the year 661, the *A.S.C.* says that a priest was sent to the Isle of Wight, on the accession of Aethilwalh to the throne of Wight, by Wulfhere in conjunction with Wilfrid. This seems highly improbable, however, seeing that in 661 Wilfrid was only a deacon.

CONVERSION OF THE SOUTH SAXONS. Eddius omits the picturesque story told by Bede (*H.E.* IV. 13) of how Wilfrid won the hearts of the people by helping them in the time of famine, teaching them to catch fish by means of nets, and in this manner paved the way for the acceptance of the Gospel.

COMPELLED BY THE KING'S COMMAND. There was often a measure of compulsion in the conversion of the Northern races to Christianity. Compare the conversion of the Norse under Olaf Tryggvason in 996.

SELSEY MINSTER. The spot on which this minster stood is supposed to have been about a mile to the east of the present church. It has long been submerged by the encroachments of the Channel, but Camden relates that it was still visible in his days at low water (*Britannia*, I. 199.)

CHAPTER XLII

CEADWALLA. A descendant of Ceawlin, and son of Coenbeorht, who is called a sub-regulus by Florence of Worcester (*Annals*, 661). His name is clearly British, and points to some connection by blood with the British race. He had long been striving to obtain the throne of Wessex, and it is not remarkable, after the treatment Wilfrid had received at the hands of Centwini (see ch. XL), that he should have helped Ceadwalla as much as possible; but Wilfrid, perhaps unwittingly, was laying up trouble for his friend Aethilwalh, for Ceadwalla gathered round him a crowd of adventurers and outcasts, and slew Wilfrid's friend, gaining thereby the throne of Sussex. He was driven out however by the late king's ealdormen (*H.E.* IV. 13).

Eddius discreetly says nothing about this incident. In 685 Ceadwalla became king of Wessex; but it is not quite clear whether he conquered it, or came peaceably to the throne. But on his accession he avenged himself on Sussex, and added the Isle of Wight to his domains, destroying the whole population in accordance with the vow he had made. Possibly, as Bright charitably suggests, the Apostle of Sussex used his influence to prevent this but in vain (Bright, *E.E.C.H.* 392). Ceadwalla abdicated the throne of Wessex in 689 in order to go to Rome to be baptized. He received baptism from the Pope and died within ten days, still wearing his white baptismal garment. So it is clear from Bede that Wilfrid's spiritual son was not only the murderer of Wilfrid's own patron, but not even a Christian. Again, it looks as though Eddius is deliberately exaggerating in order to emphasize the greatness of his patron.

CHAPTER XLIII

ERCONWALD. He was created Bishop of the East Saxons by Archbishop Theodore in 675 or 676. Before that, he had presided over a monastery at Chertsey which he himself had founded. He was famed for his holiness (*H.E.* IV. 6) and after his death many miracles were recorded at his shrine in St Paul's, London, right down to the Reformation. Under the guidance and advice of Theodore he greatly improved the condition of his diocese. His death may have taken place in 693. His name is mentioned in the preface to the laws of Ine, King of Wessex, where he is described by the latter as "my bishop," which apparently implies that the King of Wessex at this time exercised some sort of suzerainty over Essex.

THEODORE'S APOLOGY. Although there is no reason to believe that the incident of Theodore's reconciliation with Wilfrid is not historical, yet Eddius's partizanship undoubtedly puts into the archbishop's mouth words of self-humiliation which do not sound altogether likely. Bede says nothing about the incident.

ALDFRITH. An illegitimate son of Oswiu. During his brother Ecgfrith's reign he had been in exile in Ireland. Here he learned from Irish monks, and became famed for his piety and learning. On the death of his brother Ecgfrith in 685 at the battle of Nechtansmere, he came to the throne of Northumbria. He died in 705. Two of Aldhelm's letters are addressed to him, the first of which congratulates him on his return from Ireland and upon his learning. (Aldhelm, *Opera*, ed. Giles, pp. 91, 216.)*

* There is an interesting article by A. S. Cook on Aldfrith as the possible begetter of the O.E. poems *Beowulf* and *Widsith*, in the *Connecticut Academy of Arts and Sciences*, vol. xxv., pp. 281–346.

AELFFLED. Sister of King Aldfrith. She was with St Hild at Whitby for some years, and, on the death of the latter, she became abbess. She died at the age of 59. Eddius always speaks highly of her on account of her kindness to Wilfrid. Cf. chs. LIX, LX. The name occurs also in the *Liber Vitae* in the list of queens and abbesses (Surt. Soc. XIII. 3).

BENEDICT II. Was consecrated Pope probably in 683 and died in 685.

SERGIUS I. Was Pope from 687 to 701. We have no other record of any pronouncement of either Benedict or Sergius on Wilfrid's case. Eddius refers to their pronouncements again in ch. XLVI and the names occur in Wilfrid's petition in ch. LI. The mention of Sergius's bull here is probably a slip on the part of Eddius, judging from the date. See ch. XLVI, note.

CHAPTER XLIV

WILFRID'S RESTORATION. It is clear from Bede that Wilfrid did not receive the full diocese again. In the first place Lindsey had been lost to Mercia in 678 (*H.E.* IV. 12). In the second place the new see which had been formed in 681 at Abercorn had been reconquered by the Picts. Thirdly, Cuthbert remained at Lindisfarne. On the death of the latter in 687, Wilfrid administered the diocese for a year until his successor was consecrated. Lastly, upon Eata's death in 686, Wilfrid held Hexham for a year until John of Beverley was consecrated to it, probably in 687. Eddius seems to imply that Wilfrid's restoration to Hexham was permanent.

ST JOHN AT EPHESUS. Eusebius (*Church History*, III. 23) (Migne, XX. 259), quoting Irenaeus, declares that on the accession of Nerva, John removed from Patmos to Ephesus, reorganized the churches in Asia, and survived until the time of Trajan, roughly a period of five years.

CHAPTER XLV

THE CHURCH DEDICATED TO ST PETER. The churches at both Ripon and York were dedicated to St Peter. This however refers to Ripon as the reference to the "aforesaid monastery" just below clearly proves.

THE MONASTERY. That is Ripon.

WILFRID'S SUCCESSOR. Apparently Bosa, who had been driven from York when Wilfrid was restored, was in his turn restored to the see.

WILFRID'S QUARREL. Besides the three reasons assigned for the quarrel between Aldfrith and Wilfrid, the king's upbringing must

have contributed largely to it. Aldfrith had been educated under strong Celtic influences, and would naturally suspect the man who had been, throughout his career, so determined an opponent of the Celtic tradition.

S E X W U L F. The founder of the Medeshamstead (Peterborough) monastery and Bishop of the Mercians in succession to Winfrid (see ch. xxv and note). The incident related in this chapter cannot have taken place later than 692; so the *A.S.C.*, which puts Sexwulf's death under 705, must be wrong. Sexwulf was bishop over the whole of Mercia, but during his episcopate Theodore divided the great diocese into five. Wilfrid, according to Florence of Worcester, took over part of his diocese, having his seat at Leicester. (See Florence of Worcester, I. 242, ed. B. Thorpe, Lond. 1848.)

CHAPTER XLVI

There is a long interval between Wilfrid's retirement from the north and the council of *Ouestraefelda*. Wilfrid's departure must have taken place in 691 or 692, but the council of *Ouestraefelda* took place in 702 or 703, if we are to take literally Wilfrid's words that his enemies had been resisting the apostolic decrees for twenty-two years, that is since 680. He also declares that he has been a bishop for forty years (ch. XLVII). Eddius does not notice this interval of ten years, probably because he did not go into exile with Wilfrid, and had little or no information about it (see Introduction). We learn of two incidents which happened from Bede; first that Wilfrid consecrated Suidberht as bishop of the Frisians in 692 or 693 (*H.E.* v. 11), and secondly (IV. 17), he was present at the translation of his old friend St Aethilthryth in 695 or 696. It is possible that the bull in Wilfrid's favour which he speaks of several times (chs. XLIII, XLIV, XLVI, LI) as having been granted by Pope Sergius I, was granted during this interval.

O U E S T R A E F E L D A O R A E T S W I N A P A T H E. Generally considered to be Austerfield near Bawtry. The latter name occurs in the Doomsday Book as *Oustrefeld*. It was quite close to the Roman road called Ermine St, and would therefore be accessible and fairly central. There is apparently no place-name in the neighbourhood which corresponds exactly to the form *Aetswinapathe*, but there is a Swinnow Wood and a Swinecar Road quite close (cf. J. T. Fowler, *Memorials of Ripon*, Surt. Soc. LXXIV. 18, n. 2).

T H E C O N F E R E N C E. This conference is not mentioned by Bede, which is remarkable considering its importance and size. Bright (*E.E.C.H.* 439) calls this conference a general council as opposed to those at Hertford and *Haethfelth* (680), which he calls provincial councils, but it is difficult to see wherein the difference lies, seeing that at this time there was only one metropolitan for the

whole of Britain. The national or general councils and the provincial councils would therefore be identical.

BERHTWALD. Archbishop of Canterbury, was consecrated by the Bishop of Lyons in 693. He had previously been Abbot of Reculver (*H.E.* v. 8). Bede has little to say about him except for his dealings with Wilfrid though he declares very definitely that Berhtwald was not to be compared with Theodore (*H.E. loc. cit.*). He seems to have been a quiet and steady leader, who by his moderation guided the destinies of the Church during a critical period. He died in 731.

CHAPTER XLVII

THE CONFERENCE. It is difficult to believe that the account of the transactions at this conference has not been highly coloured by Eddius. Apparently the council was trying to find out whether Wilfrid would accept the findings of themselves and the archbishop. But Wilfrid resolutely refused to accept any ruling which was contrary to the Papal decision. In fact he put the authority of Rome before that of his own immediate spiritual chief. This is clearly seen in the answer of the king and the archbishop to his announcement that he was determined to appeal to Rome once again.

THE THEGN. Compare ch. XXI. This man would probably be one of the young men retainers whom Wilfrid had about him in the earlier days of his episcopate.

RESPONSIONS AND ANTIPHONS. The custom of chanting psalms by two choirs alternately was probably introduced at Antioch in the middle of the fourth century, though there is a much earlier reference in a letter of Pliny to Trajan, which almost certainly describes this custom (*Ep.* x. 96). Socrates, indeed, attributes its introduction at Antioch to St Ignatius who was martyred in 107 A.D. (*Hist. Eccles.* VI. 8). It was not introduced into the Roman Church until the beginning of the fifth century.

Responsory or responsion is the technical name for the psalms or portions of psalms said or sung between the lections in the various offices of the Church.

The Antiphon was originally the intercalation of some verse or short sentence between the verses of the psalms which were being sung. Both responsories and antiphons are part of the form of service enjoined by the Rule of St Benedict.

RULE OF ST BENEDICT. See ch. XIV and note.

CHAPTER L

ON FOOT OVERLAND. This was a remarkable feat for a man who was seventy years old, even though we do not take Eddius's expression "on foot" as absolutely literal. It may have been undertaken of course as a mortification.

POPE JOHN. This was Pope John VI, who was consecrated Pope in October 701, and died in January 705. He had a great reputation as a peacemaker and a ransomer of captives. (See T. Hodgkin, *Italy and her Invaders*, VI. 363.) It must have been on this journey that Wilfrid paid the visit to Willibrord which Bede mentions (*H.E.* III. 13), as Willibrord did not go to Frisia until 690. (See ch. XXVI and note.)

CHAPTER LI

UNIVERSAL POPE. Pope Gregory the Great strongly objected to this title and denounced it as foolish, blasphemous and anti-Christian. See *Epistles*, V. 18, 19, 20, 43; VII. 31, 33; VIII. 30; IX. 68.

CHAPTER LIII

WILFRID'S DEFENCE. Eddius puts into Wilfrid's mouth a much clearer account of the council at *Questraefelda* than he narrates himself in chs. XLVI and XLVII. It is clear from this that the whole test was whether he would accept Archbishop Berhtwald's authority as paramount. This he refused to do, and it was for this he was condemned.

TALK GREEK. Mabillon, according to Ducange, interprets "graecizare" as "demisse in aurem loqui." But John VI was himself a Greek by birth so there seems to be no reason why it should not be taken in its ordinary sense.

FOUR MONTHS AND SEVENTY SITTINGS. It seems somewhat extraordinary that so much energy should have been devoted to settling Wilfrid's affairs. Possibly the Pope saw the importance of this occasion for confirming the paramount authority of the Apostolic See in Britain and the necessity for great tact and care at this juncture.

THE TRUE AND CATHOLIC FAITH. See ch. XXXIII and note. The sixth Oecumenical Council, at which Wilfrid was present, condemned the heresy of Monothelitism. For an account of this heresy see *E.R.E.* s.v. Monothelitism.

BONIFACE AND SIZENTIUS. In the account of the Council held in 679 described above (ch. XXIX and note) there is mention of

a priest called Boniface and no less than five priests all called Sisinnius, which may be the same name. Nothing is known of the two men mentioned here.

FORTY YEARS AND MORE. It was in 664 that Wilfrid was consecrated according to Bede (*H.E.* v. 24), and this meeting took place almost certainly in 704, for Pope John VI died in January 705. There does not seem to be sufficient justification for dating Wilfrid's consecration in 665, as Bright does, following Mabillon (*E.E.C.H.* 241). Bede says "nearly forty years" (*H.E.* v. 19).

BONIFACE'S SPEECH. It sounds as though Eddius had been guilty of exaggeration here. Cf. Bede's account (*H.E.* v. 19).

CHAPTER LIV

POPE JOHN'S LETTER. The Pope was in a difficult position. On the one hand, the Papal authority was all too weak in Britain, as the treatment of the decrees of his predecessors had proved; he must not make his commands too emphatic, or they would stand little chance of being obeyed; and on the other hand, in view of the decrees of his predecessors, he could not afford to sacrifice Wilfrid. So, on the whole, he did a very wise thing when he ordered a council and practically referred the matter to an English synod. By this means he hoped to gain time at any rate, if nothing else was accomplished, before he finally committed himself to a definite decision.

HILD. See ch. x and note. Hild's opposition to Wilfrid may have been based partly on his attitude to the Celtic church; but as Plummer points out (*Bede*, II. 190) we must take her continued opposition into account, when we estimate Wilfrid's character and the justice of his appeal.

CHAPTER LV

CRUCIFY THE WORLD TO HIMSELF. Probably he meant to enter a monastery in Rome, perhaps the monastery of St Andrew on the Coelian Hill (see ch. v, note).

FINISH HIS LIFE THERE. St Wilfrid on each of his journeys abroad had shewn a tendency to linger in foreign parts.

CHAPTER LVI

MEAUX. Thirty miles east-north-east of Paris. There was a Benedictine monastery here founded by St Faro in the seventh century.

A CHURCH TO ST MARY. This church was afterwards built close to the earlier one. There is a description of it by Prior Richard

of Hexham (see Surt. Soc. xliv, 181, 183). In this account he describes it as being round in shape like a tower with four projecting portions on the four sides. It was to the south-east of the earlier church. This church was obviously built on the "central" plan where "a middle space is surrounded with concentric or radiating adjuncts often in two stories" (*A.A.E.* ii. 181). Possibly Wilfrid had got the idea from the church of St Lorenzo in Milan which he must have seen on his way to Rome. In the seventeenth century Wilfrid's second church was in a state of semi-ruin. Shops and houses were built encroaching upon the site, and some remains still exist built into the walls of the buildings facing the market-place.

HEZEKIAH'S FIFTEEN YEARS. For another symbolic interpretation of this passage see Bede's Commentary on 2 Kings 20 (Migne, xciii. 449). Eddius's interpretation is almost certainly Jewish in origin and a characteristic piece of Haggada, but I have so far been unable to discover its source.

CHAPTER LVII

COENRED. King of Mercia, 704–709, was the son of Wulfhere. On the death of the latter the succession passed to Wulfhere's brother, Aethilred, probably because Coenred was too young to rule. The latter, from what we learn of him in Bede and the *A.S.C.*, seems to have been a pious man more fitted for the monastery than the throne; he went to Rome where he became a monk, and remained until his death (*H.E.* v. 19, 24).

CHAPTER LVIII

BADWINI. There is a priest of the same name who attests the decree of the Council of Clovesho 716 (Haddan and Stubbs, *Ecclesiastical Documents*, iii. 301). Possibly it is the same person.

ALFRITH THE TEACHER. Presumably a master in the monastery school. He was probably the scholar who studied in Ireland, to whom Aldhelm wrote a letter attempting to prove to him the superiority of the scholarship of Theodore and the Canterbury school over that of Ireland. (Aldhelm, *Op.* ed. Giles, pp. 91–95.)

PREDECESSORS. Really of course "predecessor," namely Ecgfrith (see ch. xxxiv).

SENT FROM THE APOSTOLIC SEE. This is incorrect according to Bede, who says that Berhtwald was Abbot of Reculver before he was made archbishop (*H.E.* v. 8). See ch. xlvi and note.

AS YOU DECLARE. Compare Ecgfrith's attitude to the papal judgments in ch. xxxiv.

CHAPTER LIX

AELFFLED. See ch. XLIII and note. Eddius calls her "daughter of a king" meaning the late king Oswiu.

AETHILBERG. The name of Aethilberg occurs immediately after that of Aelffled in the *Liber Vitae* (Surt. Soc. XIII. 3). She may possibly have been that Aethilberg who was daughter of King Anna and sister of Aethilthryth, Wilfrid's friend (see note, ch. XIX). This Aethilberg was abbess of the monastery of Farmoutier-en-Brie.

EADWULF AND OSRED. Osred was only eight years old on the death of Aldfrith. Eadwulf, a relative of the king, whose lineage is unknown, seized the throne, but only held it for two months, after which he was driven out by Berhtfrith (see next ch.), who apparently acted as protector during Osred's boyhood. Osred was slain in 716 (see *A.S.C.* s.a.). He seems to have been a youth of thoroughly dissolute character as several contemporary writers testify.

EADWULF'S OWN SON. It looks from the Latin as though this might mean Wilfrid's own son. If so, it would mean his spiritual son. Cf. ch. XVIII, where Eodwald is called Bishop's Son and compare Wilfrid's relations with "Dalfinus" as described in chs. IV and VI. But it is much more probable that this refers to Eadwulf's son, Arnwini, whose death in 740 is recorded by Bede's continuator (Plummer's *Bede*, I. 362). We learn from Symeon of Durham (*Hist. Reg.* c. 40, Rolls Series, LXXV., vol. II. 38) that this Arnwini was Eadwulf's son.

CHAPTER LX

R. NIDD. The exact site of the conference is not known. Raine (*H.Y.* I. 89) suggests the village of Nidd which answers to Eddius's description.

THE SYNOD. This was far less representative than *Ouestraefelda*. At this synod Berhtwald was the only southern representative.

BERHTFRITH. "Chief man next in rank," that is the chief ealdorman. Bede (*H.E.* V. 24) calls him a "praefectus," and says that in 711 he fought against the Picts. He is also mentioned in the *A.S.C.* 710.

RIPON AND HEXHAM. Actually Wilfrid had gained nothing by his appeals to Rome. In 686 he was Bishop of York; now he was merely made Bishop of Hexham, and was restored to the monastery at Ripon. In spite of the fact that Bosa died about this time and that Wilfrid might easily have been appointed Bishop of York, John was translated from Hexham and Wilfrid was put in his place. But we must remember that Wilfrid's great churches at Hexham and Ripon made him feel that these places were specially his; besides this he recovered all his possessions, apparently both in Northumbria and Mercia.

CHAPTER LXIII

CHURCH OF ST MARY. That is the Liberian Basilica of St Mary Major, dedicated in 365 and rebuilt by Sixtus III in 432.

ST PAUL. The church of St Paul without the walls, dedicated in 324 and rebuilt 388–423, was burnt down in 1823, but is now rebuilt in the old form.

PURCHASE THE FRIENDSHIP OF KINGS AND BISHOPS. Contrast Bede's words about Aidan (*H.E.* III. 5) where he says that the saint never gave any money to worldly authorities.

TATBERHT. See Introduction and note.

CHAPTER LXIV

BELL RUNG. This would not necessarily be the bell which was rung, or the clapper which was struck, when a monk was dying (cf. the story of St Hild's death, *H.E.* IV. 21), but simply the signal to call the monks to a special meeting in the chapter-house. It was here of course that all the official business of the monastery was conducted.

CELINUS OR CAELIN. The name occurs also in the *Liber Vitae* among the names of clerics (Surt. Soc. XIII. 24).

DESERT PLACES. Hermit life was quite common in the seventh and eighth centuries. We read in Bede of the hermit life of Fursa (*H.E.* III. 19), Cuthbert (IV. 26), Hereberht (IV. 27), and Dryhthelm (V. 12). There is also extant an eighth-century life of the famous Guthlac, hermit of Crowland, by Felix of Crowland.

CEOLRED. King of the Mercians, 709–716. He was the son of Aethilred, and succeeded to the throne on the resignation of his cousin Coenred. St Boniface, writing to Aethilbald, Ceolred's successor, compares him with Osred of Northumbria in viciousness of character and complains that it was during the reigns of these two kings that the privileges of the Church were first violated. He relates how an evil spirit took possession of Ceolred while he was feasting and how he died insane. (Kylie, *English Correspondence of St Boniface*, King's Classics, pp. 86 and 169.)

THE OBEDIENCE WHICH YOU HAVE PROMISED. This is sufficient proof, if proof were needed, that Wilfrid was a regular and not a secular abbot. The solemn vow of obedience was made only to regular and never to secular abbots.

CHAPTER LXV

OUNDLE. The monastery at Oundle was apparently destroyed possibly by the Danes at the time of the destruction of the Peterborough monastery in 870. At any rate, it was not in existence when

Aethelwold, Bishop of Winchester (963–984), went to Oundle, for he found nothing but ruins there (Hugo Candidus, *Coenobii Burgensis Historia, Historiae Anglicanae Scriptores Varii*, ed. J. Sparkes, London, 1723). The abbot in Wilfrid's time was called Cuthbald.

BIRDS. Souls of men were often represented in the form of birds (cf. Kylie, *English Correspondence of St Boniface*, King's Classics, p. 82); sculptures also frequently occur on early tombs at Rome, representing the soul making its flight to heaven (cf. Aringhi, *Roma Subterranea*, Rome, 1651, II. 607); cf. also Bede: "Vel volucres sunt qui obviam Christo in aera ex mortuis sunt ituri" (Commentary on Job I. 12). Fridegoda also in his *Life* describes how Wilfrid's spirit flew away from his body "like a bird freed from the lime of the flesh" (Fridegoda, *Life of Wilfrid*, ll. 1355–9; *H.Y.* I. 147).

Somewhat similar miracles are related about the death of St Columba (Adamnan, *Vit. Col.* III. 23) and also that of St Chad (Bede, *H.E.* IV. 3).

DATE OF DEATH. October 12th is the day always kept in his honour, though this was not a Thursday in 709 but a Saturday. On the other hand, the Psalm quoted (ciii. (Vulg.) 30) occurs in the ordinary course of the Psalms for Saturday mattins in both the Roman and Benedictine breviaries. This would support the traditional date of October 12th.

Bede in his *Martyrologium Poeticum* dates it April 24th. This however does not fit in with the events. It was in fact the date of his Translation Festival. The statement which occurs in Bright and Plummer, quoted from Raine, that the obituary of the church of Durham gives October 3rd as the date of his death is inaccurate. The MS reads quite clearly iii id Oct. (MS Dunelm. B, IV. 24). The date of his death cannot really be settled on the evidence we have at present. (But see Poole's article on the subject, *E.H.R.* XXXIV. 23.)

PRIVATE MASS. That is, a mass celebrated by a priest in a private oratory or in the absence of any congregation. This is a very early reference to the custom of private masses and pious offices on behalf of the dead, and of the anniversary festival for the dead.

CHAPTER LXVI

WILFRID'S REMAINS. Wilfrid was buried on the south side of the minster, as we learn from the Commemoration of St Wilfrid in the Ripon Psalter (Surt. Soc. LXXIV. 29, 30). Afterwards, at the end of the tenth century, his remains were placed on the north side of the church by Archbishop Oswald. But according to Eadmer (*Life of Wilfrid*, ch. LVII; *H.Y.* I. 225) Odo visited Ripon and

removed what he asserted to be the remains of Wilfrid to Canterbury, and placed them under the altar, whence they were removed by Lanfranc and enshrined. If this is true, then there is no foundation for the account of the translation of his body by Archbishop Gray in 1224, as given in the Ripon Psalter (Surt. Soc. LXXIV. 49). The Northerners however declared that it was the body of Wilfrid II that was taken to Canterbury.

LENGTH OF WILFRID'S EPISCOPATE. Bede declares that Wilfrid was forty-five years a bishop. Doubtless Eddius means that he died in the forty-sixth year of his episcopate.

ECCLESIASTICAL ROBES. That is his episcopal robes. Cf. the *Anonymous Life of St Cuthbert*, ch. XLII.

CYNITHRITH. A fairly common name found several times in the list of queens and abbesses in the *Liber Vitae*.

MOERISA. This proper name arose by misunderstanding of the Greek text of Matth. 9. 20, γυνὴ αἱμορροῦσα.

CHAPTER LXVII

MIRACLES AT THE TOMB. Miracles at the tombs of saints are the commonest form of mediaeval miracle, and occur everywhere in the Lives of the Saints. They were of course, and are still, reasons for pilgrimages. For interesting descriptions of the mediaeval aspect of this subject see Jusserand, *Wayfaring Life in the Middle Ages*, passim.

CHAPTER LXVIII

ST PETER AND ST ANDREW. It was to these Apostles that St Wilfrid seems to have been specially devoted, and it was largely through his influence that they became so closely connected with the religion of the north. It was to these two saints that his great churches were dedicated (see ch. LVI). St Andrew in early times, together with SS. Peter and Paul, was always chosen out from among the other Apostles for special reverence.

THEY KEPT SILENCE. Because of the silence during the night hours which was rigidly enforced by the Benedictine Rule.

SIGN IN THE SKY. It is tempting to see in this miracle an unusual display of northern lights or a lunar rainbow. But as Fowler points out (Surt. Soc. LXXIV. 26) the description can scarcely apply to the former, and as to the latter it has been calculated that the moon could not have been shining at the time and place indicated.

GABLES. L. "cornibus." I take this to be a translation of the O.E. *horn*. See Bosworth and Toller, *Anglo-Saxon Dictionary*, s.v.

APPENDIX

The following are examples of the grammatical mistakes, and unusual constructions and uses of words to be found in Eddius. The list is by no means exhaustive. In each case the form is found in both MSS:

1. False concords:

   lapidem...benedicto (p. 28), Ceaddan...oboediens (p. 32), nulla...culpam (p. 60), concessae...iura (p. 62), archiepiscopi...misso (p. 92), episcopatus...quam (p. 92), cartula...continentem (p. 104), universo...synodo (p. 108), archiepiscopi...emisso (p. 110), archiepiscopi...directo (p. 112), Wilfrithi...spoliato (p. 112), Wilfrithus...appellantem...absolutum...constitutum (pp. 112, 114), ignis illa (p. 146).

2. Wrong or unusual forms:

   triumphum (nom. sing., p. 40), equitatui (gen. sing., p. 40), poposcens (p. 54), prodisset (p. 56), pontifici (gen. sing., p. 56), convinctum (p. 58), reciperit (p. 56), prophetas (nom. plur., p. 72), incutierunt (p. 74), aetatuli (gen. sing., p. 94), apostolis (gen. plur., p. 122), conventui (gen. sing., p. 130), concedisset (p. 132), genuflectans (p. 144).

3. Wrong or unusual cases:

   ante regalibus (p. 6), per manus impositione (p. 26), ante seculis nostris (p. 36), secundum...iudicio (p. 90), sententiam...subiacere (p. 96).

4. Wrong or unusual use of tenses:

   emisisset *for* emisit (p. 54), narratum *for* narratus est (p. 58), praevidit *for* praevidet (p. 62), considerat *for* consideret (p. 118), sedentes *for* sedent (p. 138).

5. Unusual use of words:

   patentes (p. 48), absolutum (p. 70), relegatus (p. 74), miserantem (p. 76), obeuntes (p. 124), perpetraverunt (p. 142. Cf. p. 28).

INDEX